Our English Heritage

This is an entertaining and acutely perceptive study of the English contribution to American life and the American Dream. It is without question a brilliant and thought-provoking book, and it deals with a phase of our heritage so fundamental that it is often ignored—the men who made the first beachheads against the wilderness, and the way of life they brought with them.

"The English in America," says Gerald Johnson, "have been partially defeated by their own success—that is to say, they were so very important that everyone takes them for granted and proceeds to study other people. This has gone so far that some of us seem to forget that the English had any hand in the job at all."

In setting out to correct this lapse of memory, Mr. Johnson brings to bear a wit and a sharpness of observation that provide a constant delight, and in the procession of Englishmen across the Atlantic he has rich and fascinating material to work with. The result is as colorful and absorbing as a superior novel.

For first came the Expendables, the beggars and rogues and outcasts, expelled from their homeland to die in the harsh New World with cruel speed and in appalling numbers. They were followed by the Indispensables, the anonymous but sturdy poor from rural England who fought the wilderness, survived—some of them—and built. And over both ruled the Gentlemen of Quality—the Bradfords, the Penns, the Rolfes—who set up libraries and services of silver plate within sound of the Indian warcry.

In the later chapters, Mr. Johnson describes what sort of civilization these men brought with them, and how what they brought had to be modified to survive on this side of the Atlantic. This is history at its best, told in terms of the human beings who made it, and told with wit, insight and the storyteller's skill.

OUR ENGLISH HERITAGE

GERALD W. JOHNSON

J. B. LIPPINCOTT COMPANY

PHILADELPHIA AND NEW YORK

Contents

∘⦚∘

BOOK ONE

The People

I   THE EXPENDABLES   9

II   THE INDISPENSABLES   44

III   THE GENTLEMEN OF QUALITY   82

BOOK TWO

The Institutions

I   THE LANGUAGE   115

II   THE LAW   137

III   THE FAITH   158

IV   THE ARTS   182

V   THE SCIENCES   205

VI   THE PHILOSOPHY   223

Book One

❖

THE PEOPLE

Chapter I

∘⦚∘

THE EXPENDABLES

1

In the year 1655 an English general traveling in the New World looked upon the class of emigrants sent out by his native land to the colonies and was not favorably impressed. "Rodgs and hors and such like people are those which are generally Brought heare," he wrote, drawing the inference that the colony in question—it was Barbados—was a "dunghill" on which England cast her rubbish.*

Like the reports of most travelers who spend two weeks in a country new to them and then write a book about it, this was a distorted judgment; but it cannot be dismissed as without foundation. In 1655 England had been pouring colonists into North America for forty-eight years, primarily, of course, to hold and exploit the land, but secondarily as a means of relieving the pressure of population on the food supply in England. To serve this purpose the first to be removed naturally were those who, in the judgment of the authorities, could best be spared; these included felons, of course, "rodgs and hors and such like people," but also all "lewed and lasy felowes" and "allsuch as lie on the parishes." In brief, they got rid of the wicked and the worthless.

This element constituted the mass of the first wave that hit

* He was apparently a certain General Venables, quoted by Abbot Emerson Smith in *Colonists in Bondage*, published in 1947 and probably the most careful examination ever made of this phase of the settlement of North America.

9

the beach. There is no doubt about it. The records establish it, both such letters as that of the plain-spoken General, and the more precise documents of government officials, shipmasters and the various trading companies that supported colonization. There was a scattering of different types, to be sure—adventurers such as John Smith and John Rolfe, clergymen full of missionary zeal, and the representatives of authority including Sir Thomas Dale, Lord de la Warr and their successors. In the main, however, the first Englishmen to land and remain in what is now the United States of America were anything but choice specimens. Even among the clergy were certain hedge-priests whose transfer to Virginia—from south Georgia to Penobscot Bay it was all Virginia then—tended to the benefit of the church at home rather than abroad.

Yet the fact need not embarrass modern Americans of English descent. These were not their ancestors. These were the first wave, and they met the customary fate of members of the first wave of an invasion, which is to say, they died on the beachhead. They did not conquer the wilderness and establish the country; they obtained the slightest of footholds on the edge of the continent and died in obtaining it. It was the second wave, marching over their graves, that delivered the heavy assault and achieved the conquest; and the second wave was of a very different character.

Yet if the English first-comers were a Falstaff's army, "tattered prodigals lately come from swine-keeping, from eating draff and husks," they were none the less indispensable; for someone had to open the attack and the conquest of a wilderness is a bitter, lethal business, even when it is contested by no foes other than those that nature provides. Even in the second wave something like eighty per cent died within a year after landing; in the first, the mortality was so close to one hundred per cent that it seems unlikely that any rogue, or any "lewed and lasy felowe" has a descendant living in the United States today.

Half Virginia (that is, the modern State) of course claims descent from Rolfe and Pocahontas. But, in the first place, a good many of those claims are probably apochryphal and, in the second place, Rolfe was not a felon, a vagabond, or an indentured servant, but a gentleman adventurer with money and influence, anything but typical of the great mass of the early colonists. Yet without their tattered prodigals he and the handful of others like him could never have maintained even a foothold in the savage land they invaded. It is true, therefore, that if the English set the pattern of American civilization they traced its first faint outlines in the blood of the lowly, of England's cast-off rubbish.

Biologically, this is not important, since these people were extinguished before—except in isolated cases—they could reproduce themselves. As far as the political and social history of the country is concerned it is not important, for these people had no perceptible effect upon the development of American institutions. But if there is moral authority in the Biblical injunction to "look unto the pit whence ye are digged," and if there is enlightenment in understanding the drama of the creation of the country this group should not be dismissed without a word.

We know a great deal about the gentlemen adventurers, the governors and the clergy. We know less individually about the sturdy pioneers who subdued the wilderness, but we have unbounded admiration for them and habitually idealize them beyond all recognition. But this first group we tend to ignore, for their virtues were not such as to impress the memory of succeeding generations, and their achievements were pitifully small by comparison with what was done later. But they established the beach-head. Someone had to do it, and whoever did was pretty sure to die in the process. This is deplorable and doubtless unjust, but it is a hard fact. Civilization is not achieved without casualties, nor is it maintained at no human cost. The American who has never understood that somber truth is not a competent citizen. He may not like it, indeed, it may sicken his soul, but if he doesn't face the fact and bear it in mind, he is not likely to contribute either wisdom or courage to the conduct of public affairs in his own generation.

We are too complacent in this country. The American who can say, with Paul the Apostle, "I was born free," tends to attribute that to himself as a virtue and to look a bit scornfully upon the chief captain who has to confess, "With a great sum obtained I this freedom." But we are all in the chief captain's shoes. Freedom is costly. If one generation doesn't pay its price another must. If the initial payment for ours was made by vagabonds and felons, rogues and whores, it was nevertheless paid; and we shall value it the more for realizing that it was not bestowed free of charge.

2

Sir Walter Raleigh whipped off his velvet cloak and spread it over the mud in order that the Queen might pass dry-shod.

This anecdote is expressive of Elizabethan England, without doubt, but it is usually only half interpreted. The courtliness of the knight, the vanity and the grandeur of the Queen are always emphasized; but as a rule little is said about the mud. Yet the mud is the central factor, the indispensable element without which there would have been no story. If the royal residence had not been surrounded by mud, Elizabethan England would have been wholly different, and that may be read figuratively as well as literally.

Consider the man Raleigh, first to plant a colony of English-speaking people on these shores. He has come down to us as the knight in the velvet cloak, the glass of fashion and the mould of form, so dainty a figure, indeed, that he turned Mark Twain's stomach and appears as an epicene clown in the

American's robust story of the Great Queen's court. As a school-boy Mark Twain doubtless had had the story of the cloak crammed down his throat by prissy schoolma'ams who clung to the preposterous notion that they could force it upon Missouri boys as an ideal of gentlemanly conduct; and the natural result was to make him loathe the very name of Raleigh.

Nor have the learned doctors on the college level done much more toward a true description of Raleigh than the teachers of the district schools. True, they know that he was more than a fop. They have found it of record that he could swap songs with Marlowe, witticisms with Shakespeare, learning with Francis Bacon. They have read,

> Give me my scallop-shell of quiet,
>   My staff of faith to walk upon,
> My scrip of joy, immortal diet,
>   My bottle of salvation,
> My gown of glory, hope's true gage;
> And thus I'll take my pilgrimage,

and freely admit that that wasn't written by an illiterate. They have found the accounts of his explorations and agree that they were not planned by a parochial mind. Above all, they have looked into his "History of the World," written when his whole world was comprised in a prison cell, and are forced to concede that, taking all the circumstances into consideration, it was an intellectual feat of a high order of magnitude.

So they have given us a Sir Walter Raleigh who was far indeed from being a mere popinjay—a bit of a dandy, to be sure, but also a poet, a scholar, a wit, a polished man of the world with respectable attainments as a statesman. Later generations have accorded him some standing as a philosopher, too, were it only for the great apostrophe written when he knew that his end was near and whose sheer sonority has kept it resounding down the centuries: "O eloquent, just, and mightie

Death! whom none could advise, thou hast perswaded; what none hath dared, thou hast done; and whom all the world hath flattered, thou only hast cast out of the world and despised. Thou hast drawne together all the farre stretched greatnesse, all the pride, crueltie, and ambition of man, and covered it all over with these two narrow words, *Hic jacet!*"

All this is incontestably true and it is all significant as showing the sort of man it was who has as fair a claim as any other individual to be called the original founder of America. But it is not the whole truth. For one thing it does nothing to penetrate the mystery of why King James I had off Raleigh's head. It must be admitted that Jamy the Scot was a poor creature with an ingrained dislike of excellence in any form—did he not come close to hanging his best surviving poet, Ben Jonson, for giggling at the wrong time?—but even a nincompoop does not do murder without some reason, and in this case the King had an excellent one. He was afraid of the man.

Nor is this any cause for wonder if one takes into consideration the reputation Raleigh had among his contemporaries. Under Elizabeth his chief office had been that of Captain of the Guard, and under Elizabeth in London that meant pretty much what it meant under Al Capone in Chicago. It was no job for a lad who was either squeamish or slow. Almost to the end of the reign, London swarmed with characters who would have slit the ancient virgin's throat, not merely cheerfully, but with pious exultation. Politics and religion were still almost identical, and removal of a leader of the opposition, even by steel or lead, was regarded by many as not only good partisanship, but also as an act of piety.

Yet in this turbulent capital Elizabeth reigned for forty-five years and never was touched. The idea that this was due exclusively to the loyalty of her people is nonsense; most of them were loyal, certainly, but there were plenty who were anything else, and if none of them ever reached her it was because what, in Chicago, she would have called her boys and the rest of the world would have called her hoods, were very much on the job. For years the chief gorilla was this same Walter Raleigh and he was excellent.

A stocky, black-browed individual, with massive shoulders and a powerful sword-arm, Raleigh * had come up the hard way. Lacking both wealth and family influence, he had cut his way to prominence, first as a mercenary with the Huguenot armies in France, and then in alliance with his half-brother, Sir Humphrey Gilbert, in raids upon Spanish commerce which to-day would be called piratical, but passed then by the name of buccaneering. In those days every great nobleman at every European court maintained a stable of bravoes for his own protection, and they were usually on the look-out for fresh talent. Raleigh attracted the attention of the Earl of Leicester, who brought him under the eye of the Queen; and he soon won a reputation as being the ideal choice for any spot that was too hot for an ordinary desperado.

He was sent into Ireland, at that time an even bloodier welter than China was in 1948, or Chicago during Prohibition. The law in Ireland was a mockery; the country was ruled—or devastated—by rival gangs that made their own law when they could. Whatever gang was hardest pressed at any specified time usually made loud protestations of fealty to the English Crown and frequently received assistance from London; which made the strongest of the other gangs, of course, the champion of Irish liberty. Raleigh went over to support the Butlers, at the moment noisily loyal to the Queen, against the Fitzgeralds, and proved so appallingly efficient that he not only liquidated the Geraldine influence, but nearly depopulated Munster,

---

* He usually, but not always, spelled it Ralegh; but in Elizabeth's day people were very broad-minded about the spelling of their own names. Sir Walter probably would not have objected to Raleigh, and since that is the spelling consistently followed in modern times, it is used here.

scene of the fighting. Incidentally, he made some amends by introducing the potato into Ireland.

Raleigh came back to England with a reputation in some ways much like that possessed by the New York gunman, Dutch Schultz, in his hey-day. He was so tough that he had scared the toughest spot in the realm into temporary quiet; he was the obvious choice for Captain of the Guard. However, he was a great deal more than merely a thick-witted brawler. He was as crafty as he was ruthless. In London he had swarms of enemies who could not be disposed of by strong-arm methods and against these he employed an immense talent for intrigue that was as effective as knife or gun. That he contributed to the ruin of half a dozen great nobles is beyond question, and that he brought down the lordliest of them all, Essex, the Queen's favorite, was generally assumed in London.

Elizabeth, the Queen, was a hard case, so hard that she had no doubt of her ability to handle even as formidable a servant as Raleigh, and she kept him by her constantly, except when he piqued her vanity by carrying on an affair with a lady-in-waiting, whereupon she instantly kicked him out and kept him out for four years. But James had none of the great Queen's superb courage. It is easy to believe that he never thought of Raleigh without shivering, so there is really no mystery in the fact that he seized upon a trumped-up charge to send this dangerous man to the Tower and, after long hesitation, to the scaffold. It is the most natural thing imaginable for a cowardly man in a position of authority, to do to a bold one of whom he is afraid.

Indeed, one may wonder whether it was, in fact, the trumped-up charge that historians have described. True, no convincing evidence was produced to show that Raleigh actually conspired to dethrone the King in favor of Arabella Stuart, but there is not much doubt that he would have liked to do it. Who wouldn't? James was a contemptible King, and to a man of Raleigh's extraordinary courage and intelligence his presence on the throne must have been doubly hard to bear. There is a strong possibility that he was guilty as charged; but, in morals if not in law, that is little to his discredit.

Here, though, was the mud that was covered by the velvet cloak. It is necessary to recognize its existence if one is to attain any comprehension of the forces that achieved the first settlement of America. The typical Elizabethan was a whole man, and we are such highly specialized creatures today that it is difficult for us not merely to comprehend a whole man, but to believe that one existed. Among us a poet is a poet, and not a swordsman, too. We have an idea that if he can sing,

> Even such is time, that takes in trust
>   Our youth, our joys, our all we have,
> And pays us but with earth and dust;
>   Who, in the dark and silent grave,
> When we have wandered all our ways,
> Shuts up the story of our days;
> But from this earth, this grave, this dust,
> My God shall raise me up, I trust!

then he must be incapable of coolly arranging the assassination of an inconvenient rival. We find it hard to credit that a statesman whose far-reaching vision was capable of planning and setting in train schemes that were to result in imperial grandeur would enter just as heartily into schemes for seducing ladies-in-waiting. It is beyond our understanding how a scholar might be a sacker of cities, and a philosopher also a pirate.

But all this was quite common in the Elizabethan Age. Raleigh was far from unique. His sincere delight in discovering Edmund Spenser and introducing him to the world, paralleled by his equal delight in capturing a Spanish treasureship, were both comprehensible to his contemporaries, who expected a competent man to be equally deft with rapier, pen and voice, and who did not question the sharpness of the division between art and morals. The splendor of their accomplishments has blinded us to the difficulty and the harshness of those feats. But such factors were part of the way the pattern was set that the United States of America has followed, in many important details, from Elizabeth's day to ours.

3

For three hundred years the hereditary foe of England has been whatever power threatened to conquer and dominate the continent of Europe, but this attitude is not as old as the kingdom. It was being adopted, in fact, at the moment the first attempts at American colonization were being made. Prior to that time England herself had been one of the powers seeking continental dominance. Not until Bloody Mary lost Calais in 1558 did the island kingdom surrender that ambition and replace it with determination to rule the sea. Ambitious and ruthless men, Walter Raleigh among them, deprived of all hope of carving out duchies for themselves in France or the Low Countries began to think of such harvests as might be reaped upon the sea, and the age of the great navigators began.

Some of them were direct, uncomplicated souls, whose desires were simple and usually accomplished. Notable among this group were Francis Drake, Martin Frobisher, John Hawkins. The richest sea-borne traffic in existence at that time was Spain's with her New World colonies, and they went after it, straight after it without any side issues to trouble or divert them. They got it, too. True, the traffic was so immense that the toll they levied was, from Spain's standpoint, merely annoying, not ruinous; but at that they took enough to add materially to England's wealth.

Economists have sometimes questioned this, seeing that what the raiders brought in included little that could be eaten, worn or used as implements of the crafts. The chief booty consisted of gold and silver, with an occasional prize of pearls or precious stones. But at the moment English economy—and that of all Europe, indeed—was severely handicapped by the scarcity of a good circulating medium, so the flood of gold captured from the Spaniards enormously facilitated trade of all kinds. Anything that facilitates the production and distribution of goods results in an addition to a nation's wealth; so the sea-raiders' booty did in fact make England richer.

But Raleigh, Humphrey Gilbert, and a few others, although they accepted and applied the technique of Drake to a certain extent, were not content to restrict themselves to that sort of free-booting. Drake was satisfied to appropriate the Spaniards' valuables; the others perceived the advantage of appropriating the source of the Spaniards' valuables. This germ of an idea was the starting point of the British Empire, whose first extensive land holdings were in North America.

Spain, like modern Russia, was primarily a land power. Her naval strength was formidable, but not beyond challenge, as both the Dutch and the English demonstrated; but Spanish infantry was as good then as German infantry became three hundred years later. England could dispute control of the sea with Spain, and both Drake and Raleigh raided and sacked Spanish seaports; but to attempt to eject Spain from any territory large enough to permit extensive military operations would have been suicidal.

Spain, however, was over-extended, although she had seized only those parts of the New World that offered quickest returns on the investment, which meant the tropical and subtropical areas. Fields of cane and tobacco were already becoming as important as mines in the Spanish possessions, and Spanish manpower and Spanish energy were no more than adequate for the exploitation of those she held. She had therefore not spread further north than what is now southern Georgia.

The second European land power, France, was beginning to see the point, but France had been attracted to the extreme north by the rich fur trade that was developing along the St. Lawrence, where French traders were busy for forty years before the English made any important move. The second great sea power, Holland, had been attracted to the East, to India and the East Indies. The Dutch did, indeed, appropriate the best harbor in North America; they held Manhattan Island and the valley of the Hudson River by the time the English were well established in Virginia.

But between Staten Island and Georgia at the end of the sixteenth century was an imperial domain on which no European power—or, as they put it delicately in those days, "no Christian prince"—had any grip at all. This area the English determined to make their own. Raleigh had the coast surveyed from Florida as far as North Carolina in 1584, and it was the report of one of his agents, Arthur Barlow, that led to his repeated attempts to establish a settlement on Roanoke Island. It was the courtier in him that inspired him, with reference to Elizabeth's unmarried state, to call the whole area Virginia, land of the Virgin. A maker of parables might find interesting material in the fact that the original English name of the United States, although it might be mistaken for a tribute to the Holy Mother, was in fact a tribute to a red-headed virago, coarse in speech and dubious in morals.

Arthur Barlow was presumably a good navigator—or perhaps his co-pilot, Philip Amadus was—since the expedition escaped the perils of an uncharted and particularly treacherous coast; but one need not say that "presumably" he was a good press-agent. He was. The proof still exists in his report to Raleigh. He described this part of Virginia as the "goodliest land under the cope of heaven" and from that he worked up to real enthusiasm, setting a pattern for American real-estate salesmen which is followed to this day, and which has been rivalled, perhaps, but never excelled, not even in Florida or southern California.

It hooked the Captain of the Guard, definitely and permanently. Raleigh had taken a great deal of money from the Spaniards and he had picked up even more through his perquisites around the court. He was rich enough as far as cash was concerned, but to maintain his slippery position he needed more than cash, he needed prestige. Elizabeth was a really great executive in that while she never underestimated the value of a good sword, she knew that a good idea is potentially even more valuable. She liked to have around her such swaggering buckos as Drake, Leicester and Essex, but not for a moment did she rate the glamour boys more highly than poisonous William Cecil and his hunchback son. They were men of ideas, and if they seem today to be in the main rather vicious ideas, nevertheless they worked to the profit of the Queen and the realm.

It followed that a courtier who hoped to remain in favor for any length of time at that court had to do more than strut. Every favorite had to defend his position from two different but equally dangerous threats—on the one hand, the swords of rival adventurers, and, on the other, the craft of the Cecils. William Cecil, known to history as the first Earl of Burleigh, spent his life fostering in the Tudor monarchs their already strong appreciation of economic, as opposed to military, strength; and his son Robert, "the crook-backed earl" of Salisbury, maintained the family tradition.

Because Elizabeth was a Tudor, one of the world's hardest-headed families, it was not difficult to persuade her that a rich merchant was an addition to the power of the realm no less than an able soldier. She therefore accorded royal favor to Burleigh's efforts to stimulate trade, thereby making it a respectable endeavor to attempt to strengthen the economic resources of the realm. Even as gaudy a figure as Sir Walter

Raleigh, Captain of the Guard, realized that he would stand still higher in the Queen's favor if he found means to enrich the kingdom and spread its influence. An enterprise of that kind was not beneath the dignity of any man in England, if he aspired to stand high at court; so the greatest of the great lords engaged in it actively. It was, among other things, one way of meeting the dangerous rivalry of the Cecils.

It was Spain's misfortune at this time to be ruled by a family as stubborn as the Tudors, but far less realistic. Philip II was a Hapsburg, and in some respects a very great king, but one far removed from any realistic understanding of the world in which he lived. In fact, he was not much interested in it; his real interest was in the next world, for he was a religious fanatic of the most virulent type. In a vain effort to impose his dogma upon all Europe he dissipated what was perhaps the most prodigious inheritance that had fallen to an earthly monarch up to that time; for it is doubtful that the Roman Empire at its greatest extent, as Hadrian received it from Trajan, was such a treasure as that which Charles V passed on to his son.

Spain held by far the largest and richest part of the New World, so far as it had been explored. In precious metals alone the takings of Spain in Mexico and Peru were so tremendous that they affected profoundly the economy of all Europe by the swift expansion of a medium acceptable in international trade; yet the value of all the gold and silver was inconsiderable by comparison with the far greater potential value of the agricultural products of the region, especially sugar, coffee, chocolate and tobacco.

Spain thus had an immeasurable advantage over England in the New World at the end of the first century after Columbus' discovery. Nor is it true, as many North Americans think, that her colonists made little or no use of their preferred position. Colonial administration in Spanish America was vigorous and, in general, highly successful. In certain respects it was wiser and more enlightened than English colonial administration. Juan Pablos was printing books in Mexico City thirteen years before Walter Raleigh was born; and the universities of Mexico and of San Marcos, in Peru, had been flourishing thirty years before Raleigh made his first attempt to settle colonists in North America. The Spanish pattern was ineradicably stamped upon tropical and subtropical America before the English started.

Yet in all her vast domain Spain never succeeded in establishing a nation comparable to the United States in economic and political strength. She did not succeed in establishing nations that would develop into sturdy allies, such as England has in Canada, Australia, New Zealand and South Africa. The English pattern, therefore, was clearly superior, as far as economic and political considerations go; its cultural superiority may be debatable, but not the fact that it excelled in creating wealthy and powerful nations.

Many of the differences between the two are more superficial than we are accustomed to believe. For instance, as regards morals and ethics, there is little to choose between them. Each looked upon the practices of the other with horror; and each had good reason. Most Americans have heard only the English side of it. We know all about the savagery of the Conquistadores, who butchered part of the Indians and enslaved the rest. We know all about the fanaticism of those ignorant priests who burned the priceless books of the Mayans and Aztecs and introduced the bloody Inquisition. But we know little about the scholars and artists who were publishing books and establishing universities in Spanish America while what is now the United States was unbroken wilderness. We forget that if some Spanish priests were ignorant fanatics, there were others like the great Las Casas, who came nearer to being at once scholar, statesman and saint than did any Englishman who came to America.

Las Casas lived to the extraordinary age of ninety-two, and

at that he died twenty years before the English made any serious attempt at colonizing America. He perceived the evils of
Spanish administration and fought them for fifty years with a
boldness and intelligence rare among priests or statesmen of
any age, and with a foresight that put him literally centuries
ahead of his time. Philip II was strongly influenced by clerics,
but unfortunately not by clerics of this type; if he had listened
to Bartolomé Las Casas more and to men of smaller minds less,
Spanish culture might be dominant today from the Arctic Circle to Cape Horn.

In qualities of mind and character, with one apparently
slight exception, there was not much to choose between the
Spanish and the English explorers and colonists. They were
all alike, men of the sixteenth and seventeenth centuries, which
is to say, they were little troubled by nineteenth and twentieth
century notions of the sacredness of human life and the dignity
of the individual. Certainly all typical Renaissance men were
tremendous individualists; but they respected no individuality
except their own. What they respected in another man was his
sword-arm, if that term may be construed to some extent figuratively. Everyone around the English court respected Salisbury, although on account of his deformity he could not have
been a great swordsman. But he was deadly without a sword.
People who came into collision with "the crook-backed earl"
commonly lived short lives; and the fact that more of them were
finished by the headsman's ax than by the rapier did not reduce the mortality.

The point is that both the Spanish and the English—and, for
that matter, the French, Dutch and Swedes as well—who came
to this country first were pretty consistent upholders of the
theory that might makes right. The way they dealt with the
savages and sometimes with their fellow-colonists appalls a man
of the twentieth century; and he will never understand them

until he realizes that they did what seemed right in their own eyes. The butchery of the Indians through treachery, whether by Cortes in Mexico, by Pizarro in Peru, or by Sir Thomas Dale in Virginia, really did not ruffle the consciences of the butchers, nor those of their contemporaries with rare exceptions, such as men of Las Casas' type.

The conspicuous difference between the two patterns was not intellectual, moral, or ethical. It goes back beyond the colonists. It was one facet of the character of the rising empire. The court of England granted a dignity to work (one may no longer employ the term "labor" because to most of us that now connotes artisans and craftsmen only) that was never accorded it at the court of Philip of Spain. Hereditary aristocracy exploited both countries ruthlessly; but the great merchants of London attained a dignity and an influence, under Henry VIII and Elizabeth, never matched by the equally great merchants of Amsterdam, whose sovereign was Philip. As for bold navigators, Elizabeth held them in an esteem that scandalized her more conservative fellow-monarchs. For a great sea-captain to be knighted was almost a matter of course in England; which made it quite correct for men of birth to go to sea and even engage in foreign trade. In the frail, small ships of those days any emergency meant that all hands must bend their backs to severe manual labor to save the ship; and in such cases a gentleman, or even a nobleman, did not debase himself if he hauled on a rope with the common sailors. Even commerce, in the turbulent ports and on the pirate-infested seas could not be conducted successfully by gentry too dainty to risk blisters on their hands. But a successful English trader was not debarred from high dignities by the fact that he had lived a rough life in order to wrest a fortune from the Spaniards or the heathen.

At Jamestown, in a period of emergency, Captain John Smith drove gentlemen by threats and violence, to labor in the fields.

That was a little extreme, even for England; but since it was plainly necessary for the common safety, Smith was sustained by public opinion. The rights of gentlemen were not unimportant in English eyes, but they were less important than the success of the enterprise; if that success were dependent upon labor, then labor must be done, and no English gentleman lost caste by doing it. On the contrary, he lost caste—and under a leader as tough as John Smith, he would have lost his life—by refusing to do it.

Thus the English pattern included from the very beginning the idea of the creation of values, which is accomplished only by the application of labor to raw materials, whereas the Spanish looked rather to values already existing. It was the difference between the development and the exploitation of a new region. Even where the Spanish developed agriculture and mining, they did it by exploiting the labor of the native population. Exploitation was more rapidly successful, as is evidenced by the fact that Spain won enormous wealth from the New World before England started; but development lasts longer and is more profitable in the end.

It was not a question of energy. The Spaniards performed prodigies of hard physical labor in connection with their military campaigns. Their exploits, indeed, would be incredible to this generation were they not attested by unquestionable records, including geography itself. But the English colonist lost nothing by working with his own hands at any sort of useful task, while the Spaniard was looked at a little askance if he could not contrive to have his menial work done by slaves, or at least by his social inferiors.

To contemporaries this difference was so unimportant that many of them were hardly aware of its existence; but the fact that the dignity of labor was established from the very beginning in the territory that became the United States of America is certainly one of the basic factors in the creation of the republic as it exists today.*

4

Yet the phrase "the dignity of labor" used in this connection may be very misleading. It meant only that an Englishman of the upper classes could engage in economically productive activity with much less risk to his social position than a Spaniard would have incurred by doing the same thing. As yet nobody in England, with the exception of a handful of poets, philosophers, and other odd fish, had developed the idea that a man may be dignified by labor. To be sure, "Piers Plowman" was already more than two hundred years old and it was a common fashion among writers to speak glowingly of the worth of the honest husbandman; but the notion that the workman, as a worker, has rights that a gentleman is bound to respect was still in the formative stage. As a tenant, an appanage of the land, he had rights recognized and carefully defined by the law; and as a guildsman in the towns he might have rights, extorted from the rulers by the collective strength of the guilds. But merely as an individual worker, endowed with nothing but his hands and his muscular strength, he was so far from having rights that the burden was upon him to show cause why he should be permitted to clutter up the world.

At the beginning of the seventeenth century England was suffering from what the authorities considered over-population. It was, in fact, the effect of a disastrous land policy, the so-called "enclosures" whereby immense tracts were expropriated by great proprietors and the people driven from the fields to

---

* Two hundred years later this part of the pattern was temporarily erased and certain forms of labor degraded in one section of the country, the Southern States in which Negro slavery had become concentrated. The erasure endured only for a matter of fifty years, but that section is still feeling the effects in a lower economic level than that of the rest of the country.

huddle in the towns or to wander about begging. At the time, however, these precursors of the American "Okies" of three hundred years later were regarded as responsible for their own condition and the problem of government was, quite simply, to get rid of them. The mercantilist theory, which regarded the nation's working force as an asset to be conserved, was still half a century ahead. The Parliament of 1572, enacting the famous statute lawyers refer to as "39 Eliz. c.4," had not the dimmest notion that government is under any obligation to care for rogues and vagabonds. On the contrary, it empowered justices of the peace at quarter sessions to banish them out of the realm, "Yf any of the said Rogues shall appeare to be dangerous to the inferior sorte of People where they shalbe taken, or otherwyse be such as will not be reformed of their rogish kinde of lyfe." As to what might happen to them after banishment, Parliament was serenely indifferent.

So to expend them upon the development of a new country seemed to the men of Elizabeth's time both reasonable and right. If the process resulted in sending them to death with great speed, they were no loss, for their removal lessened the pressure upon the food supply at home. It was two hundred years later that Thomas Robert Malthus elaborated this into a philosophical system, but they had grasped the idea in 1572, and they acted upon it. Our generation has been much entertained by the law's careful enumeration of the classes that Parliament thought England could well spare. They included:

All persons calling themselves Schollers going about begging, all Seafaring men pretending losses of their Shippes or goods on the sea going about the Country begging, all idle persons going about in any Cuntry eyther begging or using any subtile Crafte or unlawful Games or Playes, or fayning themselves to have knowledge in Phisiognomye Palmestry or other like crafty Scyence, or pretending that they can tell Destenyes Fortunes or such other like fantasticall Imagynacons; all persons that be or utter themselves to be Proctors Procurers Patent Gatherers or Collectors for Gaoles Prisons or Hospitalls; all Fencers Bearewards comon Players of Enterludes and Minstrells wandring abroade (other then Players of Enterludes belonging to any Baron of this Realme . . .); all Juglers Tynkers Pedlers and Petty Chapmen wandring abroade; all wandring persons and comon Labourers being persons able in bodye using loytering and refusing to worcke for such reasonable wages as is taxed or comonly given in such Parts where such persons do or shall happen to dwell or abide, not having lyving otherwyse to maynteyne themselves; all persons delivered out of Gaoles that begg for their Fees, or otherwise do travayle begging; all such persons as shall wander abroade begging pretending losses by Fyre or otherwise; and all such persons not being Fellons wandering and pretending themselves to be Egipcyans, or wandering in the Habite Forme or Attyre of counterfayte Egipcians.*

With slight modifications, largely in spelling and pronunciation, this statute remained the basic law of England for a matter of two hundred years, and under its provisions a large number of the first English settlers in America were bundled into this country very much against their wishes. One may reasonably describe it as a sort of selective service by contrary, an effort to select the unfit and undesirable; and the death rate among those selected is evidence that in that respect it worked.

The death rate, however, is not to be ascribed solely to the poor physical condition of the immigrants. It was a deadly country, even for the able-bodied. The very first colonists in the first successful English settlement in America were not guttersnipes rounded up by the police, but hardy adventurers. These were the one hundred and eight men brought by Christopher Newport to Jamestown in 1607. Newport was a bold and successful sea-captain with long experience of adventuring in remote places. On this voyage he had the assistance of the celebrated John Smith, a soldier of fortune also of long experi-

* This is the wording as given by A. E. Smith in *Colonists in Bondage* and was taken by him from Ribton-Turner's *History of Vagrants and Vagrancy*.

ence. Such men unquestionably would weed out the more obviously unfit before undertaking a project so hazardous; hence it may reasonably be assumed that the original hundred and eight were, or at least appeared to be, sturdy fellows capable of enduring hardships of some severity.

Yet Virginia mowed them down. Newport landed his colonists in April and hung around until they had erected habitable shelters and had planted food crops. He sailed for England on June 22, and later Captain John Smith wrote, "God (being angry with us) plagued us with such famine and sickness that the living were scarce able to bury the dead—our want of sufficient and good victuals, with continual watching, four or five each night at three bulwarks, being the chief cause. . . . About the 10th of September there were about forty-six of our men dead." A mortality rate of forty-two and a half per cent in less than ninety days, and that among picked men, was savage indeed. It is to be noted that the forty-six died of "natural" causes, for the Indians, up to this time, were disposed to be friendly, so friendly that they repeatedly came to the relief of the colonists with food.

Captain John Smith was no biometrician. All that interested him about a dead man was his utter uselessness, and as for the instrumentality that removed him, why, the wrath of God was explanation enough. The pious Captain did not inquire further. From other sources, however, we learn that a little later and therefore probably in 1607 also, the four chief avenues to death among the colonists—excluding the homicidal attentions of the Indians—were chills and fever, the bloody flux, consumption and the dry gripes, which medical men identify as malaria, dysentery, tuberculosis and lead poisoning. Smith does mention one other cause of death. For a time, the only food plentiful in Jamestown was fish from the river, particularly sturgeon, "whereon our men would so greedily surfeit as it cost many lives," which suggests ptomaine poisoning, since there is nothing the matter with sturgeon as a food as long as it is kept in good condition.

One of these deadly agencies, "the dry gripes," is not attributable to the colonists' hardships in the New World, but to commercial greed in their native land. The prevalence of lead poisoning throughout Europe at this period had led to investigation and legislation in many lands. It was due to the habit of brewers and vintners of using lead carbonate (white lead) and lead acetate (sugar of lead) as a preservative in beer and wine. In the hold of a small ship on a long voyage such beverages were unusually difficult to preserve in good condition, so it would be natural for the shippers to give them an unusually large load of the deadly preservative. In any event, the malady was prevalent and lethal not in Virginia only, but in the West Indies and other English colonies as well.

But without the intervention of adulterators, the land itself would have taken a heavy toll. To a modern American it seems odd to describe Virginia as a conspicuously savage region. Most people regard Virginia as rather the opposite—a conspicuously mild and hospitable land. In our schooldays we learned to regard the "stern and rock-bound coast" of New England as the really hard country and Virginia as the easy one; but a look at the death record is enough to show that the reverse was true. The significant figure is the rate, not the number of fatalities. In the first fifty years after the Jamestown settlement vastly greater numbers of people came to the Chesapeake Bay region than to New England, so it is the less significant that more English died in Virginia than came to New England in the early days. The significant fact is that of the Massachusetts settlers a majority survived, while in Virginia a very large majority died.

Yet the reason is not far to seek. The change of environment from England to Massachusetts was not nearly as violent as the change from England to Virginia. Furthermore, the travelers on the *Mayflower* had the benefit of what had been learned through nearly forty years' effort at settlement in Virginia, the last thirteen successful years. Finally, the Pilgrims and Puritans included a large proportion of religious fanatics already committed to an austerity of life that comported well with the inevitable austerity of life in a wilderness.

The Virginian country did become mild and hospitable, but not until after it had been subdued. The later immigrants to New England perhaps found the going rougher than the later immigrants to Virginia, but in the very earliest days the southern country was the more appalling, if only on account of the greater density of the forest. Modern Americans are likely to think of the forest as a pleasant and beautiful place, but that is because the forests we know are, as a rule, tamed and domesticated. But it was no such forest that Captain Newport's company met. It was the difference between a house-cat, purring by the hearth, and a Bengal tiger, sniffing around the tent in the darkness of a jungle night.

The forest of 1607 crowded down to the very water's edge and stretched westward for distances that were literally illimitable, for they went beyond the knowledge of any geographer on earth. The forest was dark, dismal, evil, itself a foe and the lurking-place of countless other foes of the settlers—savage beasts and far more savage men, venomous serpents, stinging insects, miasmas whose clammy touch was not figuratively but in sober truth the kiss of death. But the forest itself was enough, for, disregarding the perils it hid of fang and claw and tomahawk, the forest itself was a sleepless, relentless foe; its distances, its treacherous bogs, its thorns and thickets and falling timber, its fires started by lightning after long dry seasons, all were traps for the unwary, any of them capable of finishing the earthly career of a man fresh from the pavements of London.

From James Fenimore Cooper down American writers have

delighted to tell us how the white man learned the lore of the forest and, having learned it, lived in safety, health and relative comfort in its wildest depths. But we seldom stop to think that the first comers did not know it. There was no Deerslayer in Newport's group. Even as tough an adventurer as John Smith was hardened to the dangers of the Low Countries, the dangers of war against civilized men, which had little relation to this. Suppose he had learned, in many European campaigns, how to win to safety out of a flaming town, how to cut his way through a sudden flank attack, how to deal successfully with an Algerian corsair near the Gibraltar straits, or with a galleon on the Spanish Main, all his skill was of small avail against the forest.

It gave back slowly to a heavy frontal attack. To thrust into it only the little way required for a small patch of cultivated ground was heavy labor. The forest in eastern Virginia is dense today, especially along the banks of the tidal rivers, but it must have been far denser in 1607 when it had never been touched except for the inconsiderable clearings made by the Indians. Every contemporary writer who described the country mentioned the immense number of vines; most of them, writing as propagandists, stressed the profusion of wild grapes, but there were many other vines, thorny, tough and useless, that made the forests edging the streams all but impenetrable. Where the land rose slightly and the underbrush thinned out, the early settler's problem was little less formidable, for where the growth was less tangled it was far heavier.

The pines, in particular, were the admiration and despair of the first Englishmen in America. In 1607 it is probable that the long-leaf pine, the *Pinus palustris* of the botanists, extended into Virginia, although today it is rarely found above the North Carolina line. Until the introduction of the Douglas fir, generations later, this was the finest timber for masts and yards known to lumbermen. A clear stick of ninety feet was nothing unusual among these giants, which made them invaluable to shipyards; but a log delivered at Bristol was one thing, and a 120-foot tree lying across a settler's corn patch was quite another.

It must be remembered that the logging equipment of the settlers was crude in the extreme. Power-driven saws, of course, were non-existent, as were steel cables and tackle. Hemp rope was the stoutest rigging obtainable. The settler's principal tool was a clumsy ax, which he did not know how to use very well* and his next most important a badly shaped hoe. The result was that clearing an acre in 1607 required far more muscular exertion than it did two hundred years later. This labor had to be performed by men accustomed to and clothed for the cool English summer but working under the fierce pressure of a Virginia sun in July and August. The fact that they died rapidly under these conditions is no proof at all that they were weaklings. On the contrary, the fact that any survived is strong evidence that they were iron men to begin with.

5

Christopher Newport has never received the respectful attention that is his due from American historians, probably because his characteristic virtue is an unspectacular one. He was a reliable man, and it is one of the frailties of human nature that the reliable man soon comes to be taken for granted and ignored, if not forgotten.

Yet the reliability of Christopher Newport is one of the main reasons why this book is written in English about Englishmen, instead of in Spanish about Spaniards, in French about French-

---

* Really high skill in the use of the ax was first developed during the conquest of the American forest (paralleled, to some extent, by Australian woodsmen struggling with a similar problem). The curved hickory handle of the single-bitted ax, which contributes greatly to its use as a precision instrument, was an American invention. The axes of the first settlers lacked it, as they themselves lacked their successors' remarkable skill in using the tool.

men, or, perhaps, in Dutch about Netherlanders. It is not the
only reason, certainly, and the others are more entertaining,
therefore more frequently discussed and better known. The
statesmanly vision of Raleigh, the iron discipline of John Smith,
the piety of William Bradford, the ruggedness of Miles
Standish are qualities that are far more easily romanticized, and
writers who wish to be read are well advised to lean to the romantic. Captain Newport merely went where he was told to go
and got there reasonably close to schedule. There is no story
in that, and so he has all but faded out of American history.

Yet if the Jamestown colony had failed, as all the other English attempts at colonization had failed, the Pilgrims, in Holland, would have been much less likely to look with favor upon
a removal to America. If the Pilgrims had not come in 1620 it
is unlikely that the Calverts would have brought their Catholics
over in 1634; and the success of the Calverts undoubtedly encouraged Penn to bring his Quakers in 1681. The success of the
Jamestown colony set off a sort of chain reaction that peopled
the Atlantic coast with English from Georgia to Massachusetts.

But Jamestown succeeded because Captain Newport was a
reliable man. Having planted the first group in 1607, he was
back the next year with more people and fresh supplies. He
came again, bringing five hundred this time and arrived just
soon enough to prevent abandonment of the place. His luck
ran out on the third trip, for he was wrecked on the Bermudas
and delayed for nearly a year. He arrived to find his five hundred colonists reduced to sixty, but he arrived.

To understand the remarkable character of this record, com-
pare it with that of almost any of the other early navigators.
Raleigh lost the Roanoke colony, his most ambitious effort, by
the inability of his captains to go where they were sent and to
get there on time. Half a dozen other ventures were wrecked
the same way. Had he had a man like Christopher Newport in
his service, Walter Raleigh might loom today over the history

of the United States as Cortez does over that of Mexico. But Raleigh had no luck; he had already been in prison for three years when Newport sailed for the London Company, and he never emerged save for one brief and disastrous voyage to South America. Then Jamy the Scot struck off his head, partly, no doubt, to appease the Spanish but largely because the knightly knight made the unkingly king nervous.

By the time Newport sailed with his five hundred, the catch-polls of London and of every other great town in England were hard at work, rounding up "Rodgs and hors and such like people" for transportation. Whether they caught any "comon Players of Enterludes," or any "Minstrells wandring abroade," or any "counterfayte Egipcians" the records do not say. Charity impels one to hope that the answer is no, for it is not pleasant to think what the brutal forest would have done to actors, musicians and gypsies; but the presence of some may have added a touch of gaiety to an existence that was colorful enough, in all conscience, but that could not have had much suggestion of mirth.

Still, they made headway, despite the sullen opposition of the forest and the more dangerous threat of their own inexperience and indiscipline. Sardonic old Robert Beverley, writing less than a century after the event, had all but forgotten the forest but still remembered keenly the follies of the settlers:

They found in a Neck of Land, on the Back of James-Town-Island, a fresh Stream of Water springing out of a small Bank, which wash'd down with it a yellow sort of Dust-Isinglass, which being cleansed by the fresh streaming of the Water, lay shining on the Bottom of that limpid Element, and stirr'd up in them an unseasonable and inordinate Desire after Riches: For they, taking all to be Gold that glister'd run into the utmost Distraction, neglecting both the necessary Defence of their Lives from the Indians, and the Support of their Bodies by securing of Provisions; absolutely relying, like Midas, upon the Almighty Power of Gold, thinking, that where this was in plenty nothing could be wanting: But they soon grew sensible of their Error; and found that if this gilded Dirt had been real Gold, it could have been of no Advantage to them. For, by their Negligence, they were reduced to an exceeding Scarcity of Provisions, and that little they had, was lost by the Burning of their Town, while all Hands were employ'd upon this imaginary Golden Treasure; so that they were forced to live for sometime upon the wild Fruits of the Earth, and upon Crabs, Muscles, and such like, not having a Day's Provision before-hand; as some of the laziest Indians, who have no Pleasure in Exercise, and won't be at the Pains to fish and hunt.*

More than once the colony was all but destroyed by such idiocies and it was saved from its own folly, in the first instance, by roaring old John Smith, who may have been a swashbuckler and a liar, as later historians have pretty well proved, but who must have had a basilisk glare; for he swore roundly that any fine gentleman who refused to work in the cornfields, whether to dig "gold" or for any other reason, should not eat out of the common store. He meant it, and they knew he meant it; furthermore, they believed he was man enough to make his words good. So they worked and the corn flourished.

Here was another figure in the pattern set by the English in America. John Smith traced it first and the even more ferocious Sir Thomas Dale strengthened it later; but it was actually imposed upon the Virginians less by any man's edict than by the conditions of life in the colony. Smith and Dale simply had the intelligence to see what was required and the courage to do it; but they, and the public opinion that backed them, did establish it as a principle of the English colonies that no man has a natural right to a place in America. He must make his own place. If he is no earthly good to the community, the commu-

---

* This passage is from *The History and Present State of Virginia*, by R.B., first published in 1705, but strangely neglected thereafter, possibly because R.B. (Robert Beverley) spoke his mind about the gentry and commoners of early Virginia with a frankness ill suited to propaganda. I have followed the text of a new edition edited by Louis B. Wright and published in 1947 by the University of North Carolina Press for the Institute of Early American History and Culture at Williamsburg, Va.

nity is under no obligation to support him, regardless of his rank and lineage. Here, perhaps, is the primal source of that "rugged individualism" so beloved of President Hoover more than three centuries later.

They made headway. They crept up the great River James to the falls where the city of Richmond stands now; and a little below it they established an outpost that they called Henrico. They went down to its mouth, where it debouches into the vast anchorage that could hold the fleets even of the modern world, now known as Hampton Roads; and on its northern side, on the point where a watcher once first descried his ships coming in with the supplies that meant salvation for the colony, Captain Newport laid out an estate for himself. It is still concerned with ships, but now they go out instead of coming in, for it is the location of the great ship-building yards of Newport News.

They made way against great odds, and eventually the amenities of life began to appear. Beverley has a note on the subject that might be misconstrued as alleging a biological miracle. It reads:

Anno 1609, John Laydon and Anna Burrows were marry'd together, the first Christian Marriage in that Part of the World: and the Year following the Plantation was increased to near Five Hundred Men.

Death mowed them down, but others hit the beach, strode over their graves and carried on the attack. The forest fell back, the Indians fell back, the cornfields extended farther and farther, up and down the rivers. Jamestown was no longer an outpost, it was a center to which many scattered "hundreds" looked. The "Dust-Isinglass" had been a delusion, but the ingenious Mr. Rolfe found a way to turn the tobacco plant into gold, and the colony began to load ships with cargoes that on the docks of London were worth many times the cost of their carriage across the sea.

Still, it was touch and go for a long time. Ten years after the first landing, says Beverley, "Capt. Samuel Argall was sent thither Governour, *Anno* 1617, who found the Number of People reduc'd to something more than Four Hundred, of which not above Half were fit for Labour." But shortly thereafter Lord Delawarr, as Beverley calls him, started with two hundred more; and although thirty, including his lordship, died on the voyage, the colony was reinforced, and thereafter it was never in grave danger of extinction, not even in the great Indian massacre of 1622, when the Indian emperor Opechancanough butchered more than three hundred English in a single day.

6

So the thing was done, and thereafter the grip of the English upon the North American continent never slipped. The Swedes, the Dutch and the French were all to try to break that grip, but only the French came within striking distance of success some hundred and fifty years after the Jamestown settlement.

The price, as measured in blood and suffering, is beyond computation. Even statistically, it cannot be computed, for nobody took care to preserve the figures. Smith, by rummaging through mountains of ancient documents in the archives of the London Company and the British government, has contrived to account* for 17,740 felons dumped into Virginia after 1718, and he knows that he didn't get them all. For the century prior to 1718 the records are too fragmentary to supply the basis even for an intelligent guess. But there is no doubt whatever that the numbers were large, and there is little doubt in Smith's mind that the great majority of them died speedily.

This is one item in the cost of creating what is now the

* In *Colonists in Bondage,* the book referred to earlier. See Chapters V and VI.

United States of America, and to a twentieth century mind it is sufficiently horrifying. But we shall have a distorted idea of history if we give to seventeenth-century transactions a twentieth-century significance. An Englishman of 1619 would have been honestly puzzled by our horror; to his way of thinking, this item in the account represented no cost at all. The death of Lord de la Warr he would have admitted as an item on the debit side; even John Smith's forty-six adventurers he might have entered in red ink on his ledger. But the felons had each been convicted of some one of the three hundred crimes punishable by death in England—stealing anything above the value of a shilling was one—therefore their lives were already forfeit. Whether they died on a gallows on Tyburn hill, or in a Virginia cornfield was an unimportant detail.

As for the rogues and vagabonds, they were regarded in the seventeenth century as utterly useless. Their absence meant so many fewer mouths to feed from a dwindling English food supply, and to that extent their absence was a positive gain. To exterminate them by malaria and "dry gripes" might be rather rough treatment, but certainly meant no loss to England. Hence it was not of much importance to keep a record even of the number sent to death in America; all that was of importance was that they should do something toward advancing the work before they died. This they did; so the cost of the job was, in the estimation of the seventeenth century, nothing at all as far as this item was concerned.

One phase of the conquest of the continent merged into another by imperceptible degrees, so any date for the end of one and the beginning of the next must be selected more or less arbitrarily; but, subject to this reservation, it may be argued plausibly that 1619 marks the firm establishment of the beachhead and the start of the main invasion.

Two events of this year serve as convenient mileposts marking the passage from one era to another. One was the assembling of the House of Burgesses at Jamestown, the first American legislature elected on the representative system. This was a tremendously important figure in the pattern the English set for America, yet, like many of the most revolutionary ideas the English have introduced into statecraft, nobody seems to have regarded it as extraordinary at the time. It seemed merely the sensible thing to do, so they went ahead and did it.

The "hundreds" by that time were scattered up and down the river for a matter of a hundred and fifty miles—a formidable distance, considering the means of transportation and communication available. Jamestown could not possibly have any very clear idea of what was going on at Henrico, still less could Henrico keep up with events at Kiquotan, at the river's mouth. Everyone was working more or less in the dark. Everyone was new to the country and to the job, including the Governor and his council. Hardly a day passed without the discovery that some method or procedure that served well enough in England wouldn't work at all in the new country and must be replaced by something adapted to local conditions, of soil, of climate, of geography, or of Indian relations.

The word "must" is used advisedly. In very many cases it was not simply that new ideas and new methods were preferable to old ones; the new had to be adopted on pain of death, by disease, by starvation, or by violence. When changes are proposed merely because they seem likely to produce some betterment of conditions men may debate long and carefully before adopting them and, as a rule, will not act until carefully reasoned arguments are produced to support the change. But when the decree is simply, "change or die," nobody has to work out a philosophical system to justify changing.

The Governor and his council were confronted with that decree. The system of government to which they were accustomed and which they had brought over from England would not work in the new country without radical modification. More than that, they were aware that in certain cases, and rather frequent ones, they were allowed just one trial; they had to make a change, and it had to be the right change the first time; for if they did the wrong thing, somebody would die, and it might very easily be the Governor and his council. In short, they needed all the help they could get to insure the survival of the colony.

The only rational procedure in the circumstances was the procedure they adopted. They called upon each hundred to pick out two of its most sensible men and send them to Jamestown to consult with the Governor and council on what sort of rules and regulations should be applied to all the scattered settlements to effect the safety of them all. It is unlikely that any theories as to the Rights of Man or even as to the ancient liberties of the English had much to do with it. As a President of the United States remarked centuries later, they faced a condition, not a theory, and for the protection of their lives they had to act, to act promptly, and to act sensibly the first time.

They realized that the sum total of the brains and character in all Virginia was none too great for the task in hand; and they summoned to their aid all the brains and character that could be found, regardless of the identities of the persons in possession of these qualities. So they laid the mudsill of the democratic system, if not exactly inadvertently, yet without giving much thought, in all probability, to whether it was democratic, aristocratic, oligarchic, or what not. They weren't evolving political principles; they merely wished to keep on living, and this was obviously the best way to accomplish that purpose. Nevertheless, representative government was planted in America when that first House of Burgesses assembled in August, 1619, and the plant continued to grow in spite of all subsequent efforts to uproot it. The pattern was set, and no one has since been able to change it.

In that same month another event of tremendous future significance occurred without arousing more than passing notice among the colonists. Even to Beverley, eighty-six years later, it did not seem particularly important and he gave it only a line or two:

In August a Dutch Man of War landed Twenty Negroes for Sale; which were the First of that kind that were carried into the Country.

No other contemporary writer has identified that vessel any more precisely. Why should they? It was to be more than two hundred years before that second planting in the soil of Virginia was to bear its bloody fruit; but there are few more dramatic episodes in history than this simultaneous planting of democracy and chattel slavery in American soil. Involuntary servitude was, of course, familiar enough to Virginians; was not the land swarming with rogues and vagabonds transported from England and bound to service for a term of years? But chattel slavery was something else. Bonds and indentures soon fell away, destroyed by the progress of civilization; but this evil growth flourished and came nearer to destroying the nation than did any foreign foe who assailed it from without.

So although the colonists were not interested enough to write it down, later generations find a terrific fascination in this voyage of the Nameless Ship. It is a temptation to abandon history and resort to legends of the sea, to identify her with that fearful apparition whose appearance always brought disaster, peril and endless woe to the luckless seamen who met her. Doubtless it was not the accursed Captain Vanderdecken who turned his prow up the James River that midsummer in 1619, and doubtless his ship was not the Flying Dutchman; but by the ruin and sorrow she brought to America she might have been.

Chapter II

❈

THE INDISPENSABLES

1

The London Company was a business outfit.

This is one of the basic facts that must be kept constantly in mind if one is to attain any adequate comprehension of the way the pattern was set for the development of this country.

The nobility and gentry who put their money into it may have had high politics in mind, but not the merchants who supplied the bulk of the funds. Their motive was frankly profit, and if they had not seen a chance for an excellent return on the investment they would not have gone into the venture. When profits were slow in materializing—the thing was in the red for seventeen years—they got out; but by that time the colony was so well established that the Crown was unwilling to see it collapse so in 1624 the King assumed complete governmental authority.

Nevertheless, the idea that it was incumbent upon Virginia to show a profit was not eliminated; on the contrary, it affected the thinking of both England and America throughout the colonial period, and it is not difficult to perceive traces of it in the American way of life to this day.

Idealists are given to denouncing the profit motive as the basis of a civilization because it fosters greed and ruthlessness, but they commonly fail to consider its great merit as a deterrent of certain forms of bigotry. If a man's dominant motive is to make a profit, he cannot afford to indulge in fanaticism, religious, political, or social. He must maintain a supple mind, for if one method proves unprofitable he must be able to find and adopt another. The fact that the London Company was out for a profit may have induced a certain sordidness in its dealings, but at the same time the same factor made it extremely hospitable—that is, for the seventeenth century—to willing workers, regardless of their creeds, their nationalities, or even their police records.

Fifty years ago this might have seemed to be damning the Company with faint praise, but the twentieth century has only too much reason to know that it is not faint. Fanaticism, especially political and economic fanaticism, has all but drowned this century in blood as it all but drowned the seventeenth. Today, as in the years after 1618, when the Thirty Years' War began, any authority, even a commercial company, that will accept and protect a man on the basis of his will and ability to work hard and keep the peace, regardless of the rite by which he chooses to worship, or of his racial origin, or of his economic theories, is regarded as highly enlightened—more enlightened than the government of the United States, which not only has its domestic "minority problems" but makes great difficulty about accepting any man born on foreign soil and will not accept one who holds certain political and economic opinions, any more than seventeenth-century Spain would accept a Jew or a Protestant into first-class citizenship.

As a matter of fact, Jews came to Virginia at a very early date, possibly with John Smith, certainly within a few years after 1607. The very fact that we cannot fix the date precisely is itself significant; it shows that anti-Semitism was at so low an ebb among the colonists that none of the contemporary chroniclers noticed the arrival of the first Jews. They were simply additional settlers and counted as one each, just as did settlers of other faiths. Most of the early arrivals seem to have come from

Portugal or Spain, and presumably were counted as Portuguese or Spaniards when they were listed separately at all.

Of course the tolerance of the Virginia Company was relative. It was tolerant for the seventeenth century, not for the twentieth, as far as religion was concerned; and there were lapses, as during the governorship of Samuel Argall, who imposed belief in the Trinity upon the colonists under penalty of the law. But Argall lasted only two years, and in the main the idea prevailed in Virginia that if a man could contribute skill and energy to the community, it was unwise to inquire too closely into his opinions as long as they did not lead to breaches of the peace.

Skill, especially, was needed by the company if the colony were ever to be erected into a profit-making enterprise—almost any kind of skill, but above all skill in the mechanic arts. The problem of the settlers was to feed, clothe and shelter themselves as rapidly as possible and as far as possible with the materials available in the new country. Naturally, a carpenter, a blacksmith, a wheelwright, a cooper was immensely valuable. The skill of "juglers, bearewardes and minstrells" may have been of no great value in such a community, but a tailor was worth more than a philosopher. In general, the idea was established that a man who could do anything socially useful earned, by the exercise of his skill, an unquestionable place in America. That became part of the pattern that the English imposed upon the new country, and is part of its English heritage even down to our own times.

But among the rapscallions picked up by the police, skilled men were uncommon in the seventeenth century as they are today. It has always been, as it still is, the unskilled and incompetent who are most likely to fall afoul of the law. The Company could use common laborers, to be sure, but it could use craftsmen much more profitably; therefore it could not be content with recruiting the population of the jails to fill its colony.

This led to vigorous and persistent efforts to recruit colonists of a more desirable type than those sentenced by the courts to transportation. Some of those efforts unquestionably were dubious in both law and morals, but it is by no means proved that the agents of the London Company were any more careless with the truth than is customary among men engaged in their occupation; after all, promoters of real estate booms have never been conspicuous for their exact adherence to scientific fact.

In any event, they were notably successful among the class to whom they made their principal appeal, the class of the poor but ambitious. They were aided immensely by the work of two of the ablest press-agents of the seventeenth century—all the more effective because they worked for something other than money —Captain John Smith and Thomas West, Baron de la Warr.

John Smith wrote, it must be admitted, like a man whose primary interest was the enhancement of the reputation of John Smith, but that did not lessen the value of his work * to the Company, for the more valuable he could make the new realm the more important became his services in helping establish it. In any event he did all that lay within him to present the country in a favorable light; and because he was a fine romancer his tale enchanted readers and stimulated the desire to go and see this marvelous land. Smith sent the *True Relation,* his first

---

* The full title of his first effort was *A True Relation of Such Occurrences and Accidents of Noate as Hath Hapned in Virginia since the First Planting of That Collony.* Modern historians have cut that down to *True Relation,* but it remains one of the most important sources for the history of the period. John Smith continued to write voluminously and in 1624 summed up much of his earlier work in *The Generall Historie of Virginia, New-England, and the Summer Isles;* he also turned out maps of Virginia and New England which were surprisingly accurate and proved invaluable, especially to the Pilgrims when they undertook their adventure in Massachusetts. He wrote an autobiography which historians are inclined to regard sniffishly as being largely a pack of lies (it includes the famous story of how the Indian princess Pocahontas saved his life by throwing herself upon him as the executioners were about to brain him), but if that is the case none can deny that they are colorful, indeed, gaudy lies. John Smith may have been the American Munchausen, but that did not prevent him from being a fine propagandist for America and an ornament and delight of his age.

book, from Jamestown to London in 1609 and it was published that same year, preceding by some twelve months Jourdain's account of Sir George Somers' shipwreck on Bermuda, which critics believe suggested the plot of *The Tempest* to William Shakespeare. Possibly Smith had the same distinguished reader, for everything pertaining to the new world was widely popular.

Thomas West, the other highly effective propagandist, was a man of a very different type. He was an earnest soul, with no need to blow his own horn, for he was of noble birth; but he perceived in Virginia not only potential wealth beyond measure, but also a mighty empire. His book coming two years after Smith's (1611) bore the rather formidable title of *The Relation of the Right Honourable the Lord De-la-Warre, Lord Governour and Captaine Generall of the Colonie, planted in Virginea*, but it was perhaps more effective than Smith's as it had the prestige of an official record, subscribed by a Baron of the Realm.

Delaware (to adopt the spelling in modern use and perpetuated in the name of the State) was a far less gorgeous personality than Sir Walter Raleigh, but he was a more attractive man. He had all the energy and the daring of the Captain of the Guard, but not his ruthlessness nor, it must be admitted, his genius. There is little evidence that he could have held his own among the wits of the Mermaid Tavern, nor did he write memorable verse; but he was honest and earnest, which is more than can be said of most of the wits. He was honest and earnest even in his propaganda, which undoubtedly redoubled its effectiveness. He was doubtless a visionary, but if he deceived anyone, the first person he deceived was himself.

Delaware lived only forty-one years. He died at sea on his way to bring additional settlers and supplies to the colonists; but his life was long enough to enable him to add his bit—and a distinctive bit—to the legacy that the English left to America. His contribution was the participation in the effort of a man of high birth and equally high ideals. He is to be bracketed with Cecil Calvert, also a baron, with William Penn, untitled, but the son of an admiral, son-in-law of a knight, and personal friend of the King, and with James Oglethorpe, younger son of a titled family. Serious-minded men, these all held that their wealth and rank should be made to serve the common welfare. Well-endowed idealists, they were the precursors of such American figures as Washington and Jefferson, the Roosevelts and the later generations of the Adams family. The idealistic nobleman in America was, of course, by no means exclusively an English type. Baron de Graffenried and Count Zinzindorf come to mind at once. But Delaware was the first of that particular type and through his writings a notably effective one.

With the assistance of such advocates, the London Company captured the imaginations of English artisans and laborers to an extraordinary degree. The merchant adventurers were themselves frankly business men, frankly animated by the profit motive. But they were shrewd enough to see, or soon to learn, that the profit motive in its crudest form would not secure for them the kind of people essential to the success of their enterprise. Talk of gold and pearls and precious stones might bring in the soldiers of fortune, the born gamblers and other rolling stones, whose idea of wealth was persistently involved with the idea of loot; but to the typical English farm hand or artisan such talk had not much meaning. It was pleasant and amusing, but it all sounded pretty much like fairy tales to hard-headed realists.

There was one article of value, however, which they understood perfectly as having a possible relation to their own lives. This was land. It must not be forgotten that the industrial revolution was not to begin in England for a century and a half. Even in the early seventeenth century there were such things as stocks and bonds and other evidences of indebtedness, but they were unrelated to the experience of the average man.

Money meant gold and silver, not pieces of paper, and the only real investment was in land and the improvements thereon.* A carpenter who could not possibly imagine himself as the possessor of pearls and diamonds could very easily imagine himself as the owner of his own shop in some thriving town, the master of many apprentices and a person of importance among his fellow-carpenters.

That would be wealth that really meant something, so to that form of acquisitiveness the Company made its strongest appeal. More than that, possession of land meant more than wealth in the eyes of the English lower classes. The carpenter who held his own shop, the farmer who owned his fields, as far as their experience went, was not to be browbeaten and pushed around by anyone. He was a free man. To the extent that popular suffrage existed at this time, the suffrage was universally linked to real estate. It was as a freeholder that a man counted in public affairs. The possession of land added to his dignity, as well as to his economic security.

Within a few years the Company was making a definite offer: in consideration of a certain number of years' service, to be guaranteed by a legally attested indenture, it would immediately pay the servant's passage to Virginia and at the end of his term would give him freehold of a certain number of acres— usually fifty, in the early years, although it varied somewhat from time to time and from colony to colony—subject only to a nominal quitrent paid to the Company, or, later, to the Crown.

It is hard for us to gain any conception of how alluring this proposition was to the people to whom it was made. Seven years' service—or even four years, as the term became later—for fifty acres of land seems a hard bargain and would be a hard

---

* Macaulay considers the invention of the government bond, some eighty-five years after Jamestown was established, as one of the great achievements of the reign of William III.

bargain in the twentieth century. But in the seventeenth this servitude was the road not merely to property, but to real independence, to true freedom.

Put that way, it takes on a different aspect. If men were convinced today that a certain form of slavery, endured for seven years, would bring them thereafter freedom and security it is hardly to be doubted that thousands, countless thousands, would enter into temporary bondage with joy and thankfulness.*

That was the way the London Company did it. It became the fashion, in later years, to regard this outfit as rather sordid and to rate it distinctly lower than those organizations that undertook colonization for religious or political motives. Yet the London Company's appeal to the human desire for freedom was direct and without reservation. The religious motive and the political motive may or may not be linked with respect for the principle of freedom; they may be, and they frequently were, linked with a fanatical determination, not to establish freedom but to establish domination, which is, of course, merely the substitution of one tyranny for another.

This is not to say that the London Company was a model of tolerance and fair dealing. It was not. After all, it was a creature of the seventeenth century, imbued with seventeenth-century ideals, among which tolerance and fair dealing were not conspicuous. But it did establish the belief that a man who works for it is entitled to freedom, which has since remained a part of the American pattern—more, perhaps, the pattern of ideas than the pattern of acts, but still there. It also transferred to this country the generally accepted European idea that freedom is a function of property. This is a part of the pattern that Americans have been trying to erase for many generations, but not as yet with unqualified success.

---

* This is, in fact, precisely what a volunteer soldier does when he enters the army at the outbreak of war.

2

As to the quality of the thousands, soon to grow into tens of thousands, of people brought over under indentures, our information has to be obtained by inference, rather than through specific documentation. After all that has been said about the relatively enlightened policy of the London Company, it is perhaps advisable to repeat that this was the seventeenth century, when the dignity of the individual was not yet commonly accepted. Contemporary writers recognized the immense importance of indentured servants as a labor force, and the Company perceived the wisdom of appealing to the love of liberty as a means of recruiting that force; but as individuals they were not important; so the records that survive usually refer to them in gross and not in detail.

However, it is clear enough that certain characteristics must have been common to the great majority, or they would never have come. It is obvious, for example, that the bulk of them must have been dissatisfied, simply because the prosperous and contented would have been insane to leave England. It is equally clear that the prime cause of their dissatisfaction must have been the prime cause of dissatisfaction at all times and in all countries, to wit, poverty. This, indeed, is no inference, for it is plainly asserted in many contemporary documents. It is self-evident, also, that the people who signed indentures must have been somewhat bolder and more energetic than the bulk of the population. Even if it was the bold energy of desperation, it had to be there, or they would have remained inert.

The typical indentured servant therefore must have been a poor man without much hope of bettering his condition in England; yet not so deeply sunk in misery as to be completely apathetic. That is to say, he was a cut above the convicts, the rogues and the vagabonds that the police propelled beyond the borders of the realm. He was without property, or influence, or prospects; but his manhood, at least, was intact.

Furthermore, he was not the brutish and abysmally ignorant serf of the Middle Ages. Literacy in Elizabethan England was much more widespread than many twentieth-century Americans realize; in fact, there is reason to believe that in, say, 1619, when the first House of Burgesses met, the literacy rate was greater in Virginia than it was a century later.

Education in the Middle Ages had been exclusively a function of the church, as the phrase "benefit of clergy" attests. The law assumed as a matter of course that anyone who could read was a cleric. Yet as early as 1432 England had at least one school not attached to any religious foundation and endowed by a business man—Sevenoaks, founded by a grocer. By the time Virginia was first settled secular schools were an old story in England, and the fact that they were not confined to the upper classes is best attested by their critics.* They were attacked as leveling influences destructive of the social system and subversive of law and order; which would not have been the case had education been restricted to the privileged classes.

As a matter of fact, the critics had no chance, for they were contending against a combination of two of the most powerful factors that influence the acts of men, profit and piety. Since the Flemish weavers discovered the merits of English wool, England had been developing more and more into a trading nation. The kingdom's greatness had steadily increased, not by successful wars, but by successful international trade, that is to

---

* An interesting example is in J. W. Adamson's modernization of *Peres the Ploughmans Crede*, quoted by Louis B. Wright in his *Middle-Class Culture in Elizabethan England*. It reads: "Now may every cobbler set his son to school, and every beggar's brat learn from the book, and become either a writer and dwell with a lord, or a false friar to serve the Devil. So that the beggar's brat becomes a bishop, to sit esteemed among the peers of the land, and lords' sons bow down to the good-for-nothing, knights bend to them and crouch full low, and this bishop's father a shoemaker, soiled with grease and his teeth as tattered as a saw with champing leather." This was written full two hundred years before the settlement at Jamestown.

say, trade conducted over long distances and considerable periods of time, which did not lend itself to the methods of simple barter, but involved the keeping of elaborate accounts and written records. It followed, therefore, that the merchant had not only to be fairly well educated himself, if he were to succeed, but that he needed large numbers of assistants, clerks, apprentices, supercargoes and factors, who were literate and well trained in arithmetic. Navigation required higher mathematics and navigators were in constantly increasing demand. Some schooling for large numbers of working people was essential to continued prosperity; which accounts for the fact that many of the guilds, notably the Mercers and the Merchant Tailors, established schools that became celebrated for their excellence, while for successful business men to do something for education in their wills became so common as to be almost a requirement of the age.

As early as 1577, that is to say, thirty years before Jamestown, William Harrison was writing,

There were a great number of Grammer schooles through out the realme, and those verie liberallie indued, for the better reliefe of poor scholers, so that there are not manie corporat townes now vnder the queenes dominion, that hain not one Gramar schoole at the least, with a sufficient liuing for a maister and vsher appointed to the same.*

In this the merchants were acting in their own economic interest, but their interest in education was reinforced by doctrinal considerations. The central idea of the Protestant Reformation was that of individual accountability to God. The Anglican Church accepted it, and the rising Puritan influence redoubled the emphasis upon it. It followed that if the individual could not shift his responsibility to priest or church, he must acquaint himself with the requirements of the divine law

* This, too, is quoted in Wright's book which, incidentally, is one of the best studies of the period now available.

which, in the Protestant view, were authoritatively stated in the Bible and nowhere else. Consequently a man's eternal salvation might well hang upon his ability to read the Scriptures, and to develop that ability, especially among the poor, became a work of piety of a high order of importance.

This accounts for the endowment of St. John's College at Oxford by Thomas White, a merchant tailor, and subsequent large gifts to that college by other members of White's guild. The emphasis at St. John's was upon theology. It was not intended to turn out book-keepers and commercial agents, as the grammar schools were, but theologians; but it was not inappropriate for it to be supported by members of the Merchant Taylors Company, for the merchants accepted without reservation John Brinsley's observation that,

there is indeed a place of euerlasting happinesse, and glorie prepared for all those, who in witnesse of their loue & thankfulnesse to Iesus Christ, and to their countries, shall employ their studies, and their wealth, to the greatest aduancement of all heauenly learning, and vnto the vertuous education of youth, the hope of succeeding ages.

In short, it was the sincere belief of the business men who composed the London Company—a belief undoubtedly accepted by the vast majority of their indentured servants—that education was the best assurance of a man's welfare in this world and the next. In Spain at the same period learning was still regarded, to a much larger extent, as a clerical prerogative. Certainly we have the word of Cervantes for it that the reading of romances in Spain was a popular diversion sometimes amounting to mania; but in Spain the Church relieved the communicant of the responsibility of reading the Bible for himself, and the merchants constituted a very tight caste, rarely irrupting into social groups either above or below their own.

The English attitude toward popular education was therefore distinctive, as far as America was concerned. It may have been shared by other North European countries, but not by France or Spain, England's chief competitors in the New World. It was therefore part of the pattern set by the English; and this is one figure in that pattern that has not faded in the slightest degree in the three hundred years that have followed.

Learning is handmaiden to both gain and godliness—that is a principle accepted and defended, firmly and even fiercely, by Americans in the twentieth century. The colossal endowments of private American colleges and universities attest its acceptance by the rich; and the even more prodigious plant and equipment of tax-supported schools, from pre-kindergarten to State University attest its acceptance by the poor.

The pattern was set in Virginia—not as is commonly asserted, in New England. As early as 1609, more than ten years before the Pilgrims embarked, the Virginians were making arrangements for a land grant to a "collidge" which was to be a public institution. It is true that it was a long time—not until 1693, in fact—before the College of William and Mary actually came into being and Harvard was then fifty-seven years old. It is true also that Sir William Berkeley, when he was Governor fifty years later, publicly thanked God that there was not a free school in Virginia. But Sir William, on the whole a good governor who ruined excellent work by talking too much, in this instance made a flatly false statement; there were at least two such schools and probably more.

The development of a rural rather than an urban way of life, accompanied by the evolution of the plantation system, hampered the growth of a system of public education in Virginia, so that eventually New England took the lead and held it. But the pattern was set before the foundation of New England. It was an English, not primarily a Puritan attitude.

Nor was it—and this is the point most worth emphasis—exclusively the attitude of the nobility and gentry. To an important extent it was shared by the indentured servants. This is not to imply that they were a cultivated group. They were not. They were, for the most part, artisans and laborers with the intellectual outlook of artisans and laborers, who are not commonly intellectual giants. But they had their quota of men of unusual capacity. There were schoolmasters among them, and craftsmen whose work was of an excellence that lifted it to the level of artistry. William Buckland, the architect who designed the Hammond House at Annapolis, one of the most exquisite examples of its kind in America, was an indentured servant. So was Benjamin Franklin's maternal grandmother. So were Charles Thomson, secretary of the Continental Congress, Matthew Thornton, a signer of the Declaration of Independence, Matthew Lyon, the fiery Connecticut Congressman who did much to smash the Alien and Sedition laws, and Daniel Dulany, a celebrated lawyer of early Maryland.*

Apparently, therefore, the typical indentured servant recruited by the London Company was a reasonably good specimen of humanity. He must have been discouraged, or he would never have taken the plunge; but it is equally plain that he must have had a dogged courage to do it. As a rule, he was a man inured to hard physical labor, who expected to work all his life and who therefore had but a languid interest in the graces and amenities of existence. He came to Virginia first because he wanted to eat and his chances of being able to do that in England were none too good; but a strong, if secondary, motive was the chance that at the end of seven years he might find himself the owner of fifty acres of land. Land, be it remembered, was not merely property to him; naturally, he had but a dim notion of what it meant in America, but he was

---

* Consult *Colonists in Bondage*, a book already referred to, for an impressive list of indentured servants who made good. The author rates the proportion at about ten per cent, but when one man in ten of any group achieves a real success in life, that is no bad record.

keenly aware that in England ownership of fifty acres of land meant dignity, security, independence. His avid desire of land, therefore, was not pure avarice; he desired it for its monetary value, certainly, but he desired it also, and perhaps more strongly, for its symbolic value. The English lower classes have always had a passion for respectability; and to be an owner of land was the best possible guarantee of respectability.

The English indentured servant, therefore, was not wholly a materialist; he strove to make his materialism serve a non-material end. He believed that the cultivation of the mind is one of the avenues to a better life; and he frankly regarded the possession of material property, specifically land, as a cachet of respectability. Material possessions also meant ease and luxury, which he was far from despising; but their great value was as the stamp of success, the evidence, in the eyes of others, of his value as a man.

Unquestionably, this has remained a figure in the pattern of American life, a figure that some have deplored, but that none has overlooked. Sometimes it is taken for granted that this figure was imposed upon our way of thinking by fiat of the successful; but the chances are that it was imbedded in the minds of the great mass of indentured servants and redemptioners who came to this country before there were any successful Americans, when the English had but the slightest and most precarious of holds on the edge of the continent, and it was highly uncertain that they would ever have more.

These were the people who made the first great break into the wilderness, expanding the beach-head won by the soldiers of fortune, the convicts, the rogues and vagabonds. They, too, had no easy conquest. The mortality rate among them was appalling; but a minority survived long enough to become thoroughly acclimated, and once that was accomplished they flourished and multiplied in a fashion that might have startled the world even in those days when birthrates everywhere were astonishing.

They were the ancestors of the group that sociologists now classify as "old American." It is a phase of the truth not much emphasized by modern Virginians who prefer, not unnaturally, to regard as typical of their ancestry the rare man of rank who appeared in the colony—a Delaware, a Baltimore, a Penn, or at least a John Rolfe—rather than the sturdy, but anonymous, ploughmen, blacksmiths, carpenters and brickmasons who really populated the continent. But it is, in fact, an ancestry with its own form of distinction. The people who actually made Virginia, meaning the whole string of settlements from Charleston to Philadelphia, were, with rare exceptions, not of the privileged class; but they were brave, they were durable, and they were probably at least as honest as the nobility and gentry. As far as the general welfare is concerned, such qualities among the progenitors were vastly more important than a coat of arms with sixteen quarterings.

3

The second, the third and the fourth English invasions in force were made in Massachusetts, in Maryland, and in Pennsylvania, in that order. They differed in personnel and in method, but they had in common a primary motive that was subordinate in the settlement of Virginia. This was religious sectarianism.

Romantic historians have idealized the Pilgrims, the Maryland Catholics and the Quakers into protagonists of religious freedom, but they were nothing of the sort. All alike were refugees from religious tyranny but, except perhaps for the Quakers, it was not tyranny to which they objected, but its exercise against their particular faith. To the Pilgrims—or, to be exact, to the Puritans of whom the Pilgrims were an offshoot —and to the Catholics, the doctrine of religious freedom was a heresy only less detestable than the heresy of Anglicanism, from which they fled. Their love of liberty was highly particularist; they desired it for themselves, but not at all for others. Since they were unable to enjoy it in England, where the Established Church was dominant, they retired to the wilderness; but they did not wish to be joined there by adherents of rival faiths and, as far as they could, they excluded schismatics. They sought religious freedom, in short, precisely in the spirit in which the Mormons sought it when they moved to Utah in 1846.

But to have any adequate comprehension of these people one must carefully avoid reading their history in a twentieth-century context. The word "religion," for example, has undergone a radical modification in its meaning in the course of three centuries. In 1620, when the Pilgrims landed in Massachusetts, religion to a very large extent was politics, and politics was religion. This amalgam was not characteristic of the Pilgrim alone; all the world accepted it as inevitable, or had accepted it until very recently. The first tentative moves toward separation of the two were in fact being made by the great commercial companies, including the London Company, who were finding that religious opinions did not necessarily affect profitable trade and were beginning to suspect that they might not necessarily affect stable and orderly government.

The Puritan movement in England, though, and its Anglican opposition, as well as the Catholic minority, still regarded any such notion as nonsensical. To all of them religion seemed an inseparable element of politics, sociology and economics. This is strongly attested by the passage of Scripture which the Pilgrims selected as the certificate of divine authority on which their movement was based; it was the thirteenth to the sixteenth verses of the eleventh chapter of Hebrews,* which patently refers to an earthly policy as well as to eternal salvation. They sought a heavenly city, but they sought it on earth; and any heavenly city, terrestrial or celestial, would naturally be one inhabited by people of their own faith and no others.

The Pilgrims, as a matter of fact, found religious freedom without coming to America. Driven by Anglican persecution, they retired to what is now the Netherlands and took up residence largely in the city of Leyden. There they were permitted to worship as they pleased, undisturbed by the law; but freedom of worship was not enough for the men who considered that religion was an integral part of politics. They conceived the idea—extraordinary to a twentieth-century mind—that the Dutch were a licentious, profligate and ungodly race, whose influence would undermine and corrupt the Pilgrim way of life. In fact, as they looked around them, it was evident that the whole human race was as far gone in corruption as the Dutch and the only thing to do was to isolate themselves from the contaminating touch of man, which was practicable only in the New World.

This was as much a political as a religious move. The Pilgrims would not have denied it for, from their standpoint, there was no essential difference between the two. Separation of church and state they would have regarded with horror, if it had occurred to them that any such thing was conceivable. A few years later, when Roger Williams did begin to propagate the notion, the Pilgrims' successors, the Puritans, regarded it

---

* The passage reads, "These all died in faith, not having received the promises, but having seen them afar off, and were persuaded of them, and embraced them, and confessed that they were strangers and pilgrims in the earth.

"For they that say such things declare plainly that they seek a country.

"And truly, if they had been mindful of that country from whence they came out, they might have had opportunity to have returned.

"But now they desire a better country, that is, an heavenly: wherefore God is not ashamed to be called their God: for he hath prepared for them a city."

with such horror that they heaved him out of the colony, promptly and enthusiastically.

When the Pilgrims applied to the London Company * for permission to make a settlement in its territory, they encountered less difficulty than might have been expected. The Company was eager for colonists and a charter was granted promptly; but the Pilgrims insisted on adding to it various religious guarantees, which aroused some of the more pious members of the Company, who blocked the whole business for a year or more. But eventually a London merchant transferred to them a charter he had already received from the Company—an obvious subterfuge which would not have been permitted had not the Company really desired to further the settlement if it could do so without precipitating a religious row.

The reasons were obvious. The Pilgrims were desirable settlers. Most of them belonged to a little group organized at the village of Scrooby. They were for the most part artisans and farmers, industrious, sober and honest. On the negative side, Scrooby had been much relieved when they left for the Netherlands, because they were regarded as an unsettling element. The Anglican majority and the Catholic minority seem to have looked upon the Separatists, as they were called before they gave themselves the name of Pilgrims, much as the older American denominations regard the Holy Rollers of the twentieth century; that is to say, they were not exactly law-breakers, but they were something of a communal scandal and nuisance, whose room was preferable to their company. Planting them in America therefore seemed an excellent idea on all counts.

But the Puritan movement did not subside in England. On the contrary, it continued to mount in numbers and in violence

* Its formal title was The Virginia Company of London, to distinguish it from the Virginia Company of Plymouth, with which it had been linked in the original charter, but from which it had cut loose in 1612. Since the Plymouth Company accomplished little, modern historical references to "the Virginia Company" usually refer to the company of London.

until it culminated in civil war and revolution; but before that happened, great numbers of Puritans crossed the Atlantic to join, and eventually to overwhelm the Pilgrims. Within ten years after the arrival of the *Mayflower,* the colony of Massachusetts took on the characteristics, not of the mild and relatively sweet-spirited Pilgrims, but of the sort of Puritans who were of the stuff of one of the most formidable military machines of the age, Cromwell's Ironsides.

In numbers this movement was relatively small, not approaching the fourteen thousand immigrants the London Company before its collapse in 1624 poured into Virginia; but the quality of this group was such that it stamped its impress upon the imagination of subsequent generations so deeply as to distort American history. Even now myriads of American schoolboys are under the impression that the voyage of the *Mayflower* marked the beginning of English settlement of the continent, and that Jamestown, if not quite abortive, was a relatively unimportant incident; and as great a historian as Arnold J. Toynbee credits the descendants of New Englanders with domination of the American scene.*

The reason is not far to seek. The Puritans were by long odds the most vocal element among all the English settlers of North America. They were theorists, and theorists are ever ready to expound their theories at indefinite length. Their entire policy rested upon a doctrinal basis that could be established only by argument. The Virginian policy, on the other hand—and that of New York, both before and after its capture from the Dutch—had a more material basis. If the colony showed a profit, no argument was needed to establish the fact that it was a success; for a profitable colony was successful by definition.

* See volume ii, pages 65-73 of Toynbee's *A Study of History* for a remarkable demonstration of William A. Dunning's theory that history is not what happened, but what men believe happened. Toynbee has there accepted history not as it was made, but as it was written by New Englanders.

The Puritans, on the other hand, while they were willing enough to turn a profit, did not feel that they could justify their existence by that alone. The "heavenly city" to be heavenly must dominate intellectually, or at least doctrinally; so from the beginning they strove for intellectual dominance. They never succeeded entirely. As a matter of fact, the Puritan theocracy had collapsed long before Jonathan Edwards was dismissed from his pulpit in 1750; but the effort developed a tough and sinewy intellectuality in New England that made it so far the most garrulous section of America as to capture the attention of the world practically to the exclusion of all other sections.

Add to this the fact that New Englanders took to the sea as notably as Virginians took to the land and thus became the traders, which is to say, the representatives of America to the rest of the world, and it is easy to see why the relatively small Puritan colony masked and concealed the development that was going on elsewhere.

This is not to be construed as referring exclusively to the leaders of the Puritan group. William Bradford, John Winthrop and their successors were notable dialecticians, to be sure, but the rank and file of the Puritans were also much given to disputation, hardly less so than Cromwell's army in which every private could preach two hours at a stretch, and on small provocation would do so. To say that they were intellectually superior to other groups is to go beyond the evidence, but that they were better debaters is unquestionable, whether the debate were oral or written.

The common people's widespread interest in non-material affairs naturally stimulated and strengthened those minds among them that actually were superior with the result that we have far better records, both in volume and in clarity, concerning New England than concerning any of the other early settlements. The pietistic flavor that permeates all the records has given later generations the impression that they were cant-ing hypocrites and no doubt a good many of them were just that. But this leaves out of account the fact that in the seven-teenth century pietism invaded the field of general ideas every-where, and especially among the Puritans of England.

Almost every intellectual concept was conveniently stated in theological terms. Far beyond this time, even as late as Dr. Samuel Johnson's day, the minister was much more than an expounder of faith and doctrine; he was an intellectual leader and his sermons, not only in New England, but wherever the English settled, included comment on every aspect of life. To the early Americans he was the equivalent of the modern essay-ist, editorial writer, columnist and radio commentator. He interpreted the news as well as the Scripture, and the police took a well-justified interest in the pulpit, for it was usually the spark-plug of every subversive movement.

The theological overtones in all early New England utter-ances therefore have not the significance they would have to-day. The extraordinary appetite for printed sermons,* also, is indicative of an interest in general ideas quite as much as in the subtleties of doctrine, for the minister held forth on what-ever subject happened to engage the interest of his congrega-tion at the moment. And why not? These were the last days of scholasticism, when it was still assumed that the way to the discovery of truth lay through metaphysical speculation. Not

---

* This taste was not confined to New England. William S. Powell, in an ar-ticle in the *William and Mary Quarterly* for April, 1948, lists among books in the Virginia Colony before 1624, that is, when Plymouth was only three years old, such formidable titles as *The Practice of Pietie, being the substance of sev-eral Sermons preached at Evesham,* by Lewis Bayly, bishop of Bangor; *The Works of that famous and worthie minister of Christ in the University of Cam-bridge, M. W. Perkins,* edited by J. Legate; *St. Augustine of the Citie of God,* translated by J. Healey; and *Ursinus his Catechisme, wherin are debated and resolved the Questions, of whatever moment, which have been or are controversed in Divinitie,* translated by H. Parrie. The other books known to have been in the colony at that date are nearly all technical—treatises on law, on husbandry, on medicine and on such esoteric subjects as the culture of silk-worms, a proj-ect that seems to have had an extraordinary fascination for the early Virginians.

until 1637 did Descartes publish the *Discourse on Method,* which is usually regarded as the starting point of the scientific age in which the experiment has displaced the syllogism as the test of truth.

Much of the pious discourse in New England may therefore be regarded as indicative of intellectual rather than strictly spiritual activity. The Puritans were religious, without doubt, but religion permeated their talk a great deal more thoroughly than it did their acts. When a certain gay dog by the name of Thomas Morton showed up among them and established a settlement which he called Merry Mount and which was far from pious, the military leader of the colony, Captain Miles Standish, took a patrol to the place and jailed the lot, Morton presently being shipped out of Massachusetts. For generations the tradition prevailed, based on the scandalized comments of contemporaries, that Morton's offense was frivolity, culminating in the high crime of dancing around a Maypole. But if the records are read with attention to their significant content, disregarding the pietistic flourishes, it is clear that he was actually banished for selling firearms and firewater to the Indians, to the peril of the whole settlement. For a similar offense men were as roughly handled in Virginia, and in every other colony.

It is evident that such a group as the Puritans, tough, resolute, intellectually as well as physically energetic, and filled with a moral certitude that made them extremely dominating, must have had an effect, and a powerful one, upon the course of events in North America. It would be fatuous to question it, and yet there are in our English heritage certain items commonly attributed to the New Englanders, but with which they had little, if anything, to do.

One of these, curiously enough, is puritanism, with a lower-case "p." The Puritans, that is to say, the historical sect, settled New England and dominated it for at least two generations; but the attitude toward life which we now call puritanism, which for a time prevailed over practically the whole country, and which still prevails in large areas, particularly where economic conditions are hard, is probably the legacy, not of the Puritans, but of the early Methodists.

It is generally conceded that the intellectual giant of the Puritans was Jonathan Edwards, a native American; but it is also conceded that Edwards was fighting a losing battle all his life. Puritanism (with a capital "P") was already dying when he came to years of discretion, and he was able to revive it only briefly and locally. The man who gave the country the one form of religion characteristic of the whole continent was an Englishman, George Whitefield. This religion was as strongly Calvinistic as Puritanism and thus is frequently identified with it and traced back to New England; but it is a matter of record that Edwards regarded Whitefield with an uneasiness that eventually mounted into undisguised horror. Whitefield's "broad" Anglicanism that led him to mingle freely and tolerantly with all sorts of Dissenters, Presbyterians, Baptists, Quakers, or what not, was no part of Puritan thinking, was, in fact, its antithesis. It is extremely doubtful, therefore, that the austerity of American Protestantism is to any important extent a legacy from New England. Whitefield apparently had more to do with it than Jonathan Edwards, Cotton Mather, or any other of the New England theologians.

The figure in the American pattern that the Englishman who came to Massachusetts had most to do with setting was educational. Indirectly, the Puritan faith had much to do with this because, as Dissenters, the Puritans could not be content with an educated ministry. In their opinion the priesthood could not absolve the laity of its duty of understanding theology, which required for every man at least enough education to enable him to read the Bible, and works of piety in general. This opinion was shared widely, but the intensity of Puritan conviction on the subject was not equalled in most of the other settlements, hence the New Englanders put a drive into their educational program that has had its effect on all American history. The schoolhouse, rather than the meeting-house, is a New England part of the pattern.

New England contributed to freedom of conscience only by the left-handed method of making martyrs to that cause. The persecution of such people as Roger Williams and Anne Hutchinson made them famous and brought them support; but that was certainly not the purpose of the persecution.

It seems probable, though, that the supremacy of the ministry over the magistracy among the Puritans, even though it lasted only a short time, may have had something to do with fixing the American belief that Jefferson voiced nearly two hundred years later in his affirmation that the will of the majority "to be rightfull must be reasonable" and to which Seward appealed with his "There is a higher law than the Constitution." The firm American opinion that the government can do wrong and that not even a Constitutional Convention can repeal the moral law, perhaps dates back to those New England clergymen who by the authority they claimed from God rebuked without hesitation magistrates as well as private citizens.

4

The second religious invasion of the English after the Pilgrims was not, like theirs, a group movement, but an individual enterprise, backed by a curious character in some ways similar to Raleigh, although he belonged to a different party. George Calvert was one of Robert Cecil's bright young men, and was something of a favorite of "the crook-backed earl." Like the Cecils, he was a smooth and sinuous customer, up to a point, but then he suddenly developed a bold obstinacy comparable to Raleigh's, and this intransigence led to his interest in America.

Starting in a rather minor clerkship, he worked up until in the course of time he became Salisbury's chief trouble-shooter and was appropriately rewarded. The hottest spots in the reigns of Kings James I and Charles I were Parliament itself, Spain and Ireland, and Calvert was employed in all three. As a Yorkshireman he held a seat in Parliament from that county and served as a sort of liaison between the King and the minister, on one hand, and Parliament on the other. He was good. Everyone recognized him as the King's man, yet he was affable enough to retain marked popularity among the members and to exercise an influence in the House that Lord Salisbury found very convenient indeed. Then he went to Spain on the difficult business of arranging a royal marriage with that Catholic dynasty, and handled it with an adroitness that won the high approval of his superiors. He was then given a commission in County Clare, Ireland and managed to hold it against the formidable opposition of Buckingham, the King's favorite. He seems to have handled that thorny problem as cleverly as he did the Spanish business. He was already Sir George Calvert, and his elevation to the peerage was the logical next step. But for some reason, possibly Buckingham's enmity, perhaps the rising partisan rancor, or perhaps for some reason lost to history, it was deemed inexpedient to make him, although a native of Yorkshire, a peer of England. So he was given a barony in the Kingdom of Ireland, although he had no drop of Irish blood. He took his title from a small fishing village near Cork, called Baltimore.

Yet at this juncture the smooth and probably somewhat slippery diplomatist and courtier developed a moral rigidity by no means to be expected in a man of his type. He had been a lifelong Anglican, that is to say a Protestant of the dominant sect, although he seems to have exhibited little more religious fervor than the average scheming politician. But the tides of religious prejudice were now beginning to run strong in England

and their first victims were the Catholics. It was plain to the dullest—and George Calvert was not dull—that the position of English Catholics, already bad, must swiftly grow worse; which was the moment that Calvert chose to announce his conversion to that faith.

Nor did he ever waver. A Catholic he was and a Catholic he remained through all the storms that followed. Yet he remained George Calvert, a born smoother-out of difficulties. He would not deny or conceal his faith, yet he had no more taste than the next man for going to the stake; he wished ardently to live a tolerable life and to die in his bed, and he thought it could be done without damning his soul. Like the Pilgrims, he looked toward America.

Owing to his high standing at court Baltimore had little difficulty in securing a charter, in spite of his being a Catholic. Indeed, the King was so anxious to oblige that he gave him three successive grants. The first one was in Newfoundland, where Baltimore settled a colony in 1620, the same year in which the Pilgrims arrived at Plymouth; but the climate proved too rugged and Baltimore asked for land further south. The King (now Charles I) accordingly gave him all the territory south of the James River and north of the Roanoke, to be called the Province of Carolina. But the Virginia Company screamed; they had their own eyes on that territory. So the King made a third grant, and by way of compensation made it twice as large. From the mouth of the James to that of the Roanoke is one degree of latitude, 37 to 36. So the third grant was two degrees, from the mouth of the Potomac, at 38 north to the 40th parallel. As a graceful acknowledgement of royal favor, the recipient named the territory after the Queen, Henrietta Maria. So Maryland came into being in 1634.

This recipient was not George, but Cecilius Calvert, his son. After the charter had been granted, but before the Great Seal could be applied, George died. Except for a short visit to

Jamestown, where they made things hot for him on account of his religion, George Calvert never set foot on the territory that is now the United States. Nevertheless, he helped set the pattern for America more effectively than did thousands of men who lived and died here.

For through his efforts a new element was introduced, by design, into the population; and a new idea, not by design, but through force of circumstances, was introduced into the thinking of America. In the three hundred years that have elapsed since, both the people and the idea, instead of diminishing have increased in importance; and that notwithstanding the fact that the idea was, in principle at least, distasteful to the people.

The people were the Roman Catholic communion; and the idea was that of complete religious tolerance, which evolved into the American political principle of separation of Church and State. Needless to say, this was not a Catholic idea; no more was it a Protestant idea in 1634, above all not a Puritan idea. Both Catholics and Protestants at the time were thoroughly committed to the theory that Church and State were inseparable, which explains why doctrinal differences in those days led promptly to military combat.

Religious tolerance was a strictly political idea, one worthy of a man who had learned politics and diplomacy from Robert Cecil. Calvert was in the position of a petitioner for royal favor; the King was in the position of one willing to grant the favor if it could be done without adding fuel to the flames of religious bigotry that were already scorching Charles' royal robes. A suspicious realm was watching for and would bitterly resent, perhaps violently resent, any frank concession to Catholics. The question then was, how could the King establish a sanctuary for Catholics without seeming to grant them anything? The answer was worked out in the charter that was finally issued to Cecilius Calvert, second baron of Baltimore, but that undoubtedly was designed by his father, that skillful negotiator. It granted Baltimore the right to establish a colony and gave him exclusive control of the area north of the Potomac to the 40th parallel, under conditions similar to those of the Palatinate of Durham which meant for all practical purposes vice-regal power. But written into the charter was a stern warning to Baltimore that under no circumstances was he to interfere with the free exercise of the Protestant religion in the province.

This enabled the King to assure his Protestant subjects that the charter of Maryland conceded nothing to Catholics; in fact, its sole mention of religion was a stiff clause protecting the Protestant faith. On the other hand, Baltimore was left free to use his own judgment with regard to Catholics; if he saw fit to treat them tenderly, that was his affair, none of the King's doing.

Of course this legerdemain fooled nobody and the charter was bitterly attacked, but its language gave Baltimore a legally defensible position, which was the object of the arrangement. At that, he was so hard put to it that he dared not leave England to take over the government of Maryland; he turned it over to his brother, Leonard, while he remained in London to guard the charter. Fortunately, he had inherited enough of his father's gift of statecraft to be equal to the job and he repelled all assaults for fifteen years, in fact, until he was overwhelmed by the Cromwellian Revolution that finished the King in 1649.

The same event seemed to have stamped out the idea of religious tolerance in Maryland. Under the Roundheads the laws were promptly revised and Catholics subjected to civil disabilities some of which lasted until the outbreak of the War of Independence. It is interesting to note that Charles Carroll of Carrollton, a signer of the Declaration of Independence, although he had been educated at the Temple, in London, the best law school in the realm, could not practice law in his native Maryland until 1776 because he was a Catholic.

Nevertheless, the idea of religious tolerance had been planted in American soil, and it had taken root. From the start Maryland had been one of the most successful of all the English colonies and its experience of fifteen years proved beyond dispute that the withdrawal of the civil authorities from religious affairs did not necessarily mean the subversion of law and order. On the contrary, Maryland under Leonard Calvert had been conspicuously orderly and prosperous, although Leonard was a decidely hard-headed and hard-fisted Governor. Men did not fail to reflect that if that rough-riding official had been able to interfere with religious affairs the province would have been in a continual uproar; hence the policy had much to recommend it to moderates.

As the passions of the Civil War subsided this figure in the American pattern appeared again and became increasingly conspicuous. The Maryland experiment was not forgotten and it became more and more attractive as the development of the country called for more and more willing workers. By 1776 the idea of complete separation of the political and ecclesiastical powers was so widely accepted that only in New England did the religious establishments fail to collapse at the first breath of the Revolutionary storm, and there they survived for a few years only.

There is an apparent irony in that the American pattern of religious freedom was set by Catholics who didn't believe in it. But the irony is more apparent than real. Among the men who did the dickering and dealing in London some were Catholics and some were Protestants, but all were practical politicians, who rarely believe in anything except consolidating their power by the most convenient and least expensive means available.

Paris, thought Henry IV, was worth a mass; and while the

pious have branded him as a cynic for that, nobody disputes that he was a great king. George Calvert and his son were trying to buy peace, security and prosperity for their persecuted co-religionists. If the price they paid was that of letting heretics go unwhipped, they too may have been cynical, but nevertheless they rank, like the French king, high among the successful builders of states.

5

Fifty years passed before the next great religious invasion. In the meantime the English expelled the Dutch from New Amsterdam, converting it into New York (1664), and settled Charleston (1670), but both these enterprises followed the pattern of the settlement of Jamestown and neither can be said to have introduced a new figure. The backers of the Carolina project tried, indeed, to introduce the most fantastic figure ever proposed for the American pattern, John Locke's "Fundamental Constitutions," but it couldn't be set and swiftly disappeared. The Dutch population of New York was taken over, not expelled, and presently French Huguenots began to pour into Charleston; both wove new figures into the pattern, but they were not English and their contribution to American life is studied in detail elsewhere in this series of books.

Maryland was settled in 1634 and forty-three years later William Penn undertook his first American enterprise of West Jersey. In that year Burlington was founded. But legal difficulties involving the title caused Penn five years later to transfer his effort across the Delaware River, so it is approximately correct to say that it was fifty years from the Catholics to the Quakers.

They were fifty tremendously significant years for the world, and especially for England. During their course the terrific apparition of Oliver Cromwell swept meteor-like across the political heavens, and England was never the same again. In-

deed, the institution of monarchy was never the same, for
Cromwell reversed the ancient theory that the lives of his subjects are at a king's disposal, and proved that the life of a king
is at his subjects' disposal so that it is at his mortal peril that he
tries their patience too far. The teaching was violently rejected
by the counter-revolution and was denied for generations, but
the very emphasis with which it was denied showed how clearly
it was remembered. Before Cromwell, Shakespeare could write,
probably in all good faith,

> There's such divinity doth hedge a king,
> That treason can but peep to what it would,

but after Cromwell a great English poet would not write such
lines except with his tongue in his cheek. Cromwell proved
that it was psychologically possible for Englishmen to reject the
whole theory of monarchy; and that made a difference in all
Englishmen, including those who had come to America.

Another event of this same half-century that profoundly affected English and therefore American life was the rise to complete dominance of the mercantilist economic theory. The
central idea of English mercantilism was that as the whole is
greater than any of its parts, the national economy should aim
at the prosperity of the nation as a whole, even when that
meant the disadvantage of one segment or another. It was a
perversion of this doctrine that at last cost Great Britain
her North American empire; for while England expanded into
Great Britain and Britain expanded into the empire, the
thoughts of Englishmen did not expand as rapidly as their
king's domain. In 1776 they were still incapable of thinking
of the empire as the whole to be served; so their mercantilism
operated against the outlying dominions and the American one
broke away.

But in the years between 1634 and 1682 it was another phase
of mercantilism that touched the colonies most intimately. This

was the changed attitude toward population. As the last remnants of feudalism were collapsing in the reign of Elizabeth, the people were regarded by the authorities as so many mouths to feed; with the rise of mercantilism, they came to be regarded as so many hands to work. Under Elizabeth many thousands of landless men were classified as "sturdy beggars," liabilities whose removal to the colonies or anywhere else was a distinct relief; but as mercantilism became dominant, the same men came to be regarded as labor units, assets whose loss was to be deplored. So the recruiting of able-bodied men for the colonies came to be regarded with increasing disfavor and transportation by judicial order was no longer applied to mere rogues and vagabonds, but was restricted to felons and sometimes to rebels.

There is small doubt that this change in attitude was hastened by the epidemic of 1665, known to history as "the Great Plague of London" that wiped out 68,000 lives in the city alone, and no one knows how many more in other parts of the kingdom as the infection spread. The social effects of this disaster were greater than the statistics would indicate because they were concentrated. The population of London at the time is estimated at 460,000, of whom two-thirds fled when the plague was recognized. Naturally, those left behind were the poorest, the common laborers; and almost half of them died. The result was a shortage of man-power that made merchants and industrialists—or, rather, the merchant-industrialists, for they were as yet one class—purse their lips over the steady drain of capable workers to the colonies.

This had a selective effect upon English emigration after the first third of the seventeenth century. Excluding convicts, the great bulk of those who went overseas were no longer thrown out of England; they were drawn out. They were still poor people, or misfits, or both, for the prosperous and contented had no reason to move. But even among the poor and discontented, vast numbers lacked the imagination to perceive opportunity, or the energy to do anything about it if they did see it. So the Englishmen who came to America—that is to say, the rank and file—came to be drawn more and more from among the active and ambitious.

Nor were they all paupers, by any means. There were many causes of discontent other than poverty in England. It was a time of savage persecution of minorities of all sorts, religious, political, social, or any other kind. More than that, in the political convulsions that racked the kingdom, the persecuting majority of today was only too likely to be the persecuted minority of tomorrow. Cynical John Byrom flourished a generation later, but even at this period the true political attitude of many well-meaning Englishmen could have been summed up in his quatrain:

> God bless the King,—I mean the faith's defender!
> God bless—no harm in blessing—the Pretender!
> But who pretender is, or who is king,—
> God bless us all!—that's quite another thing.

So the colonies saw arriving in increasing numbers people who came well equipped with household goods, implements, livestock and occasionally with considerable amounts of ready money. Incidentally, this change in the type of immigrants has added to the perplexities of the modern historian. These people commonly made their own arrangements with an individual shipmaster and so are not mentioned in official archives. It is accordingly impossible to make an intelligent guess at their number, but it is fairly evident that the qualitative improvement in the tide of immigrants was not paralleled by a quantitative increase. There were too many factors working against the movement in England.

The disturbances in England gave rise to more religious sects than even Hollywood can show in modern times. The Catholics had been driven underground, and the Anglicans, except those of the Richard Baxter type, were subjugated; but there was no unanimity among the dominant groups. Independents, Presbyterians and Baptists were the three most powerful sects, but Cromwell, an Independent, was sardonically advising the Presbyterians to pray fervently to God that He might show them that it was possible for them to be mistaken; and Presbyterians and Independents agreed in approving the imprisonment of John Bunyan, a Baptist, and the sort of man who could come out of jail with the manuscript of *The Pilgrim's Progress*.

The clashes of these warring sects naturally resulted in innumerable splinter groups. Most of these were ephemeral and some downright lunatic. The Ranters and the Muggletonians, for example, were wild enough, but there were others who were worse. As always happens at times of great social stress and insecurity, weird prophets popped up everywhere, proclaiming that salvation lay in some act or omission—to eat no meat, to drink no wine, to refuse to listen to the sound of fiddles, to wear no buttons, to shave one's head or, on the other hand, never to permit the shearing of one's locks, to wear nothing but black or gray, in extreme cases to wear nothing at all, were among the methods seriously advocated as assuring eternal welfare.

There were, as there always are, a few genuine mystics to whom all this was painful as representing the triumph of gross materialism. One was a young cobbler's apprentice named George Fox, who, on the road to Coventry had an experience comparable to that of Saul of Tarsus on the road to Damascus— a sudden revelation that a political church has little to do with true religion. He conceived the idea that this revelation must be proclaimed abroad, promptly fell afoul of the authorities and landed in jail; but nothing short of death could stop him and thereafter a large part of his life was spent behind bars.

But he was a true zealot and during his intervals of liberty he preached with a power that brought him a following not all confined to the dispossessed. Among others, he converted the son of a celebrated naval officer, one of the victors of Portland, captor of Jamaica, conqueror of the Dutch, and an important figure in the restoration of Charles II, Admiral Sir William Penn. The son, whose name was also William, proved to be a greater man than the father, although he was a sore trial to the honest old Admiral. The boy had always been introspective, with a strong religious streak, and at Oxford he contrived to get himself involved in so many freakish movements that eventually he was expelled, to the mortification of his father.

The Admiral then put him into the Navy, where he served against the Dutch, honorably enough, but without any special distinction. Apparently the Admiral realized that in William he had no Navy man, so he allowed the boy to study law in London, then sent him abroad in a diplomatic capacity, and finally to Ireland, where he did well in helping suppress a mutiny at Cork, and had his portrait painted clothed in armor. But soon he was playing with religious ideas again, for the Quaker doctrine fascinated him, and he wrote a pamphlet or two so heretical that presently he was in jail. His exasperated father got him out and brought him back to England, but to little avail, for he met George Fox and openly joined the movement that Fox called the Society of Friends.

He was a good propagandist and presently he was arguing shrewdly—greatly assisted by his legal training—for freedom of religion and of speech. Soon he was in jail again, but he continued to argue and in fact at this time produced *No Cross No Crown*, his most celebrated work. Released, he proceeded to Gracechurch Street and preached a sermon that brought the catchpolls down on him again; but this time he got an open trial and argued his own case with such skill and power that he not only won a verdict of "Not guilty," but established a legal precedent liberating English juries from the dictation of judges.* The old Admiral, though, was finished before the case; William was brought to his bedside from jail and the old man gave him his blessing, unfilial conduct, subversive views, radical associations and all.

Historians have not paid much attention to Sir William's conduct at this time, but it certainly must have made the son a milder and more tolerant man than he would have been had his father cast him off. But the patience and tolerance of William Penn were largely responsible for his success as a colonizer. The dying Admiral, therefore, may have affected the history of America far more profoundly than is generally realized.

With wealth, social position and brains Penn could not fail to become one of the leaders of the English Quakers, and when they undertook to establish a colony in America he was consulted. In fact, it is believed that the fundamental constitution of West Jersey, the famous "Concessions and Agreements" came from his pen, in large part, if not altogether.

This was by far the most liberal constitution in America up to its time. Five years later, when Penn secured a grant on the western side of the Delaware and established the colony of Pennsylvania, he transferred the essential clauses of the Concessions and Agreements to the new territory. Thus Pennsylvania, as well as West Jersey, started with a constitution guaranteeing freedom of religion and protecting freedom of speech to a degree not approached in any other colony, not even Maryland, where the first start had been made.

The significant point in this, as far as the present study is concerned, is that freedom of religion as part of the American pattern was not an American invention. It was imported from England, largely as a result of the work of George Calvert and William Penn. But it was accepted and supported by the bulk

* It is known to legal historians as "Bushell's Case" and is regarded as something of a landmark in the development of British jurisprudence.

of the colonists these two leaders introduced; not the leaders only, but the anonymous men and women who followed them, and whose brain and brawn actually did the work, believed in this principle before they ever set foot on American soil.

They acquired that belief through their experiences in the Mother Country. The disturbances that racked England between 1630 and 1688 had their repercussions in this country; but they were only repercussions, not the original impact, and their effect here was far less drastic that it was there. There was some American fighting between Roundheads and Cavaliers, especially on the Maryland-Virginia border. There was some persecution, involving imprisonment, whipping and cropping of ears, even in Massachusetts the hanging of a Quaker or two. But the real upheaval was in England which meant, of course, that the real radicals were produced in England, not here. The doctrine of freedom of religion once planted in American soil flourished as it never had in England; but it was an English idea to start with, part of the heritage we have received from that nation.

Furthermore, it was an idea of the common man, propagated and expounded by William Penn, to be sure, but tenaciously held by thousands whose names are unknown to history. So were all the other figures in the pattern that have been discussed hitherto. However, the colonists did not consist entirely of common men. There were some extraordinary individuals in the group and some of them had a traceable influence upon the course that American history was to take. Let us turn, then, from the anonymous rank and file and consider a few of the heroes.

Chapter III

∞

THE GENTLEMEN OF QUALITY

1

The great Englishmen who most profoundly influenced the history of the United States are those who never set foot on American soil. The barons who wrested the Great Charter from King John; the individual who did most to set the pattern of the language, Geoffrey Chaucer; John Wycliffe and William Tyndale, who opened the Bible to the common man; Roger Bacon and John Duns Scotus, the philosophers; the hierarchy of great judges who hammered out the Common Law; the generals and admirals from Henry V to Howard, Drake and Hawkins who whipped the Invincible Armada—all these and many others modified and largely ruled the thinking of those Englishmen who crossed the Atlantic.

Even among Englishmen of the seventeenth century, no colonial governor was to exercise a tithe of the power over the minds of Americans that was wielded by the "common player of Enterludes," William Shakespeare; nor did any minister among them shape the theology of the new country as effectively as did John Milton, nor did any judge impress them as strongly as did Francis Bacon, who never saw America. Nor has that form of remote control been entirely lost even down to our times; few native sons of this generation have persuaded as many Americans to their way of thinking as did Winston Churchill.

Thus to trace even the bare outlines of the total English influence upon the United States would be the labor of more than one lifetime and would result, not in a book, but in a library. No such hopeless attempt will be made here; so this account must be taken as a chronicle of only a part, and that much the smaller part, of the work of the English in setting the pattern of our lives.

But it is true that certain phases of British culture, having been created by the joint labor of many generations, were transplanted to this continent not by the common men who constituted the bulk of the immigration, but by a handful of very uncommon men who were their leaders.

This group may be quite roughly divided into lords spiritual, lords temporal and gentry—quite roughly because many times, especially in the early days, a leader had to be everything, warrior, priest, lawgiver and bread-winner, in his own proper person. Captain John Smith, for example, planted corn, fought Indians, explored the country, chastised shirkers, and even on occasion expounded the Scriptures to Powhatan, the red-skinned emperor. Still, it is difficult to believe that any rational historian would ever classify Smith as either priest or judge. By the same token the clergy, in the early days, had of necessity to take on many mundane labors. Father Andrew White, for example, although he was head of the ecclesiastical mission, could write a neat bit of advertising for Lord Baltimore, on the one hand, and, on the other, could swing an ax effectively in the forests about St. Mary's City in Maryland. Still, he survives in history as a priest, not as either a copy-writer or a lumberman.

But if one bears in mind the vagueness of the dividing lines, it is a general truth that the law, religion, business and politics of England were transported to America by the officials, the clergy and the merchant adventurers who came along, not by the indentured servants and redemptioners, certainly not by the convicts and vagabonds. These men stood above the anonymous mass in the estimation of their contemporaries, and their names, at least, are usually known; although we have only fragmentary accounts of the work of some of the most interesting among them.

John Rolfe is a case in point. He seems to have been a gentleman, of a good but not particularly distinguished family in Norfolk, and a man of some means. But that is very nearly the sum of our knowledge concerning him. What considerations induced him to cross to Virginia in 1609, when the situation of the colony was still precarious in the extreme, no one knows. He took his wife on that desperately dangerous voyage, which seems strange and still stranger when one reflects that he was a newly-married man, the wedding presumably having taken place in 1608. Incidentally, it was fatal to her; the poor woman died soon after her arrival in Virginia.

Nevertheless, this almost unknown man was one of the pivots on which American history turned. If one is to measure men by the results that flowed from their activities, this was the most important Englishman who came to Virginia in its first ten years, for he established the security of the colony twice, once economically and again politically. Even John Smith and Christopher Newport did less toward fixing the grip of the English upon the North American continent.

It is evident that Rolfe was an inquisitive and ingenious character, with a turn for practicality. He found the tobacco grown by the Indians very poor stuff, bitter in flavor and rasping the throat, not to be compared with the fine leaf that the Spaniards brought from the West Indies. But Rolfe took it in hand, experimented continually both in plant-breeding and in improved methods of curing, and in a remarkably short time had effected a transformation. Under his hands Virginia tobacco developed a smoothness and sweetness second to none and it remains to this day one of the varieties most highly prized.

The immediate effect was to put the colony on a solid business basis. Here was a product at once highly valuable and easily transported. It is as certain as anything human can be that the merchants of the Virginia Company would have become discouraged and quit long before 1624 had not some such discovery given them hope of great profits to come; and had the Company quit in say, 1612 or 1615, it is far from certain that the Crown would have taken over as it did a few years later. It was unquestionably Rolfe's work with tobacco that gave the project the economic base that enabled it to survive.

Incidentally, he was the first to trace out a figure that has become very prominent in American life—that of the ingenious inquirer into the secrets of nature who turns his discoveries to practical account rather than into philosophical theory. Rolfe stands at the head of a long line of Americans whom we are accustomed to regard as peculiarly representative of the spirit of the country. The most distinguished example was Benjamin Franklin, but Jefferson was of a similar mind, and Washington to some extent, while the succession has come on down into our own times in such men as Luther Burbank, "the plant wizard," and Henry A. Wallace, the grower of super corn.

Rolfe's other achievement, however, was markedly out of the line of American practice. He contracted a political marriage, an act which in 1948 might well incur the disapproval of the House Committee on Un-American Activities; but at the time it was logical, patriotic, and personally as well as politically successful. By espousing the daughter of Powhatan, he secured peace with the Indians for eight successive years, which gave the English time to establish themselves strongly; so when "another king arose which knew not Joseph," to wit, Opechancanough, successor to Powhatan, it was too late. Opechancanough did his best. He was no such sentimentalist as Powhatan and he realized clearly that the survival of the English meant the doom of the Indian way of life, certainly, and probably of the Indian race. He therefore laid careful plans to extirpate them in a single day, knowing well that he would have one chance and one only. His planning was skillful and its execution was prompt, firm and well-disciplined almost beyond anything else in Indian military history. The failure of the project is not attributable to the emperor. It was the usual failure of the human element. At the last moment the plan was betrayed and part of the English had time to throw themselves into a posture of defense. Only about three hundred and fifty out of thirteen hundred were killed.

This was as complete a disaster for the Indians as Pearl Harbor was for the Japanese three hundred and nineteen years later and for exactly the same reason. It was a case of wounding the bear without killing him. It is an ironic circumstance that one of the Indians' local successes in this affair of 1622 was at Bermuda Hundred, where John Rolfe was living with his third wife. At that place there were no survivors at all, so Rolfe presumably met his end at the hands of his kin-in-law.

The massacre gave the surviving English the best possible moral sanction for breaking the Indian power forever and they went about it with relentless ferocity. Eight years later, when Opechancanough was finally rounded up, he was mortally ill, utterly destitute and a fugitive in every way as forlorn as King Lear at the end of his days. It is interesting to observe that this first big war upon the North American continent set a pattern for beginning wars that has been faithfully followed by the American republic. It is the policy of the United States never to strike the first blow; at Lexington in 1775, at Matamoros in 1846, at Sumter in 1861, on the high seas in 1917 and at Pearl Harbor in 1941, the enemy fired first, and this fact in all cases gave the Americans a moral certainty that greatly assisted them in carrying on until they could strike the last blow. Even when the case is as doubtful as that of the destruction of the battleship *Maine* in 1898 we assume that the enemy attacked us and are greatly stimulated by the assumption. Only in 1812 was it out of the question to prove that we were attacked and that is the one war we fought to a doubtful conclusion and ended by a negotiated peace.

It was stated earlier that the romance of the Englishman and the Indian princess was not part of the pattern of American life set by the English, which is true in the sense that the political marriage, or even the marriage of convenience, has never won popular approval here. Yet in another sense it is not true at all, for any incident that becomes part of the legends of a people does have an effect on their manner of thinking and living.

Pocahontas has become such a legend, one of the most gracious in the country's annals. She first comes into history as a child of perhaps twelve, and she comes in dancing in the light of a council-fire around which her father and his grave-faced chiefs sat in amicable converse with a group of English explorers. The little princess led a group of companions of her own age in a sort of sylvan ballet for the entertainment of the guests,* and this dance of the forest maidens is one of the few really charming pictures of the relations of white and red that have come down to us.

She grew up into an extraordinarily sweet-spirited young woman who managed to combine loyalty to her father and unwavering friendliness to the colonists. As to this all accounts agree, which is significant because they were, in general, a sharply critical and suspicious set. Nor is there any good reason to doubt that her marriage to Rolfe, frankly political as it was, had also a basis of affection and respect on both sides. Rolfe, in his petition to Governor Dale to sanction the marriage, has left an avowal whose quaint sincerity is hardly to be challenged. "My harte and best thoughts," he wrote, "are, and have a long

---

* Incidentally, they turned cartwheels with nothing on but a brief, tassled skirt, to the scandal of some of the vinegar-visaged old prudes among the chroniclers.

time bin so intangled, and inthralled in so intricate a laborinth, that I was even awearied to unwinde myselfe there out." When a young woman has "intangled and inthralled" a man's "best thoughts" as well as his "harte," the case is fairly complete. She has made a conquest and political considerations are likely to be an afterthought.

Rolfe took his wife to England, where she was presented at court by Lady Delaware; and she bore herself with a dignity and a quiet good sense that persuaded the English that she was indeed of royal blood and they accorded her the rank of the Lady Rebecca (the English name she had assumed at her baptism) as if she had been one of the King's nieces. She was the best sort of ambassador of good will and her visit to England materially softened the popular attitude toward the American natives; it may have had some effect upon official acts, too, although that is more difficult to establish. But certainly it did no harm.

Then to supply the last romantic touch, as she was preparing to return to Virginia and had, in fact, proceeded to Gravesend to take ship, she fell ill and died; so the dust of the woodland princess lies to this day mingled with English soil in the chancel of Gravesend church. John Smith, getting a little too old for exploring and sword-play, wrote in his *Generall Historie,* a dismissal that may seem a bit unctuous now, but that was certainly meant to be sincere and appropriate: "She made not more sorrow for her Vnexpected death, than ioy to the beholders to heare and see her make so religious and godly an end."*

Rolfe left his infant son, Thomas, in England in care of Lady Stukly, while he returned to meet his end in the massacre of 1622. So Pocahontas' son survived to go to Virginia himself

---

* Note for the rigidly exact: her original name was Matoaka. Pocohontas seems to have been a nickname, meaning "playful one," applied to more than one of Powhatan's daughters. Rebecca was given to her at her baptism, apparently on the theory that an Indian soul received into the Christian communion would remain in peril if it brought its Indian name along.

years later and found a family that flourished exceedingly. The startling John Randolph of Roanoke, perhaps the most brilliant and certainly the most bitter of American statesmen, was one of his descendants, and Virginia is full of them still.

2

Among the gentlemen of quality John Rolfe is certainly to be listed as one of the lords temporal, in that his influence was exerted upon the economic and political affairs of the colony. So were most of the colonial governors, both those commissioned by the Company and those commissioned by the Crown. Samuel Argall might seem to be an exception by reason of his insistence upon belief in the Trinity as a qualification for citizenship; but the exception is more apparent than real, for he lasted only about two years and his Trinitarianism vanished with him. Almost all of the early Governors, in fact, were simply officials, ranking as good, bad, or indifferent according to their success in maintaining peace and order in the colony, but having little perceptible effect upon the way in which it developed.

The real exception to the rule of unimportant Governors was not Argall but William Berkeley (which the English, for inscrutable reasons of their own, insist on pronouncing "Barclay"). Berkeley was a man who had the misfortune to live too long, and in so doing he made Americans acquainted with the British colonial official at his best and at his worst, compelling them to learn what to do about it.

Berkeley's career in Virginia was divided into two segments by the English civil war. The latter segment was so spectacularly bad that the world has almost forgotten the first, which was excellent. Berkeley, nephew of a lord and himself a knight, seems to have been something of a Wonder Boy in the reign of Charles I. At an early age he wangled an appointment as com-

missioner for Canadian affairs, which he handled with a combination of efficiency and good judgment that won the approval
of the King. But he also acquired a reputation as a polished
courtier, a wit, and, to some extent, as a man of letters. His
tragi-comedy, *The Lost Lady*, was, if not a smash hit at least a
fair success. His appointment at the age of thirty-six to be governor of Virginia was therefore regarded as a good one.

And so in fact it was. Sir William on his arrival in 1642
found the colony torn by factional strife and its affairs in great
disorder. He went briskly to work to straighten things out,
carefully avoided taking sides in the factional disputes, worked
for an accommodation tactfully and intelligently, and soon had
the colony's affairs moving more smoothly than they ever had
before.

Then he undertook to improve Virginia's economic position,
and for some years made a record that remains distinguished
even on the roster of British colonial administrators, which includes many great proconsuls. He studied the needs of the
colony assiduously and devised intelligent methods of supplying
them. He appreciated the danger of the one-crop system and
used his own land as a demonstration farm to stimulate the cultivation of flax, cotton, rice. He experimented with silk-worms
and on one occasion sent three hundred pounds of silk produced
in Virginia as a present to the King. He encouraged such
diversified industries as weaving and brick-making. When the
Indians became troublesome again two years after his arrival he
assembled a small army, took personal command, and in a fast,
energetic and skillful campaign smashed them so badly that
they remained quiet for a generation.

He studied the political situation of the colonists and saw
clearly that it was modified from the situation of Englishmen at
home by both geographical and psychological factors. He set
himself to understand these factors and to interpret them to the
home government, and with considerable success. He went so

far as to consent to being set aside as the final court of appeal in Virginia, approving the transfer of that function to the General Assembly. His conception of the office of Governor was not that of a mere revenue collector for the King, but that of a true vicegerent, obligated to defend the rights and interest of the colony as the King was obligated to defend those of the realm. In short, he was a brilliant success, and for ten years Virginia flourished under his rule and the Virginians came to regard him as a great Governor.

Even in these years they had, however, one warning-bell to which they should have given more heed. For all his extraordinary ability as an administrator, Sir William Berkeley was a fanatical authoritarian. He showed it by his relentless persecution of Quakers and Puritans, not that he cared much—or, probably, knew much—about their doctrinal views, but because they presumed to question the ecclesiastical authority approved and supported by the King. It is unlikely that a fashionable playwright considered himself or cared to be considered an authority on men's relation to God, but a polished courtier had very definite ideas on a subject's relation to the King, whether as monarch or as head of the church. Berkeley was not the man to tolerate any wavering in allegiance to the King or to the King's appointed officers, clerical or lay, because of a claim that allegiance to God was superior.

This he made abundantly plain by his treatment of Quakers and Puritans. Virginians should have drawn the inference that if he would not admit the claim of conscience certainly he would admit no other claim to justify any questioning of the King's authority. But in Virginia the Quakers and Puritans were weak in numbers and still weaker in influence; if the Governor was unduly rough on them, nevertheless he was in other respects an excellent Governor, so the majority of Virginians shrugged and ignored what seemed to them a peccadillo. They had not yet learned that liberty is a unit; either all men hold it securely, or none holds it securely, and when Berkeley attacked the religious freedom of Quakers and Puritans he was threatening the political freedom of Anglicans.

Naturally, upon such a man the civil war in England had a shattering effect. His first move was to open Virginia as a sanctuary for royalists and it was in grateful acknowledgement of this that the fugitive King designated the colony as the Old Dominion. But in 1652 a Parliamentary fleet appeared in the Chesapeake and Berkeley gave way to overwhelming force. He was dismissed from office, but not otherwise molested, and as England by this time was no place for royalists he remained quietly in the colony, conducting his plantation as a private citizen for eight years.

But his sense of outrage did not diminish with the passage of time. On the contrary, it festered and ate so deeply into him that it altered his character. Yet he gave no outward sign of this and few suspected it; so when the royalists triumphed at last and Charles II was restored, the colony as a whole approved the reappointment of Sir William Berkeley as Governor.

But he came back a different man. Virginians, as a matter of fact, had been conspicuously loyal to Charles I, but after his head had fallen and the Parliamentary fleet was in Hampton Roads, they deemed that further resistance would be suicide. As far as that goes, so did Berkeley. But many Virginians accepted the new order and proceeded to collaborate with it, and this Berkeley never forgave. When he was restored to power he went after the collaborators with a sanguinary fury that drenched the land with blood and, in fact, disgusted London, where the policy was to heal the wounds of war with all possible speed. "Why," said the King contemptuously, "the old fool has killed more people in that naked country than I have done here for the murder of my father!"

Nor did Sir William stop with the liquidation of collaborators. He also liquidated all the free institutions that had been established in Virginia. He refused to call the Assembly into session or to issue writs for the election of a new one. Not only did he reconstitute himself the final court of appeals, but he gradually arrogated to himself the function of all the courts. Far from standing up in defense of the rights of the colonists he grew increasingly careless of their physical safety. Where once he had vigorously explored the country and striven to thrust the wilderness ever further back, now he not only refused to do so himself, but irritably refused to permit anyone else to do so. He quibbled and delayed over the granting of land titles, even in the most plainly meritorious cases. He seemed determined to do whatever lay in his power to hold back the colony, geographically, politically, and every other way. It was at this time that he made his famous—and false—boast that there was not a printing press or a free school in all Virginia.

In brief, he faithfully reproduced in Virginia all the errors made by his former master King Charles I in England, and in the end like causes produced a like effect—civil war and the ruin of the autocrat. The Cromwell of the Virginia revolt was a man named Nathaniel Bacon, by no means an immaculate character himself, but a vigorous and resolute man. When the Indians committed depredations in his west-country neighborhood, and the Governor would do nothing, Bacon raised a force on his own responsibility and thrashed them soundly. The Governor was infuriated, but Bacon's popularity forced him to dissimulate for a while; but when the frontiersman raised a second force, proposing to finish his campaign, Berkeley denounced him as a traitor and ordered his arrest; whereupon Bacon marched, not against the Indians, but against Jamestown and took it, forcing the Governor to retire to a ship. But Berkeley was not to be disposed of easily. Assembling a naval force, he returned and attacked Bacon; a furious combat followed in which Jamestown was burned, but in the end the royal Governor was repulsed.

But then Bacon died, and with that the spirit went out of the revolt. Berkeley came back to Jamestown practically unopposed, and entered upon a career of vengeance so direful that London was shocked. He was suspended and ordered to England to explain his course; but he died before the case was adjudicated.

Here, then, is a man who set one figure in the American pattern, not wittingly, but quite strongly. Bacon's rebellion was never forgotten in Virginia. Especially vivid was the memory that it was defeated, not by the royal Governor, but by the death of its leader; up to that event it had been highly successful. All Virginia, therefore, knew not by hearsay but by experience that the royal authority was not invulnerable. It was entirely feasible to eject a Governor by force and violence, if he became quite intolerable.

This memory became important exactly a hundred years later, when the colonies once more found the royal Governors becoming intolerable. In this case Virginia was not the chief sufferer. It was Massachusetts. By that time Virginia was much the most populous and wealthiest of the colonies and might have been expected to be the most conservative. That she gave ready support to Massachusetts is certainly attributable in some measure, perhaps in large measure to her consciousness that she had once thrown out a Governor without provoking the wrath of heaven. Resistance to tyrannous rulers was already a part of the American pattern a century before the Declaration of Independence; and Sir William Berkeley is the man who provoked the resistance and thereby set the pattern.

3

If John Rolfe and William Berkeley outlined the first faint traces of the economic and political patterns of America, William Bradford and William Penn had as much to do with the intellectual and ethical patterns, as far as these were set by any Englishman. They therefore belong in the list of the lords spiritual.

The division, be it repeated for emphasis, was never absolute. In his own eyes William Penn was very decidedly a temporal ruler, and if William Bradford sought a heavenly city, yet he sought to build it on earth. Nevertheless, the lasting influence of both men was wielded in the realm of the mind and the spirit, rather than in the realm of business and politics.

Bradford was the first Governor of Plymouth colony, the second successful English settlement in what is now the United States. Plymouth eventually was overshadowed by the colony of Massachusetts Bay, and Bradford by its Governor, John Winthrop, a much more vigorous and aggressive man. Winthrop was in fact the moulder of New England to a much larger extent than Bradford; but on the lasting pattern of American life it was the quieter and simpler man who had the greater influence.

This is easily demonstrated by citing two expressions which students agree embodied the fundamental thinking of the two men. It was John Winthrop who wrote:

Democratie is, among most Civill nations accounted the meanest & worst of all formes of Governm't: & therefore in writers, it is branded w'th Reproachfull Epithets . . .: & Historyes doe recorde, that it hath been allwayes of least continuance & fullest of trouble.

It was William Bradford who, arguing for fellowship of all the churches when the world was rent by intolerant factions, wrote:

It is too great arrogancie for any man or church to thinke that he or they have so sounded the word of God to the bottome.

Three hundred years later there is no question at all as to which of these utterances set the lasting pattern of American life.

This has no bearing whatever on which was the greater man. The object here is not to balance merits, but to identify those Englishmen who first propounded ideas that were found acceptable by the American spirit in the American environment and so fixed the direction in which the nation was to proceed. The greater man was not necessarily always the more effective man in moulding America. John Locke was unquestionably a greater man than John Smith. Both undertook to guide the future of the country; but what Smith did had a profound and lasting effect, while what Locke did proved to be utterly futile;* in this study, accordingly, the smaller man demands more careful attention than the greater.

As an administrative officer William Bradford was good. This is sufficiently attested by the survival of his colony. He began with a more carefully selected group than the one that came to Virginia. The Pilgrims were accustomed to hard labor—Bradford himself was a yeoman, who afterward developed notable skill as a weaver—but they were far from being paupers or vagabonds. They brought with them much more and much better chosen equipment that the Virginians had; but at that the rigors of the wilderness came appallingly close to finishing them. By the end of the first year thirteen out of twenty-four heads of families had died and all but four of their wives. A mortality rate of sixty-eight per cent was not quite as bad as that among the indentured servants and convicts of Virginia, but it was bad enough to appall any but an extremely resolute man. Yet Bradford stuck it out, and he lived long enough to see his colony on a firm, solid footing.

John Winthrop's most effective contribution to the development of the American idea was his bringing the headquarters of his company from London to Massachusetts. Bradford ef-

---

* This refers, of course, to the fantastic scheme of government he worked out for the colony of Carolina, not to his philosophy, which had the same effect on Americans that it had upon thinkers elsewhere.

fected the same purpose by buying out his London stockholders. The result in each case was to reduce the absentee landlord handicap relatively early and to divest the colonies of part of their purely English character.

However, his economic and political devices do not constitute the great contribution made by William Bradford to the body of ideas that we inherited from the English. The great thing is to be found in his writings, which would have struck him as ironical since he made not the faintest pretense of being a literary man. Winthrop far surpassed him as a stylist, as he surpassed him in education and general culture.

But in everything Bradford wrote there is a reasonableness and lack of arrogance not equalled by the product of any other chronicler. Bradford indeed introduced an ideal that the United States of America has not realized, but to which it has paid at least lip service for three hundred years. This ideal is sometimes described as tolerance, but it was not tolerance; it was something greater that comprehended tolerance but went far beyond it. Bradford pleaded for religious fellowship, which later generations have translated into human fellowship, and which remains the far-off but radiant goal of all our hopes.

Of course he spoke the language of the seventeenth century, and in three hundred years words have changed their values so far that it is easy to misunderstand him even when we have his original manuscript before us. Were a man to employ the same phraseology today we should suspect him of cant and bigotry; but in William Bradford's day religion and politics were not merely entangled with each other; to a large extent they coalesced, they were locked in a relation resembling that which the zoologists call a syzygy, so close that men, with rare exceptions, could not think of them separately. Thus when Bradford argued for religious fellowship, he was arguing for the same thing that modern idealists sum up in the expression "One World."

That this is and has been from the beginning part of the

American pattern may seem a recklessly bold claim to those who are accustomed to thinking of internationalism as having begun with Woodrow Wilson, but the evidence to sustain the claim is abundant. Of course, it has always been an ideal, never realized in practice. It has always stood in contrast to another and bolder figure in the same pattern, that of a nationalism occasionally aggressive and always bombastic. But nations, like men, have often found it possible to believe simultaneously two contradictory doctrines, which explains why severely logical historians usually drift into the despair of Brooks and Henry Adams.

"We have erected a standard," said Washington, "to which the wise and honest can repair." "The world's best hope," said Jefferson of this government. "Dedicated to the proposition that all men are created equal," said Lincoln. In all these utterances, made long before Wilson or any of his advisers appeared, is the germ of William Bradford's belief that truth is not a monopoly of any one group and that all men must be heard if all the wisdom available in a community, or in a nation, or in a world, is to be utilized.

It is perfectly true that the seventeenth-century Pilgrim's view was a narrow one. He accepted in principle the theory that even the pagan Indians were human, but while they remained pagan they were enemies of God, hence necessarily enemies of the state. The infidel Turk came under the same condemnation. But his belief in human brotherhood was as broad as his conception of genuine humanity. The twentieth century's conception of humanity has widened, and it has not, in principle, repudiated his belief in brotherhood.

Even Bradford's philosophy could not always stand the test of living conditions. When Thomas Morton began to pass out brandy and gunpowder to the savages, then and there fellowship broke down, so Miles Standish went over under orders and threw Morton out of the colony. Yet it must be borne in mind that Morton forfeited his claim to consideration by his acts, not by his opinions, distasteful as those opinions were to the Pilgrim Governor. The fact is that William Bradford's idea has never been eradicated from the minds of the American people.

4

The diversity of paths by which men may reach the same goal has not often been better demonstrated than in the lives of William Bradford and William Penn. They were alike in being deeply religious men and adherents of minority sects; but otherwise the gulf was immense between the simple yeoman of Scrooby village, and the brilliant young cosmopolitan, lawyer, soldier, diplomat, personal friend of the Duke of York, who later became the King, and son of a famous admiral who was the friend of another King.

Penn was also one who sought to build a heavenly city upon an earthly site. He was more ostentatious about it than Bradford, carrying the idea even into the name of his city, which he called Brotherly Love; but his worldly shrewdness taught him that such a name, standing before the vulgar in raw English, was likely to produce more guffaws than genuflections, so he translated it into Greek. As Philadelphia it was, and is, taken with complete seriousness, even by its own crudest materialists.

But it was characteristic of Penn that he could whip the devil around the stump yet really give him a whipping. Behind the Greek façade the policy of Brotherly Love really existed and really was taken seriously by the early rulers of the city. Behind the frank desire to make money, Penn cherished a genuine desire to extend civilization which, like his contemporaries, he identified with the Christian religion. The curious thing, the thing that many strict logicians deem utterly impossible, is that he did both with marked success.

So he too set a pattern that has persisted in American thinking and has had some effect on American living. It is a figure that maddens extremists on both sides, for it confutes their basic doctrine. There are reactionaries who hold that for a business man to permit himself to become deeply concerned with social amelioration and the elevation of ethical standards reduces and is likely to destroy his efficiency as a business man; but Penn made more money out of his colony than any of the other proprietors except the Calverts and perhaps Lord Granville. There are idealists who hold that the profit motive cannot be pursued without attendant extortion and oppression, rarely without downright robbery; yet Penn acquired profit without enslaving the Indians at all, and without treating them as murderously as either the materialist Virginians or the religious New Englanders. By demonstration, not by argument, he stuck in the American mind, so firmly that it has never been shaken out, the idea that the Good Neighbor policy can be made to pay.

This was strictly an individual contribution. It was not simply because he was a Quaker. There have been many thousands of Quakers who were not Penns. The city of Brotherly Love itself in later years produced Quaker business men every whit as hard-fisted and hard-hearted as any Boston landlord or Virginia slave-driver.

But the founder and eponym of Pennsylvania was completely sincere in both his manifestations of profit-seeker and pietist.* Incidentally, it was the King who insisted that he give his own name to the colony; his own idea was to call it simply Sylvania, the forest country, an investment, not a monument. It does not appear that he troubled his head much about the philosophy of the affair. He simply appreciated the obvious fact that contention and strife are expensive as well as immoral, and

---

* Macaulay's furious denunciation of Penn as a hypocrite and thorough-paced scoundrel has not stood the test of critical examination in the hundred years since the *History of England* was published, although it still damns the Quaker in many minds.

most expensive in their most extreme form, which is full-scale war. To eliminate the causes of strife seemed, therefore, to serve both profit and piety; and he could not perceive, and never did perceive any inconsistency in that position.

In this connection it is necessary always to bear in mind one point: the Quaker position, as George Fox established it, is that war is the fruit, not the root, of evil. The roots of evil are the conditions that inevitably lead to war. The fact, therefore, that Penn, as a young man in Ireland, fought in a war which he had had no hand in bringing about involved no mortal sin; but as Governor of a colony his responsibility for war would have been direct and inescapable.

Nor have the Quakers ever advocated the doctrine of non-resistance to evil. On the contrary, all possible resistance short of murderous violence is enjoined upon them as a moral duty. The Calverts discovered this from William Penn himself. The Merry Monarch was never more gay and carefree than when he was dealing with such trifling matters as land boundaries. He had granted Cecil Calvert all the land north of the Potomac from the mouth of the river to the Fortieth parallel; then he proceeded to grant Penn territory north of Maryland, as everyone supposed; but when the charter was drawn up it included a stretch of land considerably below the Fortieth. In fact, that line runs squarely through the modern city of Philadelphia.

Baltimore naturally stuck to the terms of his original grant, but in Penn he encountered anything but a non-resister. Their legal battles raged for years and in the end Baltimore suffered defeat; so Maryland lost not only half of Philadelphia, but the whole of Chester, York, Gettysburg and many other towns in southern Pennsylvania. Without doubt it seemed to Penn that for so much land to go to Catholics was not only bad business but moral evil; and he resisted that evil as sturdily as any professional battler of his age.

He had to defend his proprietary interest against many other assaults, some of them arising from the disturbed condition of the times rather than from any specific dispute. For example, Penn's personal friend, when he came to the throne as James II, contrived to make himself so odious to his people that eventually he was thrown out. Naturally his friends, including Penn, were under a cloud and many of them lost everything; but Penn, after two strenuous years, managed to clear himself of all charges, including the strange one that he was a Jesuit in disguise. Toward the close of his life factional politics, not ordinary commercial losses, all but ruined him; yet to the end he managed to hold on to his title and to pass it to his sons. This record leaves no possible doubt that as a business man he was both astute and forceful. Had he been less, he would not have survived; yet it was consistently, almost monotonously true that when the clash of interests came, it was the pacifist Quaker who survived and his opponent who was extinguished.

All this contributed to the prosperity of the colony of Pennsylvania, but otherwise had little perceptible effect on the future of the United States. It was through what he did not do, rather than by what he did that Penn played a notable part in setting the American pattern.

For one thing, he did not oppress his colonists, yet he did not abdicate. He had plenty of trouble with ebullient and aggressive spirits in Pennsylvania, and while he was in England more than once he added to his own troubles by making bad choices for the office of Governor in his absence. Nevertheless, Penn had his full share of the aptitude that has been the salvation of the English aristocracy for ten generations—an apparently instinctive knowledge of just when and just how much to surrender.

The English aristocrat has not won an important victory over the English commoner for at least three hundred years. In practically every clash of wills for all that time the aristocrat eventually has knuckled under. Yet today, when the German aristocrats are for the most part buried, and French, Russian, Italian and Austrian noblemen are writing for newspapers, giving dancing lessons, driving taxicabs and washing dishes in foreign cities to keep body and soul together, the English lord remains an English lord in England. If he is a trifle out-at-elbows, so is the empire itself a trifle out-at-elbows. The fiery and bloody twentieth century has severely damaged the whole institution of aristocracy; but such remnants as survive belong to the English aristocrat as to no other. When driven to it he has been willing to surrender anything and everything, with one exception—his status as a member of the ruling class. The answer is, of course, that as long as he retained the status of a ruler, he had not surrendered anything that couldn't be regained if it was worth regaining.

Penn exhibited this trait with extraordinary clarity in his dealings with his colony. The original charter he granted them was somewhat less democratic than the one he had written for West Jersey; but when objections were raised to a specific point, Penn was always ready to negotiate. The result was that Pennsylvania made the transition from the feudal to the modern world, not through a revolutionary upheaval, but by a series of small steps, none of which was worth a first-class fight. Penn never stood upon his dignity. No request of the colonists was refused on the sole ground that it infringed the honor of the proprietor; but the result was not that he lost, but that he retained in increasing measure the respect of the colonists.

Unfortunately for England, the man on the throne a hundred years later was not an English aristocrat, but a German prince, to whom the art of judicious surrender was a closed book. George III could have learned from Penn how to preserve an empire; but it would have been beneath his dignity to learn statecraft from a simple gentleman, with no title at all. So, deservedly, he lost both his dominion and his dignity—in the end, even his wits.

Unfortunately for America, this figure in the pattern, although it was traced by Penn, has been filled in by his successors only indifferently well. Too often our adjustments have been delayed too long, and so had to be made in violence and bitterness—once by a titanic civil war that all but destroyed the country and did leave a third of it scarred and crippled for eighty years.

But it was Penn's policy in dealing with the Indians, his foreign policy, so to speak, that stamped an idea in the American mind which has been ignored frequently and for long periods, but which nevertheless remained. The taking of oaths was and is contrary to Quaker doctrine, so the arrangements made by the proprietor of Pennsylvania with the natives of the region were unsupported save by simple affirmation; yet, as some sardonic commentator has remarked, they were the only treaties between whites and Indians that were never sworn to and never violated. As a matter of fact, that statement is inexact; there were "incidents," not a few. But when it could be clearly proved that a white man had instigated the trouble, the white Governor took stern measures; and the result—quite incredible to most white men—was that ere long when it could be clearly proved that an Indian had started the trouble, the Indian chiefs took even sterner measures. There was no Indian war in Pennsylvania until William Penn had been in his grave for years.

He had few imitators. In general the record of the English in dealing with the Indians can be summed up in a word—extermination. It was not exclusively butchery; banishment served the purpose as well. But the Indian had to move or die. It is true that two hundred years later there was a revulsion of feeling that made the small remnant of the race wards of the nation, and so carefully have they been looked after since that some ethnologists hold that there are more Indians alive in the United States today than there were in the same territory in 1607.

But even as the conquest was proceeding there were Americans who believed it was all wrong, and who cried out against it unceasingly. Their great argument was the record of William Penn, who advanced civilization without a sword, and the outcry fixed that figure in the pattern of American thought. Even Henry Clay, "War Hawk" though he was, talked, at least in public, of a moral, not a military hegemony over the western hemisphere; and William McKinley, in the act of establishing a far eastern empire, insisted that the only excuse for our taking over the Philippines, was to lead the Filipinos to liberty under law.

If Wilson could pay for Panama even at the risk of seeming to repudiate one of his predecessors it was because in the pattern of American thought the figure traced by William Penn was still clear. The second Roosevelt's plea for his Good Neighbor policy was comprehensible to the average American in part because as a schoolboy he had been taught that William Penn had tried such a policy in the early days and it worked.

5

An important fact, a fact so important that its comprehension is essential to any real understanding of American history, is the apparent paradox that the pattern set by the English was not an English pattern.

English minds devised it, to be sure, and those minds were conditioned by English experience. It was applied by Englishmen with no other thought than to reproduce English institutions. Nevertheless, the result was not English. Of course, this became conspicuously true after there was a considerable infiltration of immigrants from other countries. But it was true before that. Bermuda Hundred, in Virginia, was never an English village. Neither was Salem, in Massachusetts, not even when John Winthrop was Governor and every white inhabitant either was born in England, or born of English parents in this country.

Geography and climate modified the pattern. The forest modified it profoundly. The very sea was not quite that "silver sea" in which "this precious stone . . . this England" was set, and the difference was felt in the pattern of life. The presence of savage neighbors modified it, but if there had not been an Indian in North America, still the pattern would have been not quite English.

This was imperfectly understood for a long time. As late as the time of the Revolution the colonists were laboring under the impression that they were still essentially English, or at any rate British. They spent much time and energy protesting that the utmost limit of their desire was to be treated as Englishmen, and there is no reason to doubt their sincerity. But there is every reason to doubt their accuracy. They were not Englishmen. Crèvecoeur noted the fact, but he attributed it to the mixture of races, whereas it went beyond that. George Washington was not the product of a mixture of races, but he was no Englishman, even though he thought he was. The land itself had shaped him and moulded him into a different sort of man, regardless of his English blood.

Some of the greatest of Englishmen fell into the error of supposing that the land, if not exactly a vacuum, was certainly no more than an instrumentality to be handled by the settlers for their own purposes; they did not suspect that the land itself might handle the settlers, if not for its purposes, at least according to its own nature. But the land—any land—is malleable only to a limited extent; to a very large extent it is the people who live on it who must bend to conform themselves to the land.

This is clearly demonstrated by what happened to ideas when they were devised by Englishmen who knew nothing of the country and had no share in applying their notions. The most celebrated case is that of the "Fundamental Constitutions" drawn up by the philosopher, John Locke, to serve as the organic law of the territory held jointly by eight British noblemen and called by them Carolina. It must be remembered that Locke was regarded by his own generation as what ours would describe as "a parlor pink," if not an outright Red. Although he had been brought up in a Puritan household, he was a strong protagonist of religious tolerance, which was radical doctrine at the time, and in general he received recognition as the philosopher of liberty.

It was just this reputation that induced the Lords Proprietors of Carolina to commission him to draw up a scheme for the perfect government. They assumed, and so did Locke, that in a practically empty country they could set up pretty much any kind of government they saw fit to choose. Apparently it never crossed their minds that any government that would work in America had to be American to an important degree. So Locke drew up a scheme, not, indeed, English, but not anything else, certainly not in the least American. He divided the territory into eight counties (the number of the proprietors) and the counties into seigniories, baronies, precincts and colonies. The supreme ruler was to be the Palatine, and under him were three orders of nobility, Landgraves, Caciques and Barons, while the common people were to be serfs.

Of course the project got nowhere. The territory itself could not hold together, much less Mr. Locke's ingenious and elaborate scheme of government. The northern part had from the beginning been closely allied to Virginia and the northern colonies, while the southern part was oriented toward the West Indies and had, in fact, closer connection with London than with Jamestown or Philadelphia. Between them was a wide stretch of swampy, heavily-forested country, which settlers fought shy of for generations. It soon became impracticable to govern both from any one central point, so they had to be divided into North and South Carolina, and the two colonies developed separately pretty much as did all the others. When the Crown bought out the proprietors in 1729 Mr. Locke's scheme ceased to be even a theory.*

Somewhat more effective than Philosopher Locke was another gentlemanly intellectual who flourished a generation later. This was James Edward Oglethorpe, one of the most attractive and at the same time one of the most baffling figures among all the Englishmen who came to America in the early days. Oglethorpe was an aristocrat, an intellectual, a soldier—he served under Prince Eugene and won the accolade of that brilliant commander's approbation—a politician, holding his seat in the Commons for thirty-two consecutive years, and withal a moralist and an energetic uplifter. He had the combination of military skill and mysticism that characterized "Chinese" Gordon. He had the combination of political shrewdness and rather spectacular piety that characterized W. J. Bryan. He was at once an imperialist and a Utopian. He believed in the empire, prohibition, abolition and prison reform. He welcomed to America the brothers Charles and John Wesley, Moravians, Salzburg Lutherans, Swiss and Highland Scotch Presbyterians. The Moravians were conscientious objectors to any war, and the Highlanders were equally conscientious participants in every war.

---

* Indirectly, however, it had the curious result of creating what was probably the largest landed estate (in theory) held by a private individual in human history—unless Adam, proprietor of the whole earth, be accounted an exception. When the King bought out the rest of the proprietors one stubborn member, John Carteret, Earl Granville, refused to sell and demanded that his one-eighth be laid out and conveyed to him. Accordingly, he was solemnly given a title to all the land from the Virginia line, at thirty-six degrees thirty minutes, south to thirty-five degrees thirty-four minutes, and running west to the "South Sea." Lord Granville's heirs held this title until the Revolution, which made them legal owners of an estate having at its eastern edge Kill-Devil Hill, where the Wright brothers made their first airplane flight, and at its western edge the site of the city of Monterey, on the California coast, a trifle of something over 85,-000,000 acres. It is sometimes claimed that the Van Rensselaer holdings, of some 700,000 acres in New York State, constituted the largest estate in America; but Van Rensselaer was to Granville as a postage-stamp is to a barn-door.

These were the disparate and frequently antipathetic elements that made up the colony of Georgia, last of the thirteen to be chartered (1732), and a colony not quite like any of the others. Where the Carolinas, Virginia, New Jersey and New York were primarily commercial ventures although they had religious overtones, while Maryland, Pennsylvania and New England were primarily religious enterprises with commercial overtones, Georgia's primary reason for existence was neither profit nor piety. It was deliberately designed as a buffer state, to stand between South Carolina and her formidable neighbor Spain, owner of Florida. For this reason Oglethorpe took great satisfaction in rounding up the Scots, for while they were usually pious and thrifty they were almost without exception very tough fighting men.

This was Oglethorpe the empire-builder; but it was Oglethorpe the uplifter who conceived the idea of employing the buffer state as at the same time a sanctuary for oppressed minorities. He had in mind especially the inmates of the English debtors' prisons, but he extended his tolerance to all the persecuted, even to Moravian pacifists. These, however, did not long remain with him, for the buffer state proved to be just that at the outbreak of the War of the Austrian Succession in 1740. The principal town of the colony was Savannah, with Frederica, on the Altamaha River, as an outpost. From Frederica Oglethorpe marched against Florida, but was thrown back; then the Spaniards marched against Frederica, but were thrown back in their turn. The buffer state served its purpose, but the nerve-strain was too much for the Moravians who decamped, most of them to Pennsylvania.

Unlike Locke, Oglethorpe came to Georgia as Governor and observed with his own eyes the working, and particularly the failures, of his system. He began to modify it immediately and continued to make adjustments one by one until he surrendered his rights to the Crown in 1753 and retired to spend the

remaining thirty years of his life in the literary circle that included Samuel Johnson, Boswell, Goldsmith, Horace Walpole
and Burke. It must be admitted, therefore, that his system was
appreciably more viable than Locke's Fundamental Constitutions, but it lasted as long as it did only because its creator
made timely changes to adjust it to local conditions, which is to
say, to make it more American. The gentry, no matter how
able, could not fashion in England a scheme that would fit
America.

At that, Oglethorpe throttled the colony and eventually had
to give it up on account of his stubborn adherence to two
highly moral concepts; these were the prohibition of slavery
and liquor. A century and a half later it became practicable by
heavy fighting to enforce one of these ideas; but after three centuries the other is still too advanced for America. Another
difficulty that hampered Oglethorpe was his system of land
tenure. No settler was permitted to hold land in fee simple,
but in what is known in law by the weird term of "tail male,"
which has no reference to a caudal appendage, but made the
conveyance of real estate next to impossible.

Here was another "great social experiment, noble in motive
and far-reaching in purpose" which had the effect of provoking
disorder and undermining the law. Without doubt what Oglethorpe had in mind was to prevent the development of *lati-
fundia,* the enormous landholdings that helped ruin Rome and
for two hundred years were a curse to New York State. Tail
male meant that small owners could not be inveigled into selling their holdings to speculators or agents of great landlords by
making it conveyable only to heirs male; but in practice it
prevented them from selling at all. In England this might have
been a secondary consideration, but Georgia was not England.
It was wilderness country, in process of being settled; the land
had to be first cleared and then tilled, and the more rapid the
process the faster the development of the colony. But the best

woodsman was not necessarily the best husbandman; hence it was to the interest of the community that the expert at felling timber should be able to dispose of his cleared ground to an expert farmer, while the woodsman went on to clear more land. Oglethorpe's noble ideal thus proved to be a handicap upon the colony which American conditions compelled it to reject.

Charles Wesley was Oglethorpe's secretary for a few months, and Charles' brother, John, was not only made welcome in the colony, but was encouraged in his missionary endeavors. Between them, they planted Methodism in America, although their own experience was none too happy, owing in part to temperamental difficulties and in part to unfortunate entanglements with women. These entanglements, be it hastily explained, were less amorous than militant; John had an unlucky love affair, but the main trouble was the spite of certain viragoes, who made life a burden to the brothers. The seedling plant of Methodism might have withered after the Wesleys left had it not been for the timely arrival of George Whitefield, under whose ministrations it sprang up and flourished exceedingly.

The part of the American pattern set by Oglethorpe is less easily traced than that contributed by some of the other gentlemen of quality who came to these shores from England. His great material accomplishment was his success in blocking the advance of Spain, to which the establishment of a thirteenth flourishing colony was secondary. But certain mental and spiritual qualities of the man took root in American soil and still survive. To say that he had any important part in moulding the American spirit is to go too far; but he gave the world a preview of some of its phases.

Oglethorpe had the sort of idealism that places an exaggerated value upon motive. He never entirely comprehended the important qualification that St. Paul put upon his own claim to exemption from the old law; all things were lawful to him, said the Apostle, "but all things are not expedient." Oglethorpe was one of those who believed that anything that seemed to him right and good should be done forthwith; and none will deny that he has had a host of successors in the United States. One of our weaknesses as a people has been a tendency to rush into righteousness with small regard for who or what may be trampled in our haste. Emancipation at the price of a ruinous war and a Draconian peace, prohibition at the price of fourteen years of orgiastic crime, self-determination at the price of the fragmentation of Europe, all, at one time or another, have seemed quite worth while to a majority of the American people.

A great American who was temperamentally the reverse of Oglethorpe commented on this with his tale of the time when he paid sixpence for a penny whistle. Since the days of James Edward Oglethorpe it has been part of the American pattern to pay too much for our whistle. And this truth remains, no matter how ardently we insist that the whistle has been both sweet and shrill.

Book Two

❦

THE INSTITUTIONS

Chapter I

✥

THE LANGUAGE

1

If the Englishman himself underwent a perceptible transformation by the mere fact of transferring his residence to
America, English culture underwent a much more profound
modification. The basis, or at least the preservative of that culture, the language, was altered so radically that some scholars,
notably H. L. Mencken,* contend that it has become a distinct
language, merely affiliated to the King's English.

The distinction, however, is philological. The ordinary American can understand what people are saying in London and can
make himself understood. He runs into difficulties, but hardly
greater difficulties than a white man from Minnesota and a
black man from Georgia, neither particularly well educated,
would encounter in trying to converse.

The King's English is now, of course, a subsidiary dialect. Of
the 270,000,000 people who speak some variety of English,
nearly 140,000,000 inhabit the continental United States and
11,000,000 are Canadians, while the United Kingdom (England,
Scotland, Wales, North Ireland, Isle of Man and Channel Islands) has less than fifty million inhabitants. Without North
America, Hawaii and the Philippines, English would now be

---

* See his *The American Language,* the most careful and elaborate, as well as
the most brilliant existing study of our variety of English.

115

spoken by fewer people than Russian or Spanish, not to mention the great Oriental languages, Hindi and Chinese.

Yet while it seems to be true that in this deal England has lost control of her own language, it is incontestably true that through it she has exercised dominion over American thought to an incalculable extent. It is not difficult to see why, when one considers that this is probably the most powerful linguistic instrument in human history. To begin with, English is by far the largest of all languages. There are seven hundred thousand English words recognized by respectable lexicographers, while if one adds the vulgar, the profane and the obscene, it is estimated that the total would run above a million.

It is the most hospitable of all languages. Its enormous growth is due, not to coinages, but to adoptions; there is hardly a living language and few dead ones from which English has not adopted some words. This process was facilitated by its loose grammatical structure; Mencken, in fact, has argued that there is no English grammar, properly speaking, and that such rules as exist are not native to the language, but were borrowed largely from Latin, and imposed upon the vernacular by scholars who customarily wrote in Latin.

A language so flexible was superbly adapted to the needs of a country that was to be inhabited by people of innumerable racial origins. English is difficult, perhaps the most difficult of all languages, because the significance of an English word frequently depends, not only upon the characters with which it is written, or the syllables with which it is pronounced, but upon its position in a sentence, or even the stress with which it is spoken. Take, for example, the four words, "She only said no," and give each in turn a little more stress than you give the other three. You will get four statements of markedly different significance; when stress is laid on the third and then on the fourth, in fact, you get statements of flatly contradictory significance. It is no wonder that the language is frequently the despair of students whose mother tongue is not English.

But its resources are proportionate to its difficulty. For instance, there are three hundred thousand scientific and technical terms recognized by English dictionaries, as many as there are all told in Kurschner's *Universal-Konversations-Lexikon,* a standard German word-book. Most of these are English strictly by adoption, being built on foreign roots, usually Latin or Greek, as are most English nouns for new things, *bicycle* and *telephone,* for instance. American English seems to take classical roots even more readily than the King's English—*elevator,* for example, instead of *lift, suspenders* instead of *braces,* and *radio* instead of *wireless.* Presumably this is attributable to the fact that the majority of Americans today are not of Anglo-Saxon origin and have no special feeling for Anglo-Saxon words; if so, it is another indication of the length to which the divergence from the parent stock has gone.

English maintained its dominance because of the successful defense of North America against the Spanish and the successive expulsions of the Swedes, the Dutch and the French. Before the Revolution the infiltration of peoples of other stocks was too slight to have any perceptible influence upon the language except locally and temporarily, as in New York, where Dutch survived for some time after the English conquest, not only in sermons, but in legal documents. Six years after the treaty of peace the explosion occurred in France, followed swiftly by the Napoleonic wars, which practically suspended European immigration for twenty years. Even as late as 1820, when official immigration figures began to be kept, the influx was only a little over eight thousand, largely British.

But in the thirty years from 1790 to 1820 the total population of the country increased from less than four millions to well over nine and a half millions, which gives some idea of the procreativeness of the colonial population—a rather faint idea, because the infant mortality rate was prodigious. The birthrate nevertheless was such as to absorb that mortality and still provide an annual increase in the order of a hundred and ninety thousand a year. Against this flood a trickle of less than ten thousand immigrants was nothing. Even if none of the early immigrants had spoken English, as most of them did, their linguistic influence would have been negligible.

These are some of the reasons why the dominance of English as the language of the country has never been seriously threatened. Efforts to establish a secondary language were made in many places, other than the efforts of the New York Dutch, already mentioned. In the churches, especially, one hears of sermons preached in every modern European language and in Latin. But invariably within a few years the congregations that were hearing a Sunday sermon in Dutch, or German, or French, or Gaelic, were hearing an afternoon sermon in English; and the foreign-language sermon usually disappeared with the rise of the second generation.

Not until after the Civil War did immigration from non-English-speaking countries become massive; and by that time the English-speaking population was so tremendous that not even a million immigrants a year could make much impression on the language. Except in areas already settled and taken over, such as New York, Louisiana and California, there has been no serious attempt to establish an auxiliary language that would be accepted by the courts of law. Parish registers in other languages exist in many places; but after the Revolution these, even though they might be accepted in evidence, were not strictly speaking official. With the negligible exceptions already mentioned, English has always been the language of the governments and the courts.

It is one of history's little ironies that no polyglot empire of the old world has dared be as ruthless in imposing a single language upon its whole population as was the liberal republic

"dedicated to the proposition that all men are created equal."
Austro-Hungary, czarist Russia, even Turkey, tyrannies though
they were, maintained bi-lingual schools and courts in many
parts of their domains. Switzerland remains tri-lingual to this
day. Even France, more nearly monolithic than the British
Isles, was compelled to tolerate the *langue d'oc* for centuries,
while one of the counts against imperial Germany was its ty-
rannical imposition of German upon Alsace and Lorraine.
But the idea that Charleston, for instance, was duty bound to
maintain French public schools for Huguenot children, or New
York Italian schools for Italian children, has never been seriously entertained.*

The question did not arise here for the simple reason that
it was useless for the immigrant to raise it. Even in those
areas where the concentration of non-English-speaking people
was great—in the Hudson River valley, for instance, in western
Pennsylvania, later in Minnesota and, of course, in all the great
cities, the overwhelming mass of the surrounding population
spoke English and the necessity of doing business with the
English-speakers made it very much to the interest of the new-
comers to learn English as rapidly as possible.

Furthermore, after the Revolution, there was no outer com-
pulsion to act as a solidifying influence upon those whose
mother tongue was not English. The Germans of western
Pennsylvania, for instance, were subjected to no sort of legal
pressure to abandon their language, therefore it never became
a point of honor with them to maintain it. If they chose to
speak German, the law was not interested. Therefore, in rejecting English they merely handicapped themselves without
even the inner consolation of feeling that they defied tyrannous
authority.

The result was that English, as the language of the United
States and of Canada, except for one small corner, became es-

* The slight recognition of Spanish in New Mexico is one small exception.

tablished over a larger contiguous area supporting a greater population than was covered by any other single language in the history of the world. The Latin of imperial Rome and the Mandarin of imperial China, were official languages of immense areas, but they were never more than official. Both were legally established over continuous land masses comparable to the North American continent, but for official purposes only. On the other hand, the resident of Vancouver, British Columbia, addresses not only the judge on the bench, but also his wife, or his horse, in words easily understood by the resident of Jacksonville, Florida.

Perhaps this has had an influence stronger even than the absence of political frontiers in creating the economic solidarity of the continent. This is suggested by the fact that the presence of one political frontier, the Canadian boundary, has by no means destroyed that solidarity, because it is not paralleled by a language frontier. In any event, the dominance of a single language over the whole territory of the United States has had an incalculably powerful effect in setting the pattern of American life.

2

It is difficult to believe that anyone will deny that the effect of having a single language has been fortunate for the country. Few will deny the further proposition that it is, on the whole, fortunate that this single language happened to be English. In view of its peculiar problems and conditions, this country has found the merits of the English language far outweigh its demerits; but in considering the influence of the English people upon America, the defects of their language are no more to be overlooked than its obvious advantages.

From the dim beginning of their history the English have been a foot-loose people, or, rather, a conglomerate of foot-loose peoples. The original Britons may have been a home-keeping folk. We do not know, because long before there was anything properly describable as England they were overwhelmed by a succession of rambling tribes, Angles, Saxons, Jutes, Danes and, finally, Normans. Restlessness was a prominent characteristic of all these peoples. They went everywhere, they poked into everything. The Emperor of Byzantium had a contingent of them among his bodyguard. They had establishments in Kiev while Moscow was still a collection of hovels. They were in Sicily and North Africa and, of course, at every European court. But they did not simply go out. Large numbers of them came back and went away again; and on every return they brought home, among other things, new words and new turns of speech.

So by the time their island kingdom developed into a maritime, trading nation, their language already had some kinship with every form of speech known to man, or at least European man and the Levantines. It was a traders' speech, readily adaptable to the expression of new ideas as well as the description of new products. What could have been better suited to the purposes of people engaged in erecting a new nation in a new world? The English language picked up such words as *potato, tomato, tobacco, moccasin* and *tomahawk* as readily as the English colonist picked up knowledge of the proper use of these thitherto unknown articles; which was very readily indeed.

Perhaps from the standpoint of the trader, even its great defect might be turned to profitable account. English is not an exact language. It is all but impossible to make a statement in English that is susceptible of but one interpretation. In an inflected language, such as Latin, a statement once put in proper form, is immutable. As some ingenious grammarian has pointed out, the Latin *Caesar interfecit Pompeium* and *Pompeium interfecit Caesar* mean exactly the same, but the English "Caesar killed **Pompey**" is not quite the same as "Pompey killed Caesar."

The result is that to draw a contract in English, if the agreement is at all complex, is a matter of such extreme difficulty that the legal profession has thrived on it for centuries. Yet it is going far to assert that this is altogether deplorable in the eyes of a shrewd trader. "What good, Mawruss," asked one of Montague Glass' characters, "is a lawyer that can't get us out of a contract he drew himself?" There is small doubt that the ambiguity of his language has many a time been the salvation of a Yankee skipper whose position had been materially altered by wind and weather and the passage of time, leaving calculated dishonesty aside.

The usefulness of this characteristic in the wide realm of politics is too obvious to need stress. The platform of any political party may be cited as evidence. Such documents are drawn frankly for the purpose of pleasing the largest possible number of voters, which means that they must seem to be all things to all men. In this respect they are usually masterly. The opposition party has, of course, an expert body of faultfinders whose task is to riddle the platform, but only in the rarest instances do they achieve any real success. As a rule the platform is so impervious to assault that it is easy for a party speaker in Maine to claim that the party stands for one thing, while simultaneously another speaker in Georgia is claiming that it stands for the diametrically opposite policy, both citing the platform as authority. Indeed, it is not unheard-of for the candidate himself to interpret the platform in opposite ways when he is speaking in Wisconsin and when he is speaking in Texas.

It is true, of course, that there is no language as yet devised that a devious man cannot use in devious ways, but English seems to lend itself to that sort of thing exceptionally well. Serious-minded commentators are accustomed to regard the effect that this has had upon the pattern of our political life as deplorable without reservation.

Yet it is possible to argue that the fact that written English is ambiguous has had an effect not altogether deleterious. The average voter learned long ago that the platform, because it seems to mean all things, really means nothing, and therefore pays little attention to it. He is thus forced to give more attention to the candidates, and this works to the advantage of the country, for the people are notoriously better judges of men than of measures.

It is easy to confuse the voters with regard to measures, but much more difficult to deceive them when their attention is concentrated on men. The most flagrant errors made by the American electorate have been made when public attention was concentrated on measures, rather than on men. In 1868 and again in 1872 the fight was over Reconstruction, a policy, and the most blatantly corrupt administrations in our history followed. Grant was never studied as a man; he was a lay-figure, the symbol of military victory. In similar fashion, the issue in 1920 was the League of Nations, and the voters were assured by figures as respectable as William H. Taft and Elihu Root that the way to assure our entrance into the League was to elect Harding. The candidate himself was subjected to no real scrutiny and neither was his opponent. The election was decided on a measure, not on the character of a man. The result was an orgy of corruption that ranks next to Grant's as the worst we ever suffered.

The very fact, therefore, that ordinarily nobody pays much attention to party platforms because they mean nothing, tends to concentrate attention upon the men who are candidates for public office; and whatever impels the people to study men, rather than measures, tends to produce wiser decisions than would otherwise be made. In politics, therefore, the ambiguity of the English language has its advantages as well as its disadvantages.

Possession of the English language has made the American people heirs to one of the great literatures of the world, which has been, like most large inheritances, both a help and a handicap.

What living Americans know as English literature was as yet largely uncreated when Captain Newport sailed into the mouth of the James River in 1607. Chaucer was the only one of its giants whose works might have been available to the early colonists; even the King James version of the Bible was still four years in the future. William Shakespeare was a successful producer-playwright who had gotten rich by the process of taking all the cold turkeys of the English stage, warming them over, and serving them up with a sauce of his own concoction; he had published nineteen of his plays, but a quarter of a century was to pass before some dim appreciation of the power of his magic began to spread abroad. Solicitor-general Bacon, "Sir Francis" for only three years, had published only a book of essays. The wife of a London tunesmith named Milton would give birth the next year to a son they were to call John. It was to be exactly one hundred years before Henry Fielding would appear to start the mighty line of the English novel.

The greater part of English literature thus came to Americans not by direct inheritance, nor yet through their own efforts. They were somewhat in the position of collateral heirs, cousins three thousand miles removed, and living in an environment differing from that in which the literature was produced. It was a rich cultural possession, but it probably operated to stifle native production; pioneer life is ungracious to artistic endeavor in any case, and when a literature flowering magnificently was already available, the impulse to produce one of our own was doubly discouraged.

The very fact that the production of this literature was contemporaneous with the establishment of the American nation may have emphasized the colonial status of the Americans. Perhaps had the American writer of the early days been faced with the competition of second-rate Englishmen he might have been stimulated to greater endeavors; but to raise one's voice when Shakespeare and Milton were speaking—well, one must respect the discretion of colonials who refrained.

It took a long time for Americans to discover—indeed, their realization is not yet complete—that the man who writes of America in America and writes the truth, is not and cannot be speaking Shakespeare's language, except in the sense that the greatest art cannot be utterly destroyed, even by inept translation and therefore is to a degree independent of language. Dante is impressive in Spanish, Cervantes in English, Shakespeare in German, and the man who writes in the American variety of English in measure as he is original challenges comparison with them all.

But there was a long period in American life when it was assumed that American writing must be judged, not by universal, but by English standards. Naturally, the more nearly American writers approximated those standards, the further apart they drew from their environment, and the more jejune and empty their production. Critics and public alike long accepted this intellectual right of mortmain, and the dead hand lay heavily upon such creative genuises as Melville and Whitman, to the incalculable damage of American letters.

This, note well, was not the deliberate choice of critics, public, or writers. It was nobody's fault; it was inherent in the situation. It is simply one item to be balanced against the enormous benefits accruing from the fact that the language of the country opened English literature to American readers.

3

The one item in that literature that has had the widest and most profound effect on the pattern of American life was, of course, what is known as the Authorized, or King James, version of the English Bible.

The moral and ethical concepts expressed in the Bible belong to a discussion of religion, not of language; but, partly due to fortuitous circumstances, the language of this particular version of the Scriptures was in itself a powerful influence. Because of its sacred and official character the book fixed certain foms of speech immovably. The style of any other book was subject to the vagaries of fashion and within a generation might be held in such slight esteem as to lose all authority. It is to be remembered that even Shakespeare suffered a period of relative eclipse; fifty years after his death John Dryden was esteemed so much the greater poet that when he undertook to correct and improve Shakespeare's plays nobody laughed.

But this version of the Bible was appointed to be read in churches by the King's command. It was and it remained for more than two hundred years the only version accepted as authoritative by Protestant churches using the English language; therefore much of its quality was imposed upon secular speech.

It is the good fortune of the English-speaking peoples that the translation was made at precisely the right time, from the standpoint of the language. English had just passed one of the highest peaks in its history, the tremendous outburst of creative energy that culminated in William Shakespeare. Like all supremely great periods, that one had begun to run into an efflorescence that was to degenerate into mere gaudiness; but in the year 1604 the degeneration had not proceeded far. If it had begun to decline a bit in content, in form English prose was at that moment more richly ornate than it ever was before. It was, in fact, on the verge of becoming so ornate as to be unintelligible.

In this year the King called a conference to discuss those differences between High Church and Low Church that were threatening the unity of Anglicanism. One of his recommendations was that the learned doctors try to do something about the differences in the half-dozen versions of the Bible in English that were widely accepted. The conference took this recommendation with great seriousness and the outcome was the appointment of a committee including forty-seven of the most learned men in England, who were charged with the task of comparing all existing English versions with each other and with such ancient texts as were available in Greek, Latin, Hebrew and other eastern languages, with a view to producing the best possible translation. Every bishop in England was commanded to address a letter to all scholars in his diocese ordering them to assist the work; and the universities of Oxford and Cambridge were instructed to make their facilities available.

The forty-seven committeemen were not all theologians. The best linguists in the realm were included. For instance, Sir Henry Savile, a layman but regarded as the most learned man in all England, was a member, and several lay professors of Greek and Hebrew collaborated. These men, needless to say, were affected by the spirit of the times. Their idea of the best English usage was the idea prevalent among the ablest contemporary writers, who were then enthralled by conceits and fancies, fine-drawn metaphors, flowery periods, above all by rhythm and sonority.

The translators, as men of their time, were powerfully influenced by this trend, but its debasing effect on their literary taste was largely corrected by their tremendous respect for their task. They felt a strong urge to write splendidly; but they were sworn before God and the King to write accurately, and they never doubted that jail in this world and hell in the next would be their just reward for playing tricks with the text. The result was that they wrote splendidly, but with a restraint not imposed upon secular writers of the period; and that restraint saved them from the prevalent folly of the times.

So the English language at one of its greatest periods received a Bible that soars far above the rest of the writings even of that great period. This, be it repeated for emphasis, refers strictly to its style, apart from its philosophical content. For example, the first six verses of the fifty-third chapter of Isaiah in the King James version attain a level that in its combination of majesty and grace has rarely been touched by English poetry in its highest moments; and the music of the whole book of Job makes even that of John Milton frequently sound forced and strained.

This incomparable work was given to the world in 1611, just four years after Christopher Newport had landed his first group of colonists at Jamestown, and nine years before the Pilgrims embarked in the *Mayflower*. Its reading was immediately required in all churches, and its study was enjoined upon all communicants. Americans, therefore, had it forced upon their attention from the very beginning, and its effect upon their manner of speech has been conspicuous ever since.

But it accomplished a great deal more toward setting the pattern of American life than merely establishing certain turns of phrase. The use of a single version of the Bible throughout Protestant America erected the language of that version into a sort of intellectual shorthand, a means by which a whole complex of ideas could be conveyed from speaker to hearer with a single phrase. Ethan Allen at Ticonderoga, shouting, "In the name of the great Jehovah and the Continental Congress!" instantly spread the idea of a Holy War throughout an America thoroughly familiar with "The sword of the Lord and of Gideon!" and all the ideas connected with it. A century and a half later Woodrow Wilson, saying, "We thank God and take

courage" conveyed to millions of readers of the Acts of the
Apostles a sense of calm after tempest, dry land after a stormy
sea and an encounter with a friendly envoy after long journey-
ing through hostile territory.

Naturally, this smoothing of the avenues of communication
was a great force strengthening national unity. In the early
days of the republic, when the population, almost to a man, was
well versed in the King James version, speakers and writers
could address the whole nation with a remarkable economy of
words by drawing upon this storehouse of common knowledge.
The part it played in welding thirteen disparate colonies into a
single nation is incalculable, but certainly was great.

It had other effects less advantageous. The English Bible was
a mighty creator of intellectual stereotypes. Its language,
under the ministrations of literal-minded parsons, attained a
sanctity that spread its odor over a great deal of hollow cant.
The devil's advocates learned to quote Scripture to their purpose very rapidly and to stunning effect. To this day, in many
parts of the country, the most dubious sort of proposition, put
forward in stately Scriptural language, is given faith and credit
that would never be accorded it were it described in language
not reminiscent of the Holy Book.

Furthermore, the music of the King James Bible may have
led Americans to put an exaggerated value upon the sonorous
phrase which makes them fall easy prey to bombast. If it is true
that almost all of our great state papers owe much of their
effectiveness to echoes of Biblical language, it is also true that
from the same source has sprung more bad oratory than from
any other book in the language. Little more than half a century ago the whole course of the political, and perhaps of the
economic history of the country came astonishingly close to
being changed by a single speech; and none denies that the
main impact of that speech came when the orator turned to
the New Testament for his peroration: "You shall not press

down upon the brow of labor this crown of thorns. You shall not crucify mankind upon a cross of gold."

It is questionable, however, that even a William J. Bryan could produce in 1949 as powerful an effect as he produced in 1896 with an apt allusion to the Bible. This is one part of the pattern set by the English that is fading perceptibly. Acquaintance with the Bible, and specifically with the King James version, is by no means as universal as it was only fifty years ago. What this may signify as regards morals and social institutions is not the point under consideration here; but one secondary effect deserves mention. An allusion to Scripture today frequently fails of its effect, because those to whom it is addressed do not know the Scriptures. This increases the difficulties of traders in ideas.

In 1946 H. L. Mencken complained publicly that when he described certain persons as modern Chaldeans and soothsayers, he was bombarded with inquiries from puzzled readers who did not know what he was talking about. In his youth * practically every literate man was acquainted with the second chapter of the Book of Daniel, which describes how King Nebuchadnezzar, confronted by developments that he did not understand, called for his Chaldeans exactly as a modern President in similar circumstances calls out his stable of dream-interpreters, currently known as analysts of public-opinion polls. Thus a passing reference to Chaldeans and soothsayers conveyed an idea that could not be transmitted otherwise without the employment of many more than three words.

Since there is no other writing that has ever been studied by anything like as large a proportion of the whole population, there is nothing that writers and speakers can substitute for the

---

* Another sign of the times is the fact that many persons, knowing that Mr. Mencken is distinctly not a theologian, are astonished to learn that he is a highly skilled exegete; but comprehensive knowledge of the Authorized Version was taken for granted as part of the equipment of every competent writer, lay as well as clerical, in the passing generation.

Bible in this particular function. Thus the effects of the increasing ignorance of its terminology are not by any means confined to religion and ethics; one effect is to make more difficult the circulation of ideas and the mobilization of public opinion in support of them. The English Bible has been an intellectual bond, and a strong one, making the various regions more easily comprehensible to each other.

The remarkable unity in habits of thought achieved by a continental domain is a characteristic of the republic that has impressed all thoughtful observers, native and foreign alike. The contribution of the King James Bible to the achievement of this unity is seldom stressed; but it was probably very much larger than most people realize. Certainly it was a figure in the pattern and probably it was a highly important one.

Its influence in stabilizing and standardizing English speech from Oregon to Florida was also important, but that is a point of scholarship which only philologists are competent to discuss and which, therefore, has no proper place in a general survey. There is no argument, however, over the fact that it was the great repository of English, and the effect of the language on the development of the country cannot be described without consideration of the effect of this version of the Bible.

4

An inevitable effect of the prevalence of the English language in all of the forty-eight States has been a tremendous distortion of history in the direction of British experience; but whether this has been an advantage or a disadvantage to the development of the United States is debatable.

We may safely assume that history would have been distorted anyhow, if not in the direction of Great Britain, then in some other direction. If Spanish, for instance, had been the language of the country, then it is a flat certainty that in the scale of historical importance Phillip II would stand higher and Elizabeth would stand lower; but that that would be a closer approximation of absolute truth is by no means certain.

Possession of the English language—or, if you prefer, being possessed by the English language—has loosed upon Americans the avalanche of English—and to a considerable extent of Irish, Scotch and Welsh—legendry, with which a certain amount of English history is inextricably intermixed. But the legendry magnifies the history by many diameters, and nothing can be done about it.

There is, for example, no reasonable doubt that there was a fight at the village of Otterburn in 1388. That is a historical fact about as well established as any minor incident in the fourteenth century. But there is no reasonable doubt that there were a hundred other fights scattered around Europe in the same year, even though the chronologies in the almanacs do not even list 1388 except as one year in the Hundred Years' War. In 1388 Europe was in turmoil even worse than it was in 1948, and collisions between armed bands of marauders were of daily occurrence. No doubt many of them had more military and historical significance than the brush at Otterburn. Yet they are utterly forgotten; but some unknown ballad-maker sang,

> The Persé owt of Northombarlande,
>   And a vowe to God mayd he,
> That he wolde hunte in the mountayns
>   Off Chyviat within dayes thre,
> In the mauger of doughté Dogles,
>   And all that ever with him be,

so the battle of Otterburn, under the name of "Chevy Chase," is remembered, if but dimly, by every American schoolboy who has taken a course in English literature.

The schoolboy's name may be Schiavone, or Finkelstein, or Przbylski, or De Lannoy, and his grandfather may have lived to a great age without ever suspecting that such families as Percy and Douglas existed, but Otterburn becomes a part of the boy's intellectual heritage because he lives in the United States, where the English language prevails. Furthermore, he is likely to gain the impression that Agincourt was a crucial military action, instead of what it was, a temporary success of one of the innumerable invaders of France, soon to be reversed. But dull facts stand no chance against

> Crispin Crispian shall ne'er go by,
> From this day to the ending of the world,
> But in it we shall be remembered,—
> We few, we happy few, we band of brothers . . .
> And gentlemen in England now a-bed
> Shall think themselves accurs'd they were not here,
> And hold their manhoods cheap while any speaks
> That fought with us upon Saint Crispin's day,

so to the average American Agincourt was a very important battle, regardless of what historians may say.

Averroës was a vastly greater philosopher than Roger Bacon, but the commentary on Aristotle is no part of English legend, while the Brass Head is. The idle tale of what the Friar did not do, being incorporated into the language, has preserved his name better than all the notable work that both sages actually did. Schoolboys of Polish and Greek and Lithuanian blood cherish a dim notion that a person named Gibbon invented history. They have not heard of Clarendon, because Gibbon handled the language better, but they are pretty well convinced that the art is an English art. Persons who are not schoolboys, but regard themselves as fairly well educated, frequently assume that the writing of history as we understand it is if not altogether English at least a western achievement. They are taken aback when they hear it asserted that "a philosophy of history which is undoubtedly the greatest work of its kind that has ever yet been created by any mind in any time or place" was worked out by a man named Abd-ar-Rahman ibn Muhammad ibn Khaldun al-Hadrami,* an Arab of the fourteenth century. Yet if Charles Martel had failed at Tours, and the Islamic civilization had crossed the Atlantic, Ibn Khaldun might be accepted in every little red schoolhouse as the Father of History, and Herodotus be not even a name except to some Moslem Toynbee.

Evidence might be piled up indefinitely, but why labor the point? It is clear enough that the English language has given English history, and history written by Englishmen, a greater importance in the minds of Americans than can be justified by careful study of the records. But this applies strictly to the history of England prior to 1776; since that date British history has suffered a fairly complete eclipse—or certainly since the date when the virtuous George Bancroft set out to prove the moral ascendency of the republic. The American schoolteacher has been in the Philippines for forty years, so it is not improbable that there are Spanish-speaking Filipino boys today who are under the impression that the battle of Cowpens was decidedly a more important engagement than, say, the battle of Vitoria, by which Wellington drove the French out of Spain.

This undeniable exaggeration of the importance of English history in American minds has been denounced by many commentators as unfair and deleterious. That it is unfair cannot be denied; but that it is deleterious can be established only by proving that some possible alternative would have been better. But there is no possible alternative known to man that unquestionably would have been better. History is always distorted in the direction of the country that originated the mother tongue. Latin-American history is just as badly distorted in the direction of Spain. If American history had not been twisted in the English direction, it would have been twisted in some other,

* This is Arnold J. Toynbee's estimate of the accomplishment and guess at the correct name of Ibn Khaldun. See *A Study of History*, vol. iii, p. 322.

and there is no proof that another twist would have served us better.

As far as folk-lore with a slight mixture of history is concerned, this is self-evident. "Chevy Chase" is art, not science; it is a song in praise of heroism, and the fact that the scene is Otterburn, rather than Roncesvalles or Thermopylae, is a detail of small importance. Yet one among the functions of history is to give the living generation a sense of continuity and direction.* For this purpose the identity of the landmarks in his line of sight are of less importance than their distinctness. The free man is such a landmark. Name him William Tell or Robin Hood and he will serve, if he is a free man. Courage to resist tyranny is such a landmark. Winkelried at Sempach will do, but so will the barons at Runnymede. The cruelties of Laud or of Alva will serve equally well for horrible examples. The point of importance is the continuity of experience which sustains the hope that we may learn from the past; and one line —any one line—followed continuously is more vivid than several followed simultaneously.

Finally, our political institutions did come straight from England, subject only to such modification as American experience made necessary. This is an immovable fact that must be faced. Grandfather may have lived in Bulgaria or Portugal, but grandson lives in the United States under a political system derived from England; therefore English history is more important to him than Bulgarian or Portuguese history, because it assists him to understand the government and laws under which he lives. It is a question, then, whether the distortion of history that the language effects is, in fact, a deviation from absolute truth or proper emphasis upon a phase of truth that

---

* Scandalized protests from the faculty will not persuade me to abandon this position. Rightly or wrongly, the average American believes that the teaching of history in the public school does assist the pupil to make an extrapolation of experience that is a fairly valid guide through the future. That is why he is willing to pay much money for such teaching.

for practical purposes is more important than some other phases.

So the English gave us a language marvelous in its wealth of resources and in its sinewy strength; equally marvelous in its precision in following the sinuosities of thought and in the contradictory quality of ambiguity in its terms; a language marvelously adapted alike to the exposure and the conceal-ment of what is in one's mind. Itself a language of multitu-dinous elements, it has been a strong influence toward creating unity in diversity. It is the delight and the despair of poets and philologists, the inspiration of scientists, the exaltation of phi-losophers and the ruin of grammarians. There is hardly a statement that one can conceive that is not true of English; and it remains indescribable.

Chapter II

ojo

THE LAW

1

Every American who has listened to a Fourth of July oration must be more or less vaguely aware of the existence of something called "the common law" that was imported from England in colonial times and that is supposed to be highly meritorious. But not every American has taken the trouble to find out what it is, or in what its merit consists.

A layman, indeed, runs into difficulties as soon as he undertakes to examine the subject because the term "common law" may mean any of several different things, depending upon whether it is used by counsel in a bigamy case, a jurisconsult writing a dissertation on legal principles, a historian discussing the rise of monarchy in England, or a Silver Tongue whipping up the enthusiasm of precinct workers at a political clambake. Counsel, for instance, would mean unwritten law based on decided cases with some reference to custom; the jurisconsult would mean that body of law which is distinguished from civil law and the law of equity; the historian would mean—or might mean—that law which is unmistakably English in origin and cannot be traced back to the *Pandects* of Justinian, or any other Roman authority; while the Silver Tongue, in all probability, would mean something that is not the common law by any definition, but a hodge-podge of all historical theories of the

Rights of Man, with overtones of *Magna Carta,* trial by jury and the writ of *habeas corpus.*

Yet it is what the orator has in mind that is best worth examining in a study of English influence on the pattern of American life for the heritage that most people think of when they refer to our possession of the English common law is certainly not any specific compilation of statutes, nor that body of law which is apart from civil law, canon law and equity. It is something much vaguer and more elusive—less actual law than an attitude toward the law developed both by the officers of the court and by the people of England.

It began far back when the theory of monarchy was as yet relatively undeveloped and the King was not regarded as a divinely appointed sovereign but merely as the first among the peers. The right to rule belonged to the barons, but experience and, no doubt, an innate sense of order convinced them that someone had to lead; so they agreed in principle to follow one of their number. But it was a long time before they admitted that any special sanctity attached to the King's person or to his lineage, except as they were all committed to support of the principle of inheritance.

The affair at Runnymede, for example, was an illustration of the reluctance of the barons to permit any broadening of the gap between royalty and nobility. It was a later generation that construed it as a fight to establish the liberty of the subject. To the barons themselves that liberty was not in question. It was already established, and the operation was designed merely to cut John, the King, down to what they regarded as nearer his proper size. *Magna Carta* was simply a promise in writing, since his oral promise had proved worthless, to stick strictly to his own business and let theirs alone.

More than eighty years after Runnymede Roger Bigod, earl of Norfolk, and perhaps the most powerful noble in the realm, was so little disposed to take orders from the King that their altercation has become historical and is enshrined in the *En-cyclopaedia Britannica*. Bigod, ordered to carry war into Gascony, flatly refused. "By God, earl," exploded the King, "you shall either go or hang." "By that same oath, O King," responded the earl, "I shall neither go nor hang." The record shows that he did not go and he did not hang. The King dared not press the issue, for he knew that he would not be supported by the majority of the nobles.

Yet even then it was admitted that by virtue of his position as first of the peers the King did have certain rights more general than those held by any of the rest. He was not permitted to interfere between a lord and his lieges except where his own interests were concerned. Local law was made and administered by the local lord, and an act that was a capital crime on one demesne might be no crime at all a few miles away in the territory of another lord.

But there were certain acts that touched the King's rights, as well as the lord's. Murder, for example, deprived the King of a subject. If one lord's servant robbed the servant of another lord, that was a breach of the King's peace. Such crimes, therefore, were crimes anywhere, regardless of whims of the baron on whose estate they occurred, and the laws against them were valid everywhere, that is to say, they were common to the whole realm. Judges representing the King, therefore, were said to administer the common law, while judges representing the baron administered only the local law.

But in view of the relative weakness of the King's power the common law could be enforced only with the assistance, or at least the consent, of the baron. Therefore, in the beginning, the common law applied only to acts that all men, everywhere, admitted were flagitious. That is to say, the common law had to be so obviously right that no man could seriously maintain that it was anything but just. By degrees this idea took hold so firmly upon the popular imagination that it overshadowed its origin and men came to believe that conduct revolting to the moral sense was a violation of the common law, whether or not any legislative body had dealt with it in specific terms. In case after case judges so ruled, and their rulings became precedents with the force of law. So by 1607, when the English settlement of America began, England had a tremendous body of law that Parliament had never seen.

Yet, although its formal basis was precedents set by courts, it is somewhat misleading to call it judge-made law. That term today connotes an assumption by the judiciary of the legislative power without the consent of the people or their representatives. The common law of England is better described as law made by common consent. A decision approved by the consciences of fair-minded men became a precedent with the force of law; one not so approved was over-ruled, evaded, or undermined by subsequent decisions and did not survive.

It was a muddled, illogical and haphazard method of building up a body of law, but it suited the English and served their purposes sufficiently well. It was familiar to the colonists and accepted by them, even though it was the despair of legal scholars on the continent of Europe, accustomed to the definite precision of the Roman system. But when the colonists broke away from the empire in 1776 a problem suddenly arose. They had formally repudiated all political bonds with Great Britain; but was not the law a political bond, in fact, the most important of all? If all the laws of England were repealed by the act of separation, what was to take their place? For a legislature to create at one sitting an entire code was a labor too enormous for human capacity, but something had to be done to avoid anarchy.

In most of the colonies the difficulty was met by a simple enactment that while the authority of Parliament was ended and its acts of no force in America, the common law of England should remain the law of the new State until such time as its legislature should provide otherwise. The legislatures went at the task with great assiduity, and much of the common law was swiftly replaced by specific statutes, usually embodying the same principles, but sometimes repudiating them. A case in point is the Virginia Statute of Religious Freedom, the drafting of which Thomas Jefferson considered one of his three great achievements, the other two being the writing of the Declaration of Independence and the founding of the University of Virginia—not his Governorship, his ambassadorship, his Secretaryship of State, or the Presidency.

Others were the laws, also fathered by Jefferson, disestablishing the Church of England and abolishing primogeniture in Virginia, both of which were eventually adopted by all the thirteen States. But the great body of the early legislation following the Revolution simply wrote into the statute books the legal principles gradually and often painfully evolved by the development of the English common law. It is therefore broadly true to say that American law is formal enactment of the law that grew up in England haphazardly.

There are exceptions. The law of Louisiana, for instance, is based on the *Code Napoléon*. Recent federal legislation permitting husband and wife to file for taxation each a report of half their joint income was forced because Californians enjoyed an advantage over the rest of the country by reason of the fact that their law of joint property is based on Spanish, not English, principles. But the exceptions are minor. In the main, the pattern of life represented by the law was set by the English and to this day remains largely English.

2

But what the orators have in mind when they refer to the heritage of the common law has little reference to either accumulated precedents or statutory enactments. They mean, rather, the attitude toward the law that was fostered by the way in which the common law came into existence. This attitude was stated formally by Edward Coke in the dictum, "Reason is the life of the law; nay, the Common Law itself is nothing but reason."

Americans have drawn from this the obvious inference that if it isn't reasonable, it can't be good law. Legislatures may legislate until they are black in the face, but if their legislation doesn't meet the standards of common sense and common decency, it simply isn't good law and neither Congress nor the courts can make it good.

This was first exemplified strikingly by the Alien and Sedition laws, which were never approved by the masses of the people and for that reason brought destruction upon the party that enacted them.

It was exemplified again in the various Fugitive Slave laws of the years immediately preceding the Civil War. From the strictly legalistic standpoint, these laws were perfectly sound. Not much federal legislation has been more firmly based on Constitutional authority nor more logically constructed than the acts requiring law officers and citizens of the so-called Free States to detain and return to bondage a slave who might escape into their territory.

But such laws did not seem either reasonable or right to the people of the Free States; hence these people could never be convinced that such statutes had the force and effect of real law. In England the common law had to be right in the eyes of a majority of the people before it was recognized as law. The fact that American legislatures had enacted the common law into statute law did not eradicate from the minds of the people the notion that the law acquires its validity through its reasonableness. Jefferson expressed this attitude in his First Inaugural: "though the will of the majority is in all cases to prevail, that will to be rightful must be reasonable." Unreasonable legislation he branded as oppression, and resistance to oppression he always regarded as a sacred duty.

The most recent demonstration of the survival of this attitude for more than three hundred years was the incident of the adoption and subsequent repeal of the Eighteenth Amendment to the Constitution of the United States, prohibiting the manufacture and sale of intoxicating beverages. This legislation, from the legalistic standpoint, was as sound as the Fugitive Slave laws; indeed, if repeated sanction by constituted authority had any effect, it might be called sounder, for it was cast in the form of an addition to the organic law, regularly submitted to the several States and ratified by more than three-fourths of them. Nevertheless, over large areas it was regarded as utterly unreasonable, therefore null and void. The approval of Congress, of State legislatures and of the courts, up to and including the Supreme Court of the United States, could not make it reasonable and thus, in the opinion of millions, could not make it good law. After fourteen years this opinion became so strong that the law became in itself a menace to all laws, even the most necessary, and therefore had to be abandoned.

Repeated instances of this sort have created a widespread opinion in other countries, and even among the over-educated in this one, that the American is essentially lawless. Englishmen, in particular, seem to hold to this view with great tenacity; Kipling's reference to "the cynic devil in his blood," the impulse

> That bids him flout the Law he makes,
> That bids him make the Law he flouts,

is typical. Apparently it never crossed the mind of the poet that this "cynic devil" is a profound respect for the spirit of the English common law, expressed differently, because the situation is different, but identical at bottom with the Briton's firm belief that if it isn't reasonable it isn't sound law.

The difference in the situation is that much of the English common law is the result of defiance of acts of Parliament by judges, rather than by the people. The massive array of technicalities created by the English courts prior to the last century was, in effect, the judges' way of invalidating foolish statutes. When there were three hundred crimes punishable by death in England the law was unreasonable, and every honest judge knew it. The law said that a man convicted of stealing goods to the value of thirteen pence should be hanged; but generations before the law was changed judges knew that it was bad law; therefore they sought eagerly for some technicality, were it only a misplaced comma in a bill of indictment, that would give them an excuse to refuse to convict. By skillful use of precedent and of tortuous reasoning, the judges contrived to nullify the more idiotic acts of Parliament.

But most of them were convinced of the extreme fragility of public order, which they thought would be swiftly undermined by any outward show of disrespect for constituted authority. Under no circumstances, therefore, would they say brusquely that the law was idiotic; instead they managed somehow, without questioning its righteousness, to find an excuse to say that the law did not apply to the instant case and to let the defendant go.

American judges have had no such convenient recourse. American law is relatively new and highly explicit, and there exists no immeasurable labyrinth of precedent and custom in which the courts can conveniently lose themselves in order to avoid rendering an iniquitous judgment. With no avenue of escape American judges have had to enforce to the letter statutes that were, in the opinion of a large minority, sometimes a majority, of the people unjust, unrighteous and unworthy of the respect of honest men.

There is no royal authority in the United States that must be protected from the merest breath of disrespect by such fictions as the dictum that the King can do no wrong. The highest legislative authority in the land is Congress, and Americans are of the opinion that Congress can do wrong and feel no hesitation about saying so with emphasis. They are, therefore, no respectors of the acts of Congress; but to assume that this means that they are no respectors of law is to assume that the statutes are necessarily good law, which is flatly contrary to the opinion that Englishmen have maintained stubbornly for many centuries.

This has greatly perturbed legalists in both countries ever since efforts began to be made to reduce law within the bounds of logic. Whole libraries have been written to defend the indefensible thesis that disrespect for a disreputable statute is disrespect for law. Logicians have insisted that any other theory leads straight to anarchy, for a man who feels no obligation to do anything save what is right in his own eyes is an anarchist. But these logicians will not admit the statistical factor that nevertheless enters the equation, whether they like it or not. A man who does what is right only in his own eyes may be an anarchist; but a man who does what is right in his own eyes and also in the eyes of nine-tenths of his neighbors is not an anarchist, and cannot be transformed into one by any sort of dialectic, no matter how subtle.

The English, committed to the thesis that the King can do no wrong, but confronted by the stubborn fact that wrong was obviously being done, had recourse to the theory that all wrong is attributable to the King's ministers who are quite capable of putting through Parliament legislation of the most villainous kind. But no Englishman regards such legislation as good law. It violates the British constitution and binds no man's conscience, however it may bind his acts. Only one generation ago the famous Dr. John Clifford, the Nonconformist clergyman, regularly suffered his household goods to be seized and sold by officers of the law rather than obey the statute that taxed him for the support of the Church of England. Yet a description of Dr. Clifford as having a "cynic devil in his blood" would have been regarded, even by Rudyard Kipling, as singular indeed.

The existence of frontier conditions did, of course, make inevitable a certain amount of genuine lawlessness, lawlessness in the literal sense. On any frontier the establishment of adequate and efficient agencies of law enforcement is a slow, laborious process and until such agencies are established there is, in fact, no law. The United States government announced the closing of the last frontier on this continent in 1893; so from 1607 to 1893, a period of two hundred and eighty-six years, there was an area where the edge of civilization was cutting into the wilderness, which is to say an area without law.

Since Frederick Jackson Turner made his famous study of the effect of the frontier on the civilization behind it, many writers have attributed the so-called lawlessness of America to habits acquired on the frontier. It is a questionable thesis. The spirit of the frontier was not one of contempt for all law; on the contrary, it was one of such strong, even fanatical, belief in the common law that offenses against it were suppressed with great violence. The Vigilantes of the West were frankly contemptuous of the forms of law, but in their own eyes they were enforcing the spirit of the law, which doubtless convicts them of disrespect for legalism, but strongly emphasizes their respect for law.

The man who created the legendary West confected a literary marshmallow * but it had some flavor of truth in its central tragedy, that of a man who hanged his best friend for stealing cattle. A more staggering proof of respect for law can hardly be imagined, yet things of that kind did happen on the frontier.

An intellectual stereotype of recent years is the assumption

* Owen Wister's novel, *The Virginian*, which today seems no more than a monument of honeycomb tripe, but which was a sensational success when it was published in 1902 and became the precursor of the "westerns" that still enthrall the minds of small boys from nine to ninety.

that the essential lawlessness of the American people is proved by the obsolescent crime of lynching.* Yet the fact is that lynching in its heydey, some sixty years ago, flourished mainly in the West and in the South, one a region in which no firm social order had been established, the other a region in which the existing order had been blasted by a four years' war followed by conquest and ten years' military rule by an army of occupation. In the one case there were no forms of law; in the other, the forms of law imposed by a military conqueror were regarded by the majority of the people as iniquitous. But in both cases the ancient English idea of the common law, that is, law approved by the consciences of all honest men whether or not it had been approved by Congress, was not only accepted but was supported vigorously and violently.

It is frequently asserted that the point at which the English and the Americans diverge most widely is the point of the latter's disrespect for law. Yet it may be argued plausibly that this apparent disrespect is itself a part of the pattern of American life set by the English, because it stems from the ancient English belief that acts of Parliament or of the King himself are not true law unless they are just and righteous.**

---

* In the first five years of this century lynchings, according to the Tuskegee Institute records, averaged about 104 annually; in the last five years for which figures are available (1941-6) they averaged a fraction under four annually. Even of these some are doubtful cases, bearing more resemblance to private vendettas than to true mob violence.

** If some critical reader cites against this description of the American notion of the common law the famous dictum of Mr. Justice Holmes, "The Common Law is not a brooding omnipresence in the sky but the articulate voice of some sovereign or quasi-sovereign that can be identified" (O. W. Holmes, dissent in *Southern Pacific Company vs. Jensen,* 1916), the answer is that Mr. Justice Holmes was a jurisconsult, speaking for and to the courts and the bar. In that, his voice is authoritative. But to the common man, unskilled in legal science, the common law *is* "a brooding omnipresence in the sky" or something akin to it—his own inner conviction of what is reasonable and right. In spite of the multiplicity of lawyers among us, the mass of the American people consists of common folk, and their ideas, not professional definitions, establish the manner of American thought and American life.

3

The heritage of English law thus brought with it the seeds of American liberty—not the flower and the fruit, which were to be produced only after long labor and painful struggle and which, indeed are far from having been brought to perfection yet. Nevertheless, the seeds were there and they sprouted, took root, and have continued to grow.

To this extent, the inheritance was valuable, perhaps the most valuable that the daughter owes to the mother country. But it is not to be denied that if English law gave us the seeds of liberty, it also inflicted upon us a vast amount of useless lumber that we have not swept away entirely, after three hundred years of unremitting effort.

Even the system of trial by jury, in spite of its enormous value, came to us burdened with outworn ideas and unnecessary precautions, on the one hand and, on the other, lacking adequate means of adaptation to changing conditions.

Trial by jury is, in essence, the common man's means of enforcing his notion of the common law. The court and its officers, including counsel, are there to make sure that the application of the law conforms to the sovereign authority's ideas; but the jury is there to see that it conforms to the facts. The common man has always been willing to agree that understanding what the King and Parliament (or Congress and the State Legislature) were driving at is so difficult that it calls for special educational qualifications, and he considers it necessary to intrust that part of the business to men who have studied it, judges and lawyers. But he is not willing to agree that an act of the legislature, or the royal will, or any other power whatever can alter or abolish a fact; and law that comes into collision with fact is bad law.

Authority has always struggled against this. Authority always endeavors to extend itself and the history of monarchy is in large part a long recital of the efforts of royal Canutes to impose their commands upon the tide. In the case of the kings of England, the jury was an immediate, visible obstacle in the way of this endeavor and for a thousand years they struggled to get rid of it or to reduce it to impotence. They never succeeded, but in the course of the struggle the jury system was loaded with conditions and restrictions, many of which are now archaic, but few of which have been removed.

For one thing, in the early days it was assumed that ignorance of the facts was a guarantee of impartiality in a juror. In the early days, when means of communication were few and slow, there was something to be said for the idea; but today, when literacy is almost universal and means of communication abundant and almost instantaneous, ignorance of the facts is a guarantee, not of impartiality, but of extraordinary stupidity, or of extraordinary indifference, neither of which is proof that the juror is in fact a peer of the man on trial.

The rule that a juror must be ignorant of the facts is, therefore, a rule that operates against, not for, the effort to fill the jury-box with honest men of ordinary intelligence. It has become so hopeless, indeed, that the courts long ago ceased trying to enforce it literally. It is, nevertheless, still theoretically part of the system.

In the vast field of modern commercial law the whole system of trial by jury has become so notoriously uncertain as a means of getting at the truth that the courts have devised a tremendous system of hearings by special masters and other devices calculated to clarify and restrict the issues before a jury hears them. When the Securities Exchange Commission, for example, proceeds against a giant corporation for issuing debentures based on figures arrived at by a system of accounting questioned by the Commission, the issues are frequently so intricate that Certified Public Accountants, not to mention lawyers, quarrel violently over their meaning. The chance that the butcher, the baker, the candle-stick maker and nine colleagues from their walk of life will make an accurate analysis of such a case is therefore, practically non-existent. Whether they say "Yes" or "No," the chance that justice will be served is almost exactly equal to the chance that injustice will be perpetrated. It is therefore almost unheard-of for the verdict of a jury to be accepted in such a case. The verdict is no more than a formality necessary to bring the case before a higher court where it will be heard by judges who are at least well educated and usually astute.

Hence the notion, widespread among laymen, that trial by jury is an English inheritance that is almost our sole guarantee of justice is one that requires much modification to bring it in line with the truth. It remains, however, the great bulwark of the individual against governmental persecution. There is still much force in old John Randolph's shrill declamation: "With all my abhorrence of the British government, I should not hesitate between Westminster Hall and a Middlesex jury, on the one hand, and the wood of Vincennes and a file of grenadiers, on the other. That jury trial which walked with Horne Tooke and Hardy through the fires of ministerial persecution is, I confess, more to my taste than the trial of the Duke d'Enghien."*

Far more encrusted with anachronisms than the system of trial by jury is the English law of property, especially "real property," which is the lawyers' term for land and the improvements thereon.

It would be fatuous to deny that the English system of holding land and transferring its ownership has conspicuous and peculiar merits which have been highly serviceable to this country. One of them, in particular, has acquired a romantic aura

---

* In 1804 Napoleon had the Duc d'Enghien, last prince of the House of Condé and so a possible aspirant to the French throne, seized by soldiers, tried secretly by a military tribunal, and shot by a file of grenadiers in the forest of Vincennes. It was an early demonstration of the style of justice made familiar to us by the "purges" of Hitler, Mussolini and Stalin.

that has betrayed many Americans into believing it one of the very mudsills of the common law, although it is, in fact, the reverse—it is a limitation upon the force of the common law. This is the doctrine usually expressed in the words, "An Englishman's house is his castle."

The wording gives a clue to the origin of the doctrine. The castle was the residence of the lord of the demesne; and the statement is a claim laid by the common man to one of the privileges of the lord, exemption within his castle from the operation of the King's law to which he was subject outside. But in the mind of the common man that origin was obscured two hundred years ago by Chatham's oratory: "The poorest man may in his cottage bid defiance to all the force of the Crown. It may be frail; its roof may shake; the wind may blow through it; the storms may enter, the rain may enter,—but the King of England cannot enter; all his forces dare not cross the threshold of the ruined tenement."

That statement was largely fustian when Chatham made it and it has not gained validity since. Nevertheless, it remains an ideal to which the American people cling obstinately and which has colored their attitude toward government throughout their national history. It is part of the pattern set by the English and a cherished part. It has slowed, if it has not stopped, the advance of police control of the individual citizen; and it is the basis of many judicial decisions and much legislation concerning things undreamed of by the people who originated the doctrine—wiretapping, for example, and other invasions of privacy.

Originally a doctrine of the right of security—the lord within his castle could not be touched by the King's bailiffs and, later, in America "the right of the people to be secure in their persons, houses, papers and effects, against unreasonable searches and seizures, shall not be violated" *—it has now become the

---

* The wording of the fourth amendment to the Constitution of the United States.

basis of the doctrine, still in process of formulation, of the right of privacy.

This doctrine, by the way, furnishes a striking example of the persistence in America of English habits of thought regard-ing the development of the law. The right of privacy is not yet clearly established. The subject has hardly been touched by legislative bodies, nor has the highest court yet ruled upon it; such as it is, it rests upon decisions of judges in the State courts and the inferior federal courts, notably upon one by Cobb, J., in Georgia, and another by O'Dunne, J., in Maryland. Judge Cobb ruled that a citizen's civil rights are invaded when his photograph is published without his consent in a newspaper ad-vertisement; Judge O'Dunne went a step further and applied the same reasoning to the news columns.

The point has not yet been brought before the Supreme Court of the United States, nor has Congress done anything about it one way or the other; and without action by one or both of these authorities the right cannot be regarded as estab-lished. Yet, although it may be blocked at any time, it is clearly on the way to establishment by the very process that built up the English common law, that is to say, not by formal legisla-tion but by repeated judicial decisions embodying a strong public opinion.

The establishment of this right by this typically English proc-ess may be regarded with anxiety or with satisfaction, depend-ing upon the direction of its further development. It might run into an undesirable restriction upon the freedom of the press; or it might be a bulwark protecting the individual against persecution by the press.

There are some other characteristics of the English legal sys-tem, however, and especially of the English law of property, that do not permit even a hope of benefits to come. Built as it was haphazardly, altered in character not definitely and com-pletely but piecemeal, by one judicial decision here, supplemented by another there, and by an occasional statute dealing with a specific abuse, it came to us bound, mummy-like, in all sorts of rags and tatters of superstition and mysticism surviving from the medieval conception of feud—which has nothing to do with the quarrels of West Virginia mountaineers, but refers to the basis of the feudal system of landholding.

This system regarded the serfs who tilled it as inseparable appanages of the land—as part of the "real property." The implication that money, with negotiable securities representing it, was property merely by courtesy, so to speak, is startling to a generation habituated to regard properly inscribed paper as the principal, if not the only, symbol of wealth, but the very term "real estate" surviving in modern law is proof that such was our ancestors' habit of thought. Additional proof may be found in the exceedingly cumbrous and difficult system of legally holding and legally conveying land that still exists in most States of the Union.

Yet these things were not devised simply to provide work for lawyers, as exasperated vendors and purchasers are inclined to think. When the transfer of any considerable parcel of land included the transfer of a considerable number of people, the thing had to be gone about carefully. When land was regarded as the only real property that a man could possess, its tenure had to be most zealously guarded. The clumsiness and complexity of our present system of land tenure is a penalty we pay for the extreme care of our forefathers about deals in land in the days when souls and soil were lumped together as real property.

Some of these anomalies we have stripped away. Entail and primogeniture are gone, and leasehold has been enormously simplified. In some States the conveyance of title has been made relatively simple and easy by modernized systems of registration. Even so, the American to this day has to go about the purchase of land in a ritualistic, almost reverential, way that attaches to no other sort of purchase whatsoever. It is part of the pattern the English set for us, and still a vivid part.

The corporation also arrived with the first English settlers, for the Virginia Company was itself a corporation, in the sense that it was a joint stock company in which the shareholders' liability was limited. But the corporation as we know it today is distinctly not English. It is an American modification of an English idea, and for practical purposes the modification has turned it into a different thing.

The corporation that is the characteristic type of American business organization is of very recent date. It goes back only to the middle eighties of the last century, when a decision of the Supreme Court extended to corporations the rights and immunities guaranteed to natural persons by the Fourteenth Amendment. This includes the right to equal protection of the laws in all States, and the famous "due process" clause which protects the property rights of corporations on the same basis as the property rights of natural persons.

This went far toward abolishing the federal system as far as business organizations are concerned, since it eliminated the power of individual States to favor their own business organizations above those of other States. It made possible the giantism that has been conspicuous among American corporations in the last fifty years, and thus has profoundly modified the pattern of American life. But that part of it is not English. The principle of limited liability in a joint business project is what the English gave us; the rest is our own creation.

The pattern set for us in English law relating to marriage and the family has almost completely faded out. In Virginia entail went as early as 1776 and primogeniture ten years later. Some of the States for many years clung to the English theory that divorce was properly a legislative, not a judicial process, and reserved to the legislature alone the power of granting divorces, but that theory has now been abandoned everywhere even in South Carolina, which made no provision for divorce until 1948—curious in view of the fact that South Carolina has the smallest Catholic population of any State except North Carolina.

The legal authority of the husband and father, strong in seventeenth century England, has eroded almost to the point of extinction in America. Perhaps the most completely obsolete term in legal jargon is *femme couverte*, the "protected woman." Statisticians assert that the larger part of all property in the United States is controlled by women, due largely to the fact that American wives usually outlive their husbands and inherit from them. The legal position of American women is, in fact, so radically different—whether to their advantage or disadvantage, deponent saith not, merely asserting the difference— from that of English women as to constitute a different figure in the pattern of the national life.

English canon law, of course, went down with the Established Church, and its influence upon the American way of life long since disappeared. English commercial law, always strongly influenced by the exigencies of foreign trade, has been completely transformed since the seventeenth century, in England as well as in America. The pattern of modern business law was created by modern business, and ours can hardly be traced to the English any more plausibly than theirs can be traced to us.

4

The heritage of American life brought by the importation of English law is remarkable, therefore, first of all for a certain vagueness of outline. There is no point at which the law is sharply and definitely supreme; certain rights of the citizen always take precedence. In theory, at least, the officers of the law are always accountable; they may in no case detain a citizen without being forced by a writ of *habeas corpus* to show cause, and if their excuse is patently not reasonable it is the duty of the court to free the prisoner.

This is true, of course, only when men's minds are relatively serene. When we are terrified, there will always be a Lincoln to suspend the writ of *habeas corpus,* whether or not he has the right to do so; and if we are sufficiently terrified, there will always be an Un-American Activities Committee or its equivalent to sentence men to pains and penalties without convicting them, trying them, or even indicting them. There is only one legal dictum that frightened men have ever held immutable and inviolate, and that is *Inter arma silent leges.* Even a "cold war," as recent events have amply demonstrated, can strike the law dumb.

But when we are not afraid, it is a deep American conviction that the law "to be rightful must be reasonable," for no legislature by passing statutes can convert wrong into right. This part of the pattern was set for us by the English and its importance in the pattern is denied by none.

Some decry it, and they are by no means always representatives of other nations who have come to this country since England obtained dominance over the continent. There are those of English origin who deplore the American reluctance to admit the existence of any absolute authority save the authority of the moral law or, if you prefer, the law of God. To their logical minds the absence of any unquestionable earthly authority is an invitation to anarchy. Some very eminent Americans have belonged to this school. John Adams was one; so was John Marshall; so was John C. Calhoun; and, to dispense with the Johns, so were Adams' remote descendants, Henry and Brooks Adams.

But more sanguine men, less perturbed by *lacunae* in logical thinking, and observing that the English spirit has not led us into anarchy in three hundred and forty-odd years, are persuaded that it will never do so. They may even go as far as Jefferson, who hoped for a slight rebellion about every twenty years merely to keep authority reminded that it is, after all, accountable, and that if its acts do not square with what the common man believes is right, they are not legal and cannot be made legal.

To the authoritarian this may be the very essence of anarchy. But to the libertarian it is the best hope of the survival of human freedom. For the gift of this idea he holds himself more deeply in debt to the English than he is for all the rest that they have added unto it.

Chapter III

ojo

THE FAITH

1

The ordinary American, if asked what religion the English brought to this country, would certainly say Protestantism, specifically Anglicism and its variant, Puritanism. After a moment's thought, he might add Quakerism, and if someone mentioned Roger Williams he would possibly remember the Baptists.

But the introduction of Roman Catholicism he would probably attribute, not to the English, but to the Irish. Was not Lord Baltimore, founder of the first colonial sanctuary for Catholics, an Irish peer? Was not the first Catholic bishop a descendant of Ely O'Carroll and the first Cardinal in this country a Gibbons, son of a man from County Mayo?

All this is true, but it is also true that there was nothing Irish about Baltimore but his title. The Calverts were from Yorkshire, English for generations. Furthermore, the man who actually planted the faith in English America was not his lordship, but his lordship's chaplain, the head of the ecclesiastical mission that came with the first colonists. This was Father Andrew White, born in London, educated on the continent of Europe, and having no connection whatever with Ireland.

The Irish enlarged and strengthened the Catholic communion enormously, but they did not introduce it. Even the first bishop, John Carroll, was half English, for his mother was a

Darnall, related to the Calverts. Catholicism, as well as Protestantism, was an importation of the English; of the three faiths dominant in the United States today, only one, Judaism, seems to have come from another source. The Jews who first arrived in Virginia apparently were Spanish and Portuguese, not English.

But the great religions cannot, in the nature of things, be nationalistic in themselves. Each takes on a nationalistic coloration, of course; even the most monolithic of them all, Roman Catholicism in, say, Bavaria, differs superficially from what it is in Spain. The difference is in coloration; American Protestantism would still have been Protestant had it come from Germany, Catholicism would have been Catholic had it come from Italy.

The English influence upon American religion is thus to be sought, not in the Articles of Faith, but in the relatively slight changes that the faith undergoes under the pressures of language, law and custom. It is the distinctive coloration that the English gave to Protestantism and Catholicism, not the things themselves, that constitute the unmistakably English influence.

As regards Catholicism, this influence today is almost, if not quite, imperceptible. The English Civil War of 1042-52 reduced the English Catholics to political impotence less than ten years after their first American colony was founded. The Roman Catholic Church in this country was built up by others, notably the Irish, later the Italians, and still more recently the Poles. So, while they introduced both, it is the English influence upon Protestantism, not upon Catholicism, that constitutes the important part of the religious pattern set by the English.

Most conspicuously of all, this influence was divisive. Although Anglicism was the official religion at the time of the first settlement, the Established Church remained completely dominant in English America for just thirteen years. Then came the

Pilgrims with another creed, then the Catholics, then the Quakers. Within a very few years there were Baptists, Methodists, Presbyterians, Lutherans and others, including "Seekers" —Roger Williams became one—who rejected all creeds, while accepting the fundamentals of Christianity.

This was a mirror-faithful reflection of conditions in England. German Lutheranism had its schismatics, but they were mere splinter parties. French-Swiss Calvinism was reasonably solid. But English Protestantism, almost from the beginning, divided, sub-divided and divided again. Its most conspicuous characteristic was fragmentation, and in the Civil War period this led to bloodshed. Eventually, however, the condition was recognized as incurable and a *modus vivendi* was established that seemed to many foreigners impossible but that, in the teeth of logic, continued to exist.

Voltaire perceived that this apparent incitement to war was in fact the basis of peace. "If only one religion were allowed in England," he wrote, "the government would very possibly become arbitrary; if there were but two, the people would cut one another's throats; but as there are such a multitude they all live happily and in peace."*

The French cynic's argument is certainly not to be cited as an example of close reasoning, but it is a fact that the United States is the only large and powerful nation that has never been rent by religious war. Even England had her Cromwellian incident at the moment when the multiplicity of religions was being established. But the United States has been happily free from such convulsions. This is due primarily to the policy of separation of Church and State; but it is unlikely that that policy would have been accepted as early as 1787, if ever, had it

---

* The passage is in the *Letters Concerning the English Nation*. Out of deference to Mr. Alfred Noyes' hot indignation against the wickedness of the original translator ("one of the coffee-house hacks") I have used the English version that appears in his life of Voltaire.

not been for the manifest impossibility of establishing any one sect that could command the willing adherence of a majority of the American people. If any such sect had been chosen it must have been one of the evangelical group, particularly abhorrent to the Anglican group that, in 1787, included not, indeed, a majority of the people, but a large majority of the wealthy and influential. The idea of an Established Church that excluded most of the rich and powerful was patently absurd; so the outcome was no establishment at all. Force is the argument of secular power; so with ecclesiastical authority entirely divorced from secular power the very basis of religious wars was removed, and they have not occurred.

No historian will assert seriously that this long peace is attributable to the nature of Protestantism as such. Elsewhere Protestantism has had its wars as savage and bitter as any clash between Catholic and Protestant, or as any Catholic operation against such heretics as the Albigenses. It is clearly attributable to the nature of the particular kind of Protestantism that obtained dominance in the early years of this country, to wit, English Protestantism which was, above all else, fragmentary.

Yet to base on this a claim that religious peace is part of the pattern set by the English is going too far. It is better to say that abstention from shooting war is part of that pattern. A claim that religious peace has pervaded the republic throughout its history would be a reckless claim indeed. On the contrary, America has been the field of clamorous disputation by clerics from the time of Jonathan Edwards to that of Father Coughlin. They have invaded politics, as in the campaign of 1928 when the Solid South was split because the Democratic candidate was a Catholic. They have incited to violence, as when Henry Ward Beecher sent consignments of Sharpe's rifles ("Beecher's Bibles") to Kansas, and Ralph Waldo Emerson encouraged the paranoiac John Brown to back his arguments with butchery. The Know-

Nothings, the anti-Mormon mobs, and the Ku Klux have all had their clerical fuglemen.

But these incursions into secular strife have always been individual enterprises, undertaken without the sanction, and sometimes against the express command of higher ecclesiastical authority. No American church has officially blessed violent action and as a rule they have condemned violent language. Occasionally they have set up non-ecclesiastical organizations, such as the Anti-Saloon League and the Watch and Ward Society, which operate effectively in the political field, but none has organized a private army since the Danite Band of the Mormons.*

It seems reasonable to claim, therefore, that a disposition to refrain from homicide in the name of holiness was part of the pattern set by the English. Ardent churchmen sometimes assert that this was accomplished at the price of dampening the religious spirit so far that there is danger of its complete extinction. Objective evidence to support this view is not immediately apparent. Church membership in 1947 was something over seventy-three millions, well above 50% of the total population; at the time of the first census in 1790 it was well under 40%.

If it is argued that church membership is not a reliable index of the religious spirit, it may be as plausibly argued that the process of fragmentation is an indication of the vitality of that spirit. Men do not disagree vigorously, not to say violently, on subjects about which they are indifferent. The *World Almanac* for 1948 listed in this country two hundred and twenty-eight kinds of Protestants, and there were besides Roman Catholics, eleven kinds of Greek Catholics, seven kinds of Mormons, two kinds of Jews, and organizations such as the Mayan Temple, the Baha'is, the Vedanta Society, and the Buddhist Churches of

---

* Popularly known as "The Avenging Angels." Even this, to do it justice, was a defensive guard rather than an instrument of conquest. A Mormon's life was not worth much until the Avenging Angels made it expensive to kill one.

America, whose authenticity as elements of Christendom would seem to be doubtful.

This enumerates, of course, all the subdivisions of the larger classifications. There are, for example, twenty-three kinds of Baptists, besides four kinds of German Baptists, or Dunkers, and the Fire Baptized Holiness Church. There are nineteen kinds of Methodists, fifteen kinds of Lutherans, and nine kinds of Quakers. Separation seems to have occurred on extremely closely-defined points of doctrine. Among Baptists, for instance, one group stands apart as the Two-Seed-in-the-Spirit Predestinarian Baptists, and there is an organization completely independent of all the big denominations, with a total of two hundred members and the formidable name of the House of God, Holy Church of the Living God, the Pillar and Ground of Truth, House of Prayer for All People.

From this the skeptic may reasonably gather some doubt as to the divine inspiration of all the creeds, but how can he doubt the existence of religious zeal? The preponderance of the evidence is distinctly on the other side; the fragmentation of Protestantism into multitudinous sects has not prevented it from flourishing prodigiously in the United States. Only by adopting the attitude of a strict sectarian who denies that any other sect is true religion can one argue that the English influence has worked to the detriment of religion in America. From any other standpoint it is easier to believe that the absence from this country of any religion militant to the point of resorting to the sword has been, on the whole, favorable to the propagation of the faith.

2

In spite of the multiplicity of sects in the United States five great religious groups include nearly fifty-nine of the seventy-three million communicants claimed by the churches listed in the *World Almanac*. These are, in order of size, the Roman

Catholic, the Baptist, the Methodist, the Jewish and the Lutheran groups. The Roman Catholics claim twenty-five million communicants, the Baptists fifteen, the Methodists ten; after that, the figures plunge swiftly to the Jews, with four and three-quarters and the Lutherans, with three and a half.

Three of these groups, the Roman Catholic, the Jewish and the Lutheran, although all of them, no doubt, have felt the influence of English thought, are distinctly non-English in origin, and in a discussion of the English influence on the pattern of American religious life, they may be omitted. On the other hand, two smaller, but highly influential bodies are, one distinctly English, the other partly English and partly Scottish. These are the two million Episcopalians and the three million Presbyterians. There are a million Congregationalists who trace their spiritual lineage to the English Puritans, but the modifications of Puritan polity have been so numerous and so radical that Congregationalism is now a completely different thing, an American, not an English creation—referring, of course, entirely to its mundane aspects and not to those spiritual matters which are immutable through the ages.

The religious pattern that the English set may thus best be studied by examining the Baptist and Methodist denominations, with some reference to the Episcopalians and the Presbyterians, especially in their historical roles.

Perhaps some Baptist historian may instantly file a protest against any suggestion that his denomination is of English origin. As a matter of fact, it isn't, but for that matter neither is Christianity itself of English origin. This discussion is strictly secular, confining itself to the roles the varous sects have played in the secular world; and it happens that the Baptists who established their faith in this country were English Baptists.

The antiquity of the sect is not to be denied. There is some color of truth in the claim of Baptist extremists that they are not correctly described as Protestants, since they antedate both

Martin Luther and Henry VIII. Without doubt long before the Reformation there were in existence groups holding the two characteristic tenets of the denomination, congregational government and anabaptism;* and it is difficult to prove that these were not Baptists in matters of faith and dogma.

However, the organization as a traceable influence upon secular affairs came into being almost simultaneously with the first English settlement of America. Like the Pilgrims, the first English Baptists were Separatists who removed to Holland, where they organized a church in 1608. But they did not migrate in a body to America. They came by a process of infiltration, their welcome was anything but enthusiastic and they were subjected to persecution in many areas. Their first conspicuous American leader was Roger Williams, himself an exile for his religious opinions, and although he eventually became a "Seeker," rejecting all creeds, he is still a great hero of the denomination.

On account of their strictly congregational form of government—the local Baptist church recognizes no ecclesiastical superior and affiliates with other Baptist congregations only for the more efficient conduct of joint enterprises, such as missionary work, the management of publications and the support of eleemosynary institutions—the Baptists have never been a cohesive force in secular affairs. For the same reason their polity offers little to attract ambitious men of the dominant type. There has never been a great Baptist prelate for the sufficient reason that there cannot be a Baptist prelate of any sort.** Even men as forceful as Dr. Harry Emerson Fosdick, or as learned as Dr.

* The author begs the reader to note that this is the common noun, meaning the baptism of believers only on confession of faith. It is a necessary precaution, because modern Baptists become heated to a perilous degree by attempts to identify them with the Anabaptists, a sect of Zwinglians best remembered for their seizure of Munster in 1534 and the establishment there, under their leader, John of Leiden, of various startling customs, including polygamy and polyandry, not countenanced by American Baptists.

** Bunyan was popularly called "the Baptist bishop" but it was a strictly honorary title.

Cornelius Woelfkin, can occupy no ecclesiastical rank higher than that of pastor of a single congregation, because there is no higher rank. A Baptist Richelieu is a contradiction in terms.

As a result, the impact of this group upon secular affairs is infrequently recognized. Not a few Americans, indeed, labor under the misapprehension that it is a relatively small and obscure sect without wealth or influence; and they are incredulous when they are told that it is by long odds the largest Protestant American communion, that in the matter of wealth it can show the Rockefeller family, in the matter of influence politicians as prominent as Harry S Truman among the Democrats and Harold E. Stassen among the Republicans, judges including former Chief Justice Hughes and present Associate Justice Black, and a formidable array of educators of whom the most celebrated probably was William R. Harper, stormy first president of the University of Chicago.

In a democracy a group including such leaders and voters by the million could not fail of having some effect upon public affairs, even if its influence is not recognizably sectarian. In effect, the Baptist influence is readily indentifiable if one gives some attention to the history of this religious body.

In the beginning it was a persecuted sect. The seventeenth-century Baptists were extreme radicals in matters of organization and church government. Some elements among them also became radical in matters of faith and dogma. The Anabaptists (with a capital "A") previously mentioned were a lurid case in point. But these wild fanatics seldom attracted any considerable following and never lasted long; before the end of the seventeenth century most of them had disappeared and the peculiarity of the Baptists consisted in their attitude toward ecclesiasticism rather than in their strictly theological views.

As a matter of fact, these views were and have remained curiously vague and ill-defined. In the early days the so-called General Baptists veered toward Arminianism and the Particular

Baptists toward Calvinism; the first notable invasion of this country was by General Baptists at Charleston, but the Particular Baptists flourished among the frontiersmen in the hill country. Eventually, however, the distinction disappeared, not by any formal compromise, but by a gradual melting away of the disposition to quarrel over whether the Atonement was general or particular. Even the sacrament of baptism was not, in the early days, confined to the rite of total immersion; only gradually did that become established Baptist practice.

But in their opposition to the episcopacy the Baptists were adamant from the beginning and have never wavered. This, of course, made them exceptionally vulnerable to persecution. It is a matter of great difficulty to establish in court exactly what are a man's views on such abstruse subjects as trinitarianism or prevenient grace, but it is no trouble at all to prove that he disregards the admonitions of the bishop.

Thus when a Puritan was haled before an English court, if he were a skillful dialectician he could, and frequently did, argue the court into a state of such utter confusion that he escaped altogether, or with the lightest of penalties. Not so with a Baptist; he could not argue away the fact that he repudiated the authority of the hierarchy from top to bottom, so he went certainly and promptly to jail. Even the Quaker, William Penn, won an acquittal on his second appearance at the bar; but John Bunyan did twelve long years in Bedford jail, and some less distinguished Baptists were hanged.

It is true also that the more mundane the character of the establishment, the less it bothers about spiritual heresy and the more violent it becomes toward those whose obduracy relates mainly to the payment of tithes and obedience in temporal affairs. Thus a worldly established church of whatever creed, whether the Anglicanism of Charles II, the Catholicism of James II, or, for that matter, the Greek Orthodoxy of Nicholas II, of Russia, is always particularly ferocious toward

Baptists. It is an ironical circumstance that the only country in which Baptists have ever enjoyed anything resembling privileged status is the country whose government is presumed to be most violent against all religions, Soviet Russia. Since the Russian Baptists had little organization, no hierarchy and no priesthood, it was difficult for the Soviets to grip them and they have flourished since 1917 to such an extent that they now claim some millions of Russian communicants.

Out of bitter experience, therefore, the Baptists have developed an ingrained conviction that, while others may wriggle out, a Baptist in the hands of the law has no chance whatever. In this situation there is but one reliable means of protection, which is to make sure that the law lays hands on no man for his religious beliefs. Thus Baptists were among the earliest advocates of complete separation of Church and State and are still among its most vigorous supporters.

This has not always worked to the advancement of the general welfare. Like other sects the Baptists realized the need for an educated ministry and undertook to supply it by setting up colleges under denominational control which established in the minds of many the idea that higher education is properly a religious enterprise. So when State universities began to be organized they encountered fierce opposition among the Baptists, especially in the older States, where denominational colleges were already functioning. The real opposition was to what seemed to be State interference in religious affairs; but it gave the Baptists something of a reputation as opponents of higher education.

On the other hand, they have been equally vigorous in their opposition to the appropriation of public money to parochial or other private elementary schools. The opposition is based on the same principle; but it has put the Baptists in the anomalous position of advocating State primary education and opposing State higher education.

But both attitudes have been local and sporadic. The steady, continuous pressure exerted by the Baptists on American public affairs has been in the direction of maintaining the absolute separation of Church and State.* Perhaps it may have been pushed to unwise extremes at times. In the late thirties President Roosevelt, in his last desperate efforts to maintain international peace, sent a personal representative—not a regular ambassador—to the Vatican to coordinate his efforts with those of the Pope, and was subjected to a drumfire of criticism from the Baptists. But President Truman, himself a Baptist, continued the arrangement, well aware that there was no curia, synod or council with authority to mobilize the whole power of the denomination against him.

In view of their enormous numbers and of the uncompromising Calvinism to which a majority of Baptist churches adhere, it is conceivable that the liberties of the rest of the country are safer by reason of the loose organization of the Baptists; for if they were drilled and disciplined for the conquest of temporal power they would be formidable indeed. As it is, their unrelenting opposition, even though it is exerted only individually, has played no small part in smothering at its inception every effort to establish an ecclesiastical influence in secular affairs.

It may seem ironical that the English, creators of one of the oldest and strongest religious establishments, also brought to this country one of the strongest forces operating against establishment. But this is simply part of the proof that the characteristic of English Protestantism is its fragmentation. It is unquestionably fissionable material; but in the United States up to the present it has produced power, not explosion.

---

* All American Protestants are, of course, committed to the principle of separation of Church and State; but I do not think that any other denomination has made as much of the issue as the Baptists, or has been as quick to take alarm at any suggestion of an infraction of the rule.

3

There is no question as to the English origin of the second largest Protestant group, the Methodists. They have, in fact, the largest unit, for the Baptists are still divided into Northern and Southern conventions, while the Methodist Church is a single body, claiming eight million, four hundred and thirty thousand communicants in 1948. There are about two million other Methodists separately organized, three-fourths of them belonging to Negro churches.

Because of their episcopal form of government the Methodists are a much more closely knit organization than the Baptists * and their impact upon public affairs, while it may not be heavier, is much more easily perceived. A Methodist bishop's powers are sharply limited by comparison with those of the more highly organized churches, but at that he speaks with more authority than any Baptist can claim, and an utterance of the Council of Bishops, while it may lack the force of law, has a tremendously persuasive effect upon at least eight million Americans.

Formal Methodism, that is, the schematic arrangement whereby the denomination is organized and directed, was the work primarily of that extraordinary genius John Wesley; and to the extent that the church consists of organization, law and discipline, he is unquestionably its founder. But, in this country at least, it was not Wesley who put the steam into it and made it take root and flourish prodigiously in the United States. It was a more dynamic and decidedly less conventional figure, the amazing George Whitefield.

Modern Methodists are inclined to ignore Whitefield for

---

* Again the author reminds the reader that this discussion refers to secular affairs exclusively. The doctrinal solidarity of the Baptists is, in fact, much greater than their loose organization would seem to promise and their fraternal spirit is certainly not conspicuously less than that of other sects. It is not within the province of this book to comment on any of the mysteries of the faith.

several good reasons. In the first place, he quarreled with
Wesley and became a schismatic. In the second place, before
the end of his career he turned into a violent Calvinist, while
orthodox Methodism is Arminian.* In the third place, he was
constitutionally incapable of submitting to discipline, and submission to reasonable discipline is of the very essence of Methodism. As Wesley projected it, Methodism is, in fact, no more
than a modification—Wesley, of course, would have said a recti-
fication—of Anglicanism; but because the modification was
more easily adjusted to the American spirit and environment
than the original, it has run ahead of Anglicanism, numerically,
in the ratio of five to one.

A man of Whitefield's histrionic ability could not fail of success anywhere, and his effect in England was prodigious. The
intellectual content of his sermons is not impressive, as one
reads them now, but their delivery must have been stupendous.
David Garrick, greatest actor in England of his generation,
once said that he would cheerfully pay a hundred guineas to be
able to say, "Oh!" as Mr. Whitefield said it. Even more impressive to Americans, perhaps, is Benjamin Franklin's confession
that he once went to hear Whitefield resolved not to give him a
penny; but when the sermon was over Poor Richard emptied
his pockets into the collection plate. A man whose eloquence
could stir the envy of David Garrick and charm the money out
of Franklin's pocket was eloquent indeed!

Whitefield first came to America in 1737, when the religious
revival known to history as the Great Awakening was already

* Since it is conceivable that this book might fall into the hands of a
heathen reader, it may be well to explain here that none but a skilled theologian
should presume to explain these terms precisely. Roughly, the Calvinists may
be described as those who adhere to the doctrines expounded by the French
divine, John Calvin, as they were originally set forth, while the Arminians accept them subject to certain *caveats* filed by Jacobus Arminius, or Jacob Hermansen, a Dutch theologian who wrote a commentary on Calvin's work contending that the Frenchman was too strong on predestination and too weak on
free will. Calvinism is generally regarded as the more austere form of Protestantism.

stirring, so he cannot be called its originator, but he was certainly one of its most powerful accelerators. Americans were enchanted by more than the "surge and thunder" of his oratory. He brought them a doctrine beautifully adapted to their needs. They were a relatively small population, thinly scattered over an enormous territory. Under such conditions, a man must look out for himself, simply because help is not available. With the nearest neighbor miles away, the pioneer of necessity had to be his own carpenter, stonemason, blacksmith and wainwright; he had to be his own doctor, lawyer and merchant, since there was no one to perform these services for him. He had to be judge in his own family, and not infrequently in his own neighborhood. He had to be legislator, when the need arose.

Now one of the essentials of Whitefield's doctrine was that he might be and should be his own priest, as well, at least in that part including the most momentous of all spiritual experiences, the making of the soul's peace with God. Whitefield himself in his youth had passed through a terrific psychological crisis in which he had found ritualism and priestcraft of very little help; he emerged convinced that a similar experience must be endured by all who would attain salvation. So through the backwoods of America he proclaimed the possibility of an individual approach to God without the assistance of either rite or priest. It was a convenient doctrine in a country where regularly ordained clergy were rare and difficult of access. It would have been easy to accept in any case; but when it was proclaimed with the hurricane-sweep of George Whitefield's eloquence, it was irresistible.

He visited America from time to time for thirty-three years (1737 to 1770), finally dying in this country; * but he was an indifferent organizer and never built his following into a com-

---

* He was buried in Newburyport, Mass., in ground belonging to a Presbyterian, not a Methodist church.

pact body. He was so careless of dogma, indeed, that he seems
to have been content to see his converts go into any evangelical
church, Baptist, Presbyterian, Congregational, or what not—a
strange attitude in a rigid Calvinist.

The organizational work was done by thorough-going Wes-
leyans who came after him; but the material was laid ready to
their hands by George Whitefield. He bequeathed them difficulties, as well as opportunities. It was a long and arduous
labor to eradicate the Calvinism with which he had imbued
much of American Methodism. In fact, to this day in its influence on temporal affairs and in certain passages in the Book
of Discipline the church sometimes exhibits an asceticism that
calls to mind austere John Calvin rather than Jacob Hermansen who was, after all, a reasonable Dutchman. The establishment of the episcopacy, too, was not achieved without
contention that led to many temporary and a few permanent
splits.

But in general it may be said that when such skillful con-
structive geniuses as Francis Asbury arrived, they found the
main structural elements of a great church already hewn,
squared and fitted by George Whitefield. From about 1800 its
erection proceeded with speed and today it stands as one of the
great monuments of English influence upon the religious life
of America.

In the larger English religious controversies the Methodists,
like the Baptists, were somewhat left of center, but they were
less radical. They accepted, not only the episcopacy, but
twenty-five of the Thirty-Nine Articles of the Anglican church.
A resounding controversy was precipitated among them over
the question of the apostolic succession, but the effort of the
extremists among them was not to repudiate it, but to convince
mankind that it had been duly carried on through the hands of
their leaders. Thus in the eyes of Methodists Methodism

stands, not as a substitute for Anglicanism, but as a refinement that eliminates the dross from its essential substance.

So it was in a measure a bond between the old country and the new. It did not come into existence as an organized force until after the political separation, so the American church never had even a remnant of the establishment in its organic law. At the same time, it did frankly take its inspiration from leaders who were English in every fibre, and it was thus a vigorous influence supporting English moral and ethical concepts.

Those concepts were, of course, profoundly affected by Puritanism, and Puritanism was as profoundly affected by England's position as a trading nation. A necessary condition for the existence of trade in large volume is that most men shall be reasonably honest. If it were the normal condition that most checks were bad, business would collapse within twenty-four hours; only where the bad check is the rare abnormality can business be done with speed and in volume.

But after all possible precautions are taken, the only guarantee of financial integrity is the conscience of the individual. A trading nation therefore must lay tremendous emphasis upon the conscience of the individual and a religion that redoubles this stress is well adapted to its needs. The accountability of the individual before God is accepted, of course, by Anglicanism, but it is the very heart and center of Methodism, which gave the doctrine a strong appeal to a nation of traders.

Critics of Methodism assert that its rejection of ritualism has made it an arid and joyless influence upon American life, accountable in some measure, perhaps in large measure for the artistic sterility of the country through generations. But it is possible that they have the cart before the horse. An esthetically barren environment must inevitably influence people to turn to a religion as little as possible dependent upon such adornments as color, music and rhythm. The severely rationalistic doctrine of the Methodists, far from rejecting beauty, instructed its adherents that the richest liturgy is but a faint—they called it "vain"—representation of the spiritual beauty that is the true object of the believer's quest.

The pioneers and their successors for generations lived in an environment in which the amenities of civilization had to wait upon the necessities of survival. Art is social. It cannot flourish on Robinson Crusoe's isle, nor come into full flower in a new and raw society. Only the art of living, which is independent of artifacts, can come to maturity in a region that has not inherited multitudinous skills long practiced and highly developed. That is why the chief work of art produced on the North American continent in the first three hundred years after its settlement was a product of the art of living, to wit, the government of the United States.

It is a grave error to assume that the Methodists did nothing in this *genre*. On the contrary, the most superficial acquaintance with their history produces abundant evidence of their energy and success in teaching men how to live beautifully. Of course they had their share of false prophets, preposterous mountebanks, and blind leaders of the blind. It would require no great learning or labor to fill a book with the ridiculous or pernicious activities of certain Methodists; but one could do as much regarding any other sect, taken at random. More to the purpose is the fact that they also produced their saints, men and women who attained a beauty of the spirit that demonstrated the truth of the Scriptural assurance that the kingdom of Heaven is within you.

But part of the pattern of American life set by the English through the Methodist church is an affirmation of the dignity by asserting the responsibility of the individual. The Baptists had affirmed this dignity regardless of tradition; the Methodists affirmed it with all due regard to tradition, as, in fact, a logical and necessary inference from Anglican tradition. Together, they were strongly influential in giving the sanction of religious faith to the political theory of democracy. They are still exercising that influence so powerfully that they have come near to incorporating democracy in religion. This is one part of the pattern set by the English that thus far exhibits no tendency to fade.

4

The Presbyterians and the Episcopalians in America are offshoots, respectively, of the Church of Scotland and the Church of England. But the Presbyterians should be included here because the Church of Scotland was not, as hasty persons frequently assume, the unaided work of John Knox, operating in a vacuum. It had its English roots and more conspicuously its English top. Since the accession of that James who was the Sixth of Scotland and later became the First of England, the King who reigns in London has been head of the Church of Scotland.

It is reasonable to claim, then, that the Presbyterian influence on the religious life of America has been to some extent an English influence and part of the pattern that the English set. Numerically, the Presbyterians have never been close to the Baptists and Methodists and in 1947 they were only three-fourths as numerous as the Jews; but their influence upon the life of the country has been out of all proportion to their numbers. Of the four great Protestant communions through which English influence on American life was mainly exerted, the Presbyterian is by long odds the most rigidly intellectual. The relentless logic of Calvinism developed in Presbyterian theologians a skill in forensics that made them formidable controversialists; they were frequently able to silence even those whom they could not persuade, so while the following they commanded was relatively small, the respect they commanded was universal.

The dominant intellectuality and skill in dialectics may have been Scottish in origin, as was the first great Presbyterian leader in this country, John Witherspoon; but the church in America was heavily influenced by two Americans of English descent, Jonathan Dickinson and Jonathan Edwards, first and third presidents of what is now Princeton University, the leading Presbyterian seat of learning. Dickinson was notable for his moderating influence upon the excessively rigid practice of the presbytery of Philadelphia; * and Edwards no less notable for strengthening the rigidity of Calvinistic principle.

Like the Baptists, the Presbyterians in America strongly reinforced the theory of individual accountability, and although their emphasis was less upon his dignity than upon his responsibility, they did stress the individual. Like the Methodists, they represented a link with traditionalism going back to the English crown. But more conspicuously than either of the other two, they stood for intellectual discipline as the basis of religious, as well as of political and social eminence. Respect for learning was an important Presbyterian contribution to the American pattern,** and if their influence was really Scottish, or British, rather than English, nevertheless it ran parallel to and powerfully supported the pattern set by the English for American religious life.

Like the Presbyterian, the Protestant Episcopal church has exercised an influence on American life wholly disproportion-

* He founded the College of New Jersey, afterward Princeton, in protest against the ruling of the Presbytery that only graduates of Harvard, Yale, or some European university could be considered eligible to the Presbyterian ministry. Edwards never followed Dickinson in transferring formally from the Congregational to the Presbyterian congregation, and the theological differences of the two sects in his day were slight. The philosophy of his famous sermon, *Sinners in the Hands of an Angry God,* seems to have been perfectly acceptable eighteenth-century Presbyterianism.

** Curiously, the Presbyterians gave us both the least and the most learned of Presidents in Jackson and Wilson. Buchanan and Benjamin Harrison, two of the others, were not noteworthy for either ignorance or knowledge—nor for much of anything else. Cleveland, the only Presbyterian President of English ancestry, is usually regarded as one of the strong Presidents, but he was certainly no scholar.

ate to the size of its membership, which is only a fifth that of the Methodist and hardly more than an eighth that of the Baptist communion. As the State church it was by definition the church of the privileged classes in the colonial period and all the labors of its apostles to the poor—and they have been both numerous and devoted—have never entirely divested it of that character.

While it is not altogether a reliable test, some suggestion of the influence of the Episcopalians may be gathered from the fact that they have supplied exactly one-fourth of the thirty-two men who up to 1948 had occupied the office of President of the United States.* While it is possible for a Jackson or a Lincoln to reach the White House, it is undeniable that the boy born into an influential—not necessarily a wealthy—family has a long start in the Presidential race. It is apparent, therefore, that when a communion with two and a half per cent of the church members in the country supplies twenty-five per cent of the Presidents, its influence is not to be measured altogether by its size.

The economic level of the Episcopalians has always been high. Today it is probable that the Catholics, the Baptists and the Methodists, by reason of their enormous numbers, may each control a larger share of the country's wealth than is held by Episcopalians; but in average income per family it is unlikely that they are exceeded by any American sect with the possible exception of two minor ones, the Christian Scientists and the Mormons.

The natural assumption is that this means that they are a strongly conservative influence and, in general, the assumption is justified; yet it is historical fact that the two most radical

---

* More to the point, perhaps, is the fact that of the eight Episcopal Presidents, four were memorable. These were Washington, Madison, Monroe and F. D. Roosevelt. The others were W. H. Harrison, Tyler, Taylor, Pierce and Arthur, pretty much nonentities. Five were of English ancestry, Monroe and Arthur being Scotch and Roosevelt Dutch.

asserters of the rights of the common man among the Presidents were, one, Thomas Jefferson, brought up in that faith, and the other, Franklin D. Roosevelt, an active communicant until his death.

American Episcopalianism, in fact, to the extent that it represents an English influence upon American life, is better described as traditionalist than as conservative. Conservatism, as the average man understands the term, excludes rejection of prevailing political, social and economic ideas, but traditionalism can easily accommodate widely divergent philosophies. Francis and Augustine, Bernard, Abelard and Erasmus, all fit snugly within traditionalism. Contumacy and revolt are as traditional as meekness and submission, for it was Tertullian, not a modern Communist, who observed that "The blood of the martyrs is the seed of the Church."

The Episcopal church was unquestionably one of those forces, typically English forces, that enabled the American Revolutionists to effect a transfer of sovereignty from King to people without an accompanying social upheaval. There have always been those who resented the emollient effect of English thought on this crisis and who hold that the American Revolution was half defeated because it did not overthrow more of the social order when it threw off the political order imposed upon this country by England. Some of these disappointed souls have been English—Tom Paine, for instance—and it is not without reason that they vent their bitterness on the church then known as the Church of England, but which slipped with relative smoothness into the status of the Protestant Episcopal Church. There should have been, as these people believe, more of a clash, a more complete disruption. The Americans revolted against the head of the church when they revolted against the head of the state; yet somehow, when the dust settled, American members of the church found themselves in essentially the same communion, just as the republic has found itself in the same comity of free nations as the empire.

This should not be, according to those strict logicians whose rigid adherence to logic has prevented them from understanding the history of England which has always defied logic. Unfortunately for the logicians, it happened. As in the political world after the War of 1812, when nobody conceded anything, but everybody stopped fighting, so in the religious world the Church of England conceded nothing, but declined either to fight the rebellious Americans or to repudiate the spiritual authority of their priesthood. It is illogical * for an American bishop to be received as a perfectly authentic bishop at a Lambeth Conference; but he is so received and, since a slight flurry at the beginning of the series, no serious question has been raised.

This bit of ecclesiastical history may not be of great importance in itself, but it illustrates with admirable clarity the way in which the Episcopalian faith has acted as a bond between the two nations. Its elasticity is its characteristic feature. It has chafed neither side; under sufficient pressure it can be stretched amazingly; but its own pressure has been constant, never relaxing, never becoming oppressive, but tending steadily to pull the nations together.

Its political effect cannot be measured with any assurance because it has been achieved indirectly. But it would be egregious folly to omit mention of the political influence of a group that gave us the great Virginia Dynasty in the early days—for Jefferson, although he abjured all creeds in his maturity, was by birth and early training a Church of England product—and in our own times has returned with as impressive a figure as the second Roosevelt.

---

* This was felt so strongly in 1867, the date of the first conference, that the Archbishop of York and many of his suffragans refused to attend; but at the second conference, ten years later, York preached the opening sermon.

In religious affairs, therefore, the pattern that the English set is one of interwoven figures—through the Baptists, respect for the individual, through the Methodists, respect for tradition, through the Presbyterians, respect for learning, and through the Episcopalians, respect for England. Of course, each of the four reflected in some degree the outstanding characteristics of all the others; but the brightest thread in each figure seems to be the one mentioned.

This discussion has pointedly ignored the primary business of all religions, which is the satisfaction of the spiritual needs of men. To assess the work of the various sects in that field is the business of a theologian and laymen are all well advised to let it severely alone. The learned Ursinus may debate and resolve "the Questions, of whatever moment, which have been or are controversed in Divinitie," but a mere chronicler repudiates any such ambition.

Chapter IV

❦

THE ARTS

1

Men setting out on arduous and perilous adventures do not customarily include in their baggage many examples of the fine arts. Men battling to subdue a wilderness do not turn to the amenities of civilization until they have made its necessities surely available. For these reasons it is idle to expect to find any perceptible English influence on the artistic life of America in the very early days, since there was no artistic life to be influenced.

Yet it happens that one English visitor to these shores did influence strongly a phase of the artistic life, not of America only, but of all Europe. This was John White, in descending order of ability artist, colonist, and governor, one of Raleigh's strange and unfortunate choices. White was sent to Roanoke in 1585 for the purpose of making a pictorial record of the country and its inhabitants. Again he was sent in 1587 as governor, and made then at least one more drawing, that of the Tiger Swallowtail butterfly, which was to be the means of identifying him with reasonable certainty three centuries later when people were suspecting that there were two men of the same name. This picture, found in the manuscript of an old book on insects, was dated 1587 and ascribed to *Candidus Pictor*. Since there was only one John White on the voyage of 1587, and that one the governor, and since "the brilliant

White" who drew the butterfly certainly drew the other pictures, it seems clear that there was only one John White involved in the whole adventure.

In 1593 this man sent to Richard Hakluyt an account of his "fift & last voiage to Virginia" which chronicles the somber tragedy with which the history of English America really begins. Among the colonists was White's daughter, called sometimes Ellinor and sometimes Elyoner, and her husband, Ananias Dare. Four days less than a month after the landing, on August 18, 1587, a child was born to the couple, a girl whom they named Virginia. On August 27 her grandfather, Governor White, started back to England to secure more supplies and ran straight into the Spanish War. King Philip's Invincible Armada was assembling and to meet it England had need of every ship and every seafaring man available. White might as well have asked for the moon as for a ship in that desperate crisis; not until the Armada had been shattered and scattered did his pleas receive any attention, and then he returned to America with explorers who regarded him rather as a passenger than as commander.

It was the year 1591 when he reached Roanoke Island again, to find not a trace of the colonists except for the word "Croatan" carved on the trunk of a tree. Croatan was the name of an island and of an Indian tribe somewhat farther south, but White never went there; the weather turning foul, the master of the ship refused to remain longer in the dangerous neighborhood of Cape Hatteras, and bore the governor away, willy-nilly. The first child born of English-speaking parents in America is known to have lived nine days, and that is all that is known of her to this day.*

White himself had a curiously brief span in the light of

---

* The *Dictionary of American Biography* lists Virginia Dare with the comment that she is probably the youngest person ever given a separate article in a dictionary of biography.

history. We know that he went to Virginia in 1585 and we know that he wrote to Hakluyt in 1593, but "the rest is silence." Nevertheless, in the eight years in which he emerged from obscurity he exerted a more powerful influence upon art than many painters have achieved in eighty. He was a competent draftsman and he had something of Audubon's respect for accuracy in drawing plants and animals, but his pictures of the Indians were his masterworks.

His Indians are realistic enough to satisfy ethnologists, yet remarkably successful in combining vigor and grace. White's notions of perspective may be a little odd, but his sense of the dramatic was unerring. As a result his pictures, especially when he deals with groups, are eloquent. Their success was immediate and lasting. Theodore de Bry, a first-rate craftsman, engraved twenty-three of the originals for Hariot's book on Virginia and so they were spread all over Europe at a moment when European interest in America was intense and visual representations of the New World almost non-existent.

White's Indians were copied, imitated, modified and adapted by countless illustrators in France, Italy, Spain, Holland and Germany, as well as in England. His style became and for generations remained the conventional pictorial treatment of North American Indians; and his originals remain today one of our principal sources of information regarding the inhabitants of the continent as they were when the first white men arrived.*

Here, then, was an English influence exerted upon American art twenty years before Jamestown was founded. Perhaps John White set the pattern in a more literal sense than any other Englishman of his generation. Certainly it is easier to identify than any other, simply because it is a visual pattern.

---

* Sixty-three undoubted originals and a score of questionable authenticity lay forgotten for centuries in the British Museum until 1925, when Lawrence Binyon resurrected a few and reproduced them in a work on British artists. In 1946 a very handsome (and expensive) American edition with 64 color plates was brought out in New York with a sketch of White by Stefan Lorent.

But his was the last distinctively English influence of much importance for nearly two hundred years. After all, when Jamestown was settled Titian had been dead less than thirty years and the Flemish and Dutch painters were just reaching their greatest height. Rubens was still alive, Rembrandt was one year old, Vermeer not to be born for twenty-five years. English painting was dominated, not dominant, in those years, and if any perceptible influence had been transmitted to America, it would have been derived from Italy and the Low Countries, rather than native.

England was to score, heavily, but not for four or five generations after John White made his brief appearance upon the stage of history. The one art that the mother country did transmit to the colonies in the very beginning was tonal, not graphic or plastic. English music came to America in Captain Newport's ships to become part of the first permanent settlement.

2

There are, perhaps, Americans to whom this will seem a statement of little significance, so fixed is their conviction that the English are and have always been musically second-rate. But they are in error. True, since the Monodic Revolution England has not produced a composer of the first rank, but the Monodic Revolution dates from the sixteenth century, while music is the oldest of the arts.

Georg Friedrich Händel did not introduce the English to music, but only to German music. True, Händel obliterated the older English style almost as completely as the Angles and Saxons did the ancient Britons, but some fragments survived and within recent years industrious musicologists have been digging up more and more. Only a generation ago Purcell stood as the only early English musician known to modern audiences; but the assiduous work of research men, abetted by concert performers and conductors, has brought us to realize that Byrd and Dowland were at least as great as he, while half a dozen others of Elizabeth's time crowded close.

At that, no one has as yet identified the most astonishing of all English composers, the man who wrote "Sumer is icumen in," a canon evincing a mastery of the principles of composition not in evidence elsewhere for two hundred years after this work, which is certainly not later than the year 1240.* This achievement alone would shatter the illusion that the English are a race devoid of musical genius.

On the evidence of existing records, indeed, a good case can be made out for the theory that, as far as modern music is concerned—meaning music written since the medieval period, not "modernistic" music—the English were its earliest known progenitors. Apparently the English taught the Dutch, the Dutch taught the Italians, the Italians taught the French and Germans, and the Germans, beginning with Händel, came back to teach the English, who had forgotten what they knew three hundred years earlier. By the time Händel died the colonies were within fifteen years of independence and the more recent development of American music was influenced by forces other than English.

But in the days of Queen Elizabeth English music was unquestionably great, and it is the first great music of which we have exact, unquestionable knowledge. Michelangelo could learn sculpture and Brunelleschi architecture from the Greeks and Romans because examples of their work were in existence. Abelard could refine his notions of literary style by studying the writings of ancient masters. But Hucbald, the monk of St. Amand, had no such resource. The music of the ancient world was not open to him, because no way of representing it

---

* Any interested reader can find a discussion of this, and a good deal else that will astonish him, in Donald N. Ferguson's treatment of English music in *A History of Musical Thought*. Incidentally, the book is a fine American contribution to that thought.

in an intelligible and permanent form had been devised. Even the music of his own grandfather's time was represented vaguely and uncertainly by neumes which could be read in various ways, with no certainty as to which was the right one.

Hucbald is supposed to have introduced the staff which, combined with the neumes, made it possible to represent music on paper with a precision comparable to that which the alphabet gives the representation of ideas on paper. He lived in the tenth century, and it is only since his time that music, as an art, has been subject to the process of refinement that the other arts underwent through comparison with masterworks of earlier periods. So, although it is probable that music antedates architecture, painting and sculpture, not to mention literature, by many aeons, the art, as we know it, dates back appreciably less than a thousand years.

Apparently it was in England first that music as an art form became distinguishable from music as a part of religious ceremonial. By the twelfth century it had already attained a considerable degree of elaboration; by the thirteenth it could produce such a work as "Sumer is icumen in"; by the fifteenth it had already strongly affected the Netherlands and the Dutch, in turn, were beginning their trek into Italy; by the end of the sixteenth it had attained a brilliance of creative power that was the prelude to a long decline; and this was the moment when the English settlement of America began. In 1607 England was just in process of losing leadership of the musical world to the Dutch and Italians; so the statement that English music came to America with the first English settlers is far from being insignificant.

It is noteworthy that the characteristic form of this English music was the madrigal, and it may be prudent to note also that careless use of this word has twisted its meaning out of all recognition in modern times. Even as ancient a poet as Christopher Marlowe's Passionate Shepherd promised to lead his love

> By shallow rivers, to whose falls
> Melodious birds sing madrigals,

and as recent a one as Alfred Noyes, defying the clamor of the churchbells, said that

> We'll drown it all with a madrigal
> Like this, at the Mermaid Inn,

plain implications that the madrigal was a simple ditty, or a thundering drinking song. It was neither. It was a severely intellectual musical form, complex to an extraordinary degree,* and not to be mastered except by highly trained musicians, with a phenomenal sense of balance and rhythm. The point significant in this discussion is that the form of music most admired by Englishmen of the time was an intellectual exercise.

But English music in 1607 was seeing the beginning of another movement endowed with tremendous creative energy. This was the development of hymnody, incident to the rise of Puritanism. There was little in Anglicanism to which the Puritans objected more strongly than its liturgical music, which was, in fact, developed from the mass, and seemed to the Puritan mind a particularly insidious and therefore particularly dangerous transmitter of the influence of the Church of Rome. With characteristic vigor they set about eradicating it from their own worship, and they found the best means of effecting this the development of musical forms better adapted to their theological views. They began with metrical versions of the Psalms, most of them of a formidable dreariness, so dreary, indeed, that they soon turned to the richer musical texture of the hymn. A good

---

* Perhaps only the Hopi Indians, whose rhythms are so complex that Efrem Zimbalist told the writer that he once spent a whole day listening without being able to catch them, have produced music more intricate than an English madrigal written in, say, sixty-four parts; and some went far beyond that.

hymn tune came to be valued more and more highly and for generations the musical genius of England was largely poured into that channel.

But it is to be noted that the hymn was not merely music; it was also a spiritual exercise, as the madrigal was an intellectual exercise. Thus English music came to America invested with ulterior motives. Music was not a goal, it was an avenue of approach to a goal. It was not in itself a supreme delight but a contributor to the delight of the intellect or the delight of the soul.* One may doubt that this was true of Byrd, Dowland and Purcell; probably it is not true of individual English composers of later generations; but that it was the attitude of the public is hardly to be denied and that it created an atmosphere somewhat frosty for the development of supremely great music, except in such restricted fields as hymnody and oratorio, seems more than probable.

Some critics, including as judicious a writer as Ferguson, are inclined to lay most of the blame on the Industrial Revolution, regardless of the fact that the Industrial Revolution smote the rest of Europe as well as England without producing the same effect; and the rest they attribute to the sabbatarian attitude fostered in England during the long reign of the prudish Queen Victoria. But strict sabbatarianism was a conspicuous attitude of the Puritan, as was the belief that music is unworthy of cultivating for its own sake, and justifiable only as an adjunct to spiritual improvement.

Well into the twentieth century this attitude persisted among audiences, if not among musicians. In 1922 an American sati-

* As time passed this strictly utilitarian concept of the hymn dragged it, as a musical form, into abysmal depths. Such an American Protestant as Ira David Sankey would have been inexpressibly shocked had he been accused of following Papist practices in his treatment of the hymn; yet he frankly regarded music as merely an implement with which to reinforce religious emotion, exactly as the monks who devised the predecessors of the Gregorian chants regarded it. The difference was that the monks were concerned most with the dignity of the Eternal, Sankey with the ecstasy of the rapt. Neither was primarily interested in music itself, with the result that the monk desiccated it and

rist* described the tortuous reasoning by which an American community persuaded itself that in subscribing money to support a symphony orchestra it was purchasing, not music, but an advertising medium. Favorable publicity for the town was desirable for its own sake; music was desirable if it would furnish good publicity; thus grave citizens could support music without the loss of dignity that would have attended support of music because they liked it. This strange attitude is a vestigial remainder of the utilitarian concept of music brought to us by the English. It has been a handicap; it has hindered the development of American music, and ever since the rise of the astonishing clan of Bach it has insured that English music should hold a secondary position.

Nevertheless, as long as America remained overwhelmingly English, it was English music that dominated and the music of the literate classes included more hymns than madrigals. Much of this music was traditional and much was adapted from non-English composers, but the writers of the words to which the music was set certainly had some share in shaping American musical taste. The Rev. Isaac Watts and the Rev. Charles Wesley were so unimpressive as composers that they are disdainfully omitted from Grove's *Dictionary of Music,* but it may be plausibly argued that they did more toward determining the early American's attitude toward the art than was done by Johann Sebastian Bach, who, if he was known to Americans at all, was known only through some fragment of his music attached to words by Wesley or Watts.

Charles Wesley visited these shores briefly as secretary to Governor Oglethorpe, of Georgia; but although he returned to England in less than a year, in spirit he was to abide with Americans for many generations. He became the laureate of

---

Sankey degraded it. But as Moody, the evangelist, and his singer were both native born of native parents, what they did to hymnody cannot fairly be charged against the English and so is aside from the main line of this inquiry.
  * Sinclair Lewis in his novel, *Babbitt.*

the Methodists and a great literary hero of the whole Nonconformist movement through his prolific output of hymns. He is
believed to have written no less than sixty-five hundred. It
must be admitted that most of them were pretty dismal, but it
would be folly to assert that no effect was produced on American life by the man who wrote "Hark, the herald angels sing,"
and "Jesus, lover of my soul." The music was not Wesley's, but
the effect produced by that music set to his words was certainly
his in part. When Whitefield and the Great Awakening came
together, the evangelical sects swept the country and the hymns
of Charles Wesley went with them. It is incontestably true,
then, that although he was a poet, not a musician, he represents
one strong English influence on the musical life of America.*

Another influence was English balladry, but this is much
more difficult to trace because it was largely the possession of
the unlettered, who left no documentary records. It is certain
that it came with the first settlers. When John White was making his brief search for the lost colonists of Roanoke, one of his
methods of signalling, as the boats pulled along the forested
shore, was to have his trumpeters play all the popular tunes
they could think of. He knew that his people would recognize
them, if they were heard, and would answer. But no answer
came.

In the twentieth century fragments of these ballads have been
found in isolated sections of the United States that have been
least affected by the changes of the past three hundred years,
notably in the Southern Appalachians, in the remotest fastnesses

* The statement that the association of familiar words has immense power to
modify the effect of music will not be challenged by anyone trained from youth
in the Protestant persuasion who hears for the first time the horn solo in the
overture to Weber's *Der Freischutz*. The overture is a musical synopsis of a
story all about a compact between a hunter and the Devil and it expresses this
antinomian concept admirably up to the moment when the horn insanely begins to play, "My Jesus as Thou wilt." The effect is shattering. Not only does
Benjamin Schmoltz, writer of the words, triumph over Karl von Weber, composer of the music, in that one passage, but he vaporizes the intended effect of
the whole overture.

of New England and in certain backwaters of New Jersey and Pennsylvania. It is evident that once they must have permeated the colonies, for the same ballads are found still current at widely separated spots; but they were the music of the poor, who commonly pass from the earthly scene leaving few traces that the historian can read with assurance.

Barring the bugle calls prescribed for use by the army and navy, the only piece of music officially recognized by the United States is thoroughly English in origin. This is the National Anthem, written originally as a drinking song, probably by a certain John Stafford Smith, and set to words by an American of English descent, Francis Scott Key. From the purely musical standpoint it was a questionable choice, being difficult to sing and written in a tempo that was intended to suggest burlesque stateliness. Selection of "The Star Spangled Banner" is the more curious in that there was already in existence another patriotic song with a tune more ancient and, if possible, more English since it is ascribed to Thomas à Becket. This is the ditty beginning, "Oh, Columbia the gem of the ocean," which is not only much easier to sing, but is also much more strutting, swaggering music than that of Smith and therefore more appropriate as a national anthem. How Saint Thomas came to write such a tune may be less of a mystery than it seems when one recalls that he was a soldier before he was a prelate, and it is a first-class marching song, to which a military band can add ruffles, flourishes and curlicues, world without end!

The half-century following the close of the Revolution is almost a blank in the musical history of America, and after that the Germans and Italians influenced native music far more than the English.* Yet even in this relatively barren period, at

---

* But Gottlieb Graupner, vedette of the German invasion, had reached Charleston in 1795 and Boston in 1797, while the Händel and Haydn Society had been organized in Boston in 1815; and in acknowledging the great influence of the Graupners on American music it must not be forgotten that Mrs. Graupner was born Catherine Comberford, an Englishwoman.

least two Englishmen arrived who exerted an appreciable influence on American music. One of these was James Hewitt, something of an impresario, but more important as the founder of a publishing family that figured conspicuously not only in Boston, but in New York and Philadelphia.

The other was the formidable, not to say fabulous, Dr. George K. Jackson, some three hundred pounds of the beef of Old England, an authentic Doctor of Music of Oxford, a competent organist, but above all a man conscious of his own dignity and of the dignity of his art. Dr. Jackson stood foursquare against the rising tendency to introduce what he regarded as frivolity and frippery into church music. Moreover, he was as sure that religious music should be controlled by a musician as that theology should be in the hands of a theologian; when he was organist at Boston's Trinity church and the minister, the Rev. Dr. Gardiner, instructed him to shorten his voluntaries to keep the service from running too long, Dr. Jackson observed that the object could be better achieved by shortening the sermon; which in Boston at the time was *lèse majeste* at least, and bordering on blasphemy.*

The burly Englishman was but a mediocre composer, and his influence as performer and teacher did not last long. But there is little doubt that by sheer force of character he dominated the minds of his generation much as Samuel Johnson did in London, and impressed upon the imaginations of Americans an increased respect for music and musicians. It is reasonable, therefore, to claim that he was a perceptible influence upon the musical life of America; and as an English influence he became part of the pattern that the English set.

* There is a highly entertaining account of Dr. Jackson in H. Earle Johnson's *Musical Interludes in Boston,* an examination of the period from 1795 to 1830.

3

The characteristic example of early American architecture, the log cabin, was not English, nor, in fact, does it belong to the earliest American period. It is unlikely that there was a log cabin in all of what is now the United States before 1638, that is to say, thirty-one years after Jamestown was founded, eighteen years after the landing at Plymouth, and four years after the Calverts came to Maryland. The people who brought that type of construction to America were the Swedes who settled on the banks of the Delaware River. At that, the log cabin did not meet with immediate favor; it became a conspicuous feature of the American scene only about 1710, and then it was taken up, not by the English, but by the Scotch-Irish and Germans who were streaming down the valleys through Pennsylvania and Virginia into North Carolina.* These frontiersmen and their successors carried it west all the way to the Pacific.

The log cabin was picturesque. No traveler failed to note it and to comment on it. Soon it was associated with the frontier and with pioneer life, with the early days of each western community, eventually with honest poverty and rugged individualism. "From log cabin to White House" became a slogan of democracy, and after 1840, when William Henry Harrison won an election largely on the assertion that he had been born in a log cabin—which he had not—the thing became a symbol of Americanism that romantic historians took back to the earliest settlement of the country. Imaginative artists pictured the Pilgrim Fathers as emerging from their log cabins to go to church, Bible under one arm, blunderbuss under the other.

Nevertheless, the fact is that there wasn't a log cabin in Salem, or Plymouth or Jamestown until long after the Indians had

* In 1939 the question of the origin of the log cabin was settled fairly decisively by Harold R. Shurtleff and S. E. Morrison in *The Log Cabin Myth*, which is my authority on the subject of the earliest English architecture in this country.

been driven far into the interior. The English did use squared timbers for fortifications, as did military engineers all over Europe. Quite early they protected their settlements with strong points that they called "block houses," built of squared logs dove-tailed at the corners, and loop-holed for musket fire. But these were fortifications, not residences, although they were sometimes pressed into service as dwellings.

Later in New England as settlements pushed farther and farther from the coast, it became the practice to erect one structure of this type in each new village to serve as a refuge for the women and children in case of an Indian attack. This was known as the "garrison house," or simply the "garrison," and one family was usually allowed to occupy it on the understanding that they would receive all the others in an emergency. But round logs with ends projecting beyond the notched corners were not used by the early English in building dwellings.

Ralph Hamor, writing in 1615, said of Henrico, built about 1611,

> There is in this town 3 streets of well framed howses, a hansom Church, and the foundation of a more stately one laid, of Brick . . . there are also as ornaments belonging to this Town, vpon the verge of this Riuer, fiue faire Block houses, or commanders, wherein liue the honester sort of people, . . . and there keepe continuall centinell for the townes security.

From this it is obvious that the conventional type of residence in 1615 was the frame house, the block house being primarily a fort and the log cabin nowhere in evidence. The very first shelters, of course, were tents, Indian wigwams, or huts made of poles covered with bark, but these were never regarded as anything but temporary contrivances for use while permanent houses were being built.

The frame consisted of upright corner posts resting on a heavier sill and connected at the top with a lighter plate, which supported the rafters. All these structural elements were roughly squared, usually with adz or broadax, rarely sawn, and mortised together at the joints. The better constructed frames were strengthened by studding and braces between the corner posts and the plates were connected by joists to carry ceiling or an upper floor, if there was one.

In the early days, long before there were power-driven saws, boards were obtainable only by the slow and laborious method of the saw-pit, so they were rarely used for anything but furniture. The early English houses were not weatherboarded; their walls were made by filling the intervals between the studding with materials of various sorts, sometimes brick or tile, more often wattles daubed with clay, or simply clay mixed with straw to strengthen it.

These walls were sturdier than a modern reader is likely to imagine. A well-constructed mud wall, properly dried, would harden until it was almost like stone. If it were well-protected at the top, and especially if it were given a light coat of plaster made with lime, it was dry, warm and astonishingly durable. Such houses were storm-proof, but vulnerable to fire, for the roofs in the early days were thatched, and later when time proved that in the dry American climate thatch was an invitation to disaster, they were covered with bark held down by transverse poles, finally with shingles, but not for many years with tile, slate, or other fire-proof material.

This was the pattern set by the English for American domestic architecture, but it faded swiftly once the Swedes and later the Germans had shown the highly practical Scotch-Irish how to make efficient use of the building material most abundant on the Atlantic seaboard, to wit, logs. The reluctance of the English to adopt this mode of construction is a curious example of a cultural lag. The log cabin was not practicable in England, because it used wood extravagantly, and wood was scarce in the British Isles. The fact that in America wood was the material most abundant, so abundant that its removal from arable land

was one of the pioneer's most difficult problems, could not for
many years overcome the Englishman's reluctance to use it
lavishly in building.

Eventually, however, obvious fact overcame ingrained prejudice, and the log cabin replaced the mud-walled frame house
so completely that the very existence of the latter was forgotten.
So the legend grew up that the English brought the log cabin
to this country and all the labors of historians of architecture
have not sufficed to abolish it.

Brick, at first brought from England, was a material reserved
for churches and government structures, including fortifications. But clays excellently adapted to brick-making were
quickly discovered, and even the English did not object to the
use of the abundant wood for firing kilns. As soon as the colonists attained an economic level above the struggle for bare
subsistence, the more prosperous among them began to use
brick for private as well as public structures.

Another legend has grown up around this. In all America
there is hardly a brick building more than two hundred years
old which is not said to be constructed of brick brought from
England. It is true of only a small number. The ruined church
tower at Jamestown is certainly of English brick, and there may
be one or two others. There are more that have incorporated
in their fabric small numbers of ornamental or other special
kinds of bricks that may have been imported; but when excellent brick could be made with ease in the neighborhood—
and this was proved within a very few years after the first settlements—it would have been fatuous to use precious cargo space
to haul them across the Atlantic. It is usually asserted that the
brick were used for ballast; but lead and iron bars were equally
effective, and enormously more valuable on delivery. It must
have been a rarely stupid ship captain who loaded brick.

The early architects who worked in brick had a relatively
permanent influence on American architecture. The best of

them came before the end of the century under the influence of Christopher Wren, whose ideas are perhaps the most powerful influence demonstrably English that was exerted on American architecture. William Buckland, the indentured servant who became the architect of Gunston Hall, in Virginia, and the Hammond house in Annapolis, came to this country in 1754, when Wren had been dead for thirty years.

The so-called Greek Revival of the early nineteenth century, notable examples of which still exist in the older portions of such cities as Baltimore, Philadelphia and Boston, is the last noteworthy English impression made upon American architecture. At that, its greatest exponent in this country was Benjamin H. Latrobe, born of a French-Irish father and a German-American mother, and educated in Germany. Nevertheless, he was born on English soil and, what is more important, studied architecture under English exponents of the classical revival. But there is little that is unmistakably English about his surviving masterpieces, the south wing of the Capitol at Washington and the Catholic cathedral in Baltimore.

The first genuinely original creative genius in architecture that America saw, Robert Mills, was of Scottish, not English, descent, and his mightiest achievement, the Washington Monument certainly doesn't impress the casual observer as English, or even as Greek, for that matter, although experts count it as an example of the Greek revival. The layman is likely to think of that gigantic obelisk as going all the way back to Egypt, with its colossi and its gargantuan columns.

It is not to be denied that the greatest architect of the period, the only one whose buildings are still regarded as unrivalled in their particular style, was thoroughly English as far as ancestry is concerned. This was Thomas Jefferson who, incidentally, gave Mills much of his training. But to call the University of Virginia and Monticello English is worse than dubious. The University is patently Roman in its inspiration and Monticello goes back to Palladio, the Italian, rather than to any English architect. The fact is that both are authentically American, the first great works in an art in which Americans have shown more genuine originality than in any other.

From Virginia south the English influence on American architecture was from the beginning opposed by an irresistible force, climate. To build English houses in Savannah was a rank absurdity. It has been done, but not with success. Domestic architecture, especially, had to be adapted to long, hot summers, and the most successful buildings in the region owe more to Italy and Spain than to any north European country. Of all the Southern public buildings more than a hundred years old perhaps the best, the State Capitol of North Carolina, is Italian, not English.

So the pattern that the English set in architecture has been all but obliterated. The "colonial" style, the experts say, is not colonial at all, but English Georgian. Perhaps they are right; but it takes a discriminating eye to see anything unquestionably English in such an institution as the Johns Hopkins University, in Baltimore, although the whole group of buildings is keyed on Homewood, an exquisite "colonial" house built by one of the Carroll family about the time of the War of 1812. Modern colonial, in fact, is almost as purely American as a grain elevator or locomotive roundhouse.

It is true that the country is full of highly self-conscious imitations of Perpendicular Gothic, especially in churches and colleges, but it has as many equally self-conscious imitations of every other architectural style under heaven. Unfortunately many of these are products less of inspirational suggestion than of lack of imagination—and look it.

In architecture the English set a pattern, but time and circumstance have almost eradicated it.

4

Perhaps the most celebrated instance of English influence on American sculpture was exerted when Hiram Powers made his "Greek Slave" without even a fig-leaf and in his home town of Cincinnati a sort of coroner's jury of Protestant clergymen sat on the case to judge its morality. This was in 1843.

Powers was of English descent, but he took his training in France and Italy, so his artistic influence is to be credited to the continent, rather than to England. Nevertheless, the uproar over the "Greek Slave" did have the effect of drawing public attention to sculpture and the possibility that an American might practice the art with success. It was unquestionably a surprise to many Americans to learn that a sculptor need not bear a name such as Houdon or Canova to be capable of carving a statue meritorious enough to be taken seriously by cultivated people. But here was proof; a man with as simple a name as Powers had made a figure that was the subject of agitated discussion all over the country.

It is highly probable that Powers' example encouraged the committee in charge of erecting a monument to Andrew Jackson ten years later to commission Clark Mills, another American, to create an equestrian statue in bronze. Mills—a New Yorker by birth and apparently no blood relation of Robert Mills, the architect of the Washington monument—had never seen either Jackson or an equestrian statue, nor had any bronze sculpture of comparable size ever been cast in this country. All these statements are easily believed by anyone who has seen the statue in Lafayette Square, directly in front of the White House. As sculpture it is startling; but as the triumph of an idea backed by ingenuity and unremitting labor over a myriad formidable difficulties, it is art. If the influence of Powers' English name had something to do with its creation, the fact deserves note in this chronicle. For the rest, there is little in the finer American sculpture that can fairly be claimed for the English.

Their influence on painting is much more easily traced. Disregarding John White and certain "American primitives" whose merits are apparent only to an exceptionally discriminating eye, the English influence was brought to bear on American painting through a curious process of capture and re-capture revolving around one of the most extraordinary geniuses in the history of painting, Benjamin West.

It is true that today there are vinegary critics who are ready to deny that West was a painter at all, and it is a matter of general agreement now that he was a pretty bad one. But he was a genius, nevertheless, if not as a painter, then as a diplomatist, business man, preceptor and megalomaniac. Of English ancestry but a native of Pennsylvania—he was born on what is now the campus of Swarthmore College—he studied painting in Italy and then went to England, where he blandly and easily took over. Reynolds and Gainsborough were both living, but all they could do was paint. Benjamin West knew a better trick than that—he could make aristocratic friends.

In this, at least, he was a great artist. Proof is afforded by the fact that although he was an American, and although he arrived in England in 1763 when the American troubles were coming to a head (the Stamp Act was passed in 1765), he won the tolerance, if not the friendship, of Dr. Samuel Johnson, the man who was "willing to love all mankind except an American." The fact that he became a boon companion of Edmund Burke is less impressive since Burke was an American partisan, but his really remarkable achievement was his collection of bishops. Why West should have had a fascination for prelates is one of those impenetrable mysteries of personality which a prudent analyst will not undertake to illuminate, but it is a fact that he was befriended and extolled successively by Dr. Thomas Newton, bishop of Bristol, Dr. James Johnson, bishop of Worcester, and above all by Dr. Robert Hay Drummond, archbishop of York.

The archbishop brought West to the attention of the King and the American's fortune was made. At this time, of course, Americans were loyal subjects of George III and, except for a handful of extremists, had no intentions of ever becoming anything else; so the favor accorded one by the monarch was not given to a foreigner. Within ten years after his arrival in England Benjamin West was appointed historical painter to the King at a salary of a thousand pounds a year, a post that he retained for thirty-nine years. In 1772, the year of West's appointment, a thousand pounds was opulence; Samuel Johnson lived pleasantly on a pension of three hundred a year, so West was comparatively rich, in view of the private commissions that he added to his official salary. By royal patent he was made a charter member of the Royal Academy and succeeded Reynolds as its president, in which office he served a total of twenty-eight years.

In brief, within a remarkably short time after his arrival in England—he came for a stay of a few weeks and remained for fifty-seven years—the Pennsylvanian had become rich, famous and fashionable, easily the most eminent artist in England. When he died, in 1820, his body lay in state in the Royal Academy and was buried with great pomp in St. Paul's Cathedral.

Up to this point Benjamin West's career would seem to represent an American influence on British painting, rather than the reverse. But there is more to the story. West may have been a bad painter, but the evidence is abundant that he was a remarkably decent human being. His worldly success injured him only to the extent that it made him somewhat stuffy and complacent about his own work. It did not destroy his innate amiability or his generous appreciation of other men's work. His lifelong friendship with Joshua Reynolds, a vastly better painter whom West overshadowed—Reynolds was not given a

royal commission until twelve years after West had received his
—may be more creditable to the greater man, but it proves at
least that prosperity had not made the American swell up
intolerably.

But a phase of his career that at once testifies to his fine
human quality and makes him worthy of note in a study of this
sort was his relation to young Americans. Naturally, the appointment of a Pennsylvanian as historical painter to the King
had not gone unnoticed in this country, and every young American ambitious to become a painter did all he could to make
contact with Mr. West. They streamed to London, and they
found him not merely courteous, but genuinely interested and
helpful. Even the Irishman, Copley, who might have been regarded as a rival, West received in most friendly fashion. He
helped secure a number of commissions for the Bostonian.

To innumerable younger men he gave assistance and instruction—to so many, indeed, that his pupils dominated American
painting for the next two generations. His long life enabled
him to impress his stamp on an astonishing succession of artists;
he taught Charles Wilson Peale and then his son, Rembrandt
Peale. He taught John Trumbull, born in 1750, and Charles
Robert Leslie, born in 1794. He taught Gilbert Stuart, Thomas
Sully, and S. F. B. Morse. Washington Allston, Robert Fulton,
Mather Brown, William Dunlap and Henry Sargent * were
among his pupils; and this group, taken together, pretty well
constituted American painting in the first third of the nineteenth century.

Many of West's pupils were better artists than their teacher
and learned more from others than they did from him. But he
drew them to London and through him they came into inti-
mate contact with Gainsborough, Reynolds, Romney and the
like; and back in this country they established a tradition of

* One of the Gloucester Sargents, but not a direct progenitor of J. S. Sargent,
who was subjected to English influence but not through West.

study in England, especially for portrait painters, that lasted a long time, and in Abbey and J. S. Sargent came down into the twentieth century.

It is pretty thoroughly broken now. Even in American painters with names as soundly English as Grant Wood and Thomas H. Benton it is difficult to descry any trace of the world that Benjamin West and, after him, Whistler, Abbey and Sargent invaded and enjoyed. With the change has come a tendency to scorn the English influence on American painting. Artists base their criticism on many technical points, but in the mind of the average layman the main charge against it is that it imposed upon a whole century of American painting a simpering gentility that, especially in the hands of the less competent craftsmen, removed painting leagues away from any contact with life. What they frequently ignore is the fact that if the English were over-genteel, they did, nevertheless, give the early American painters a lasting respect for sound craftsmanship and for a discipline of both hand and eye that the artist forgets at his peril.

The truth is that, literature aside, the arts in modern America are not English. The English set the pattern and the achievements following their design were better than the scornful modern generation is inclined to admit. But since the great influx of population from other countries, the pattern has been rewoven so completely that the English influence is all but lost.

Chapter V

∞

THE SCIENCES

1

The first English scientist who profoundly affected the American way of life was John Rolfe. His work in improving the culture and curing of tobacco set the Virginia colony on a firm economic basis, as was noted earlier in this book. Without some such basis the venture would have failed. The Virginia Company had expected the economic foundation of the colony to be mining, as it was in the Spanish colonies of Mexico and Peru. Rolfe's work made it agricultural instead, and thereby shifted the whole course of American history.

But it is highly doubtful that it ever crossed Rolfe's mind that he was a scientist. It is highly doubtful that he had ever encountered the word. The thing itself is so old that its origin is lost in the mists of antiquity, but the name for it is modern; if Rolfe had given a label to his studies in agronomy and the effects of heat upon certain plant structures he would have called it "natural philosophy," as Franklin and Jefferson did call similar studies. In his own eyes he was only a man of sense, doing his best to solve a problem that urgently required solving and to that end using whatever means came to hand.

Yet in this he set the pattern that American science has followed consistently for three hundred years.

To call this English, however, is to invite endless disputation. Did the creator of the pattern adopt the pragmatic attitude because he was English, or because he was Rolfe? Let every reader decide for himself. Perhaps a Spaniard, a Frenchmen, a Dutchman or an Italian, confronted with the same problem, would have done the same thing in the same way. Nevertheless, the fact remains that Rolfe did it and he was English. Americans ever since have maintained the same attitude toward science. It may not be because many of them are of English blood and others influenced by English thought, but because they are Americans, as Rolfe was American by residence when he worked on the tobacco plant. This annalist will not undertake to answer a question so perplexing; he is content merely to record the fact that the man, an Englishman, who accomplished the first notable scientific feat in the territory that is now the United States approached science in exactly the way Americans have been approaching it ever since. Intentionally or not, voluntarily or involuntarily, Rolfe set the pattern.

The Frenchman, Renée Descartes, was a child of eleven when Rolfe landed at Jamestown, and the "Discourse on Method," the essay in which it is generally agreed that Descartes announced the arrival of modern science, was not published until 1637, fifteen years after the Indians had ended Rolfe's earthly career in the massacre at Bermuda Hundred. The essay had been in print five years when Isaac Newton was born and a hundred and seventy-two years when Charles Darwin was born. It would be silly, therefore, to attribute to the colonist any trace of the mental attitude with which the great English scientists, thoroughly familiar with the Cartesian idea, approached their problems.

For that reason it is all the more interesting to note that the attitude he did adopt has persisted in the country where he adopted it, while the Cartesian predilection for pure science has made slow headway. This supports the theory that America set Rolfe's pattern, not that Rolfe set America's.

Science itself, like religion, cannot be made nationalistic

except at the price of losing its vital spirit. The investigation of phenomena, the business of science, was once regarded as an individual enterprise, but when it was so conducted it was not science. At best, it was alchemy or astrology; at worst it was a frank attempt at necromancy. Friar Bacon is said to have known how to make gunpowder, but he told nobody and the secret died with him; so he was popularly regarded as a magician, and not without reason. Houdini did not give away his tricks, and he was far more of a real magician than Roger Bacon, or even than Hasan ibn-al-Sabbah, the original Old Man of the Mountain, who pretended to have supernatural powers.

Once the study of the natural world divested itself of magic, it became international, for its success depends upon observation and measurement, and success on the grand scale depends upon an enormous number of observations and measurements, a number larger than any restricted community, even a community the size of a nation, can supply. In a sense, therefore, it is a misuse of terms to speak of "English science" or "American science," since there are and can be only two kinds of science, true and false.

But, as in the case of religion, the attitudes of various nationalities toward the central truth do vary somewhat and in that sense there can be a nationalistic science; in that sense it is possible for one nation to influence another, in science as in religion. An examination of the English influence on American science is not therefore a patent absurdity if one bears in mind that it is not the truth that is the subject but men's varying attitudes toward the truth.

Rolfe's new method of curing tobacco and Einstein's theory of relativity were both scientific achievements in the sense that each was an approach to thitherto unknown truth. But Rolfe wanted tobacco, while Einstein was content with the truth. To this day the typical American scientists want tobacco, and only here and there a rare one is content with truth. To state it in conventional terms, our strength is in applied, rather than in pure science.

This has given rise to countless animadversions upon the American mind, and it is undeniable that it sometimes betrays us into absurdities. It has led us into bestowing upon an inventor, such as Thomas A. Edison, honors and public adulation as a great scientist. Yet the error is not egregious. In Edison's case the honors and adulation were well deserved because he had done wonders to make life easier, safer and pleasanter for the public; only the title of scientist was misplaced.

It is the fixed opinion of mankind that the discovery of a universally valid principle is a greater intellectual feat than the discovery of its application to a specific problem; yet a principle unapplied, like faith without works, is dead. The mourning over the fact that the bulk of American scientific work has been in the field of applied, rather than pure, science seems less than justified as far as the intellectual discipline involved is concerned. If there is danger in this attitude it is to be found among laymen, rather than among scientists. Applied science is, after all, a superstructure raised upon foundations laid by research in pure science; if popular opinion regards the research as unimportant, research will not be supported, which would weaken the underpinnings of applied science and invention. If we develop the notion that we can have an Edison without having first a Faraday and a Helmholtz, then we shall indeed stand convicted of having but a second-rate mentality; but if this idea is propagated to a dangerous extent, it will be among laymen, not among scientists.

The pattern of American science set by an Englishman but doubtfully English is, therefore, not necessarily a bad one. It has its dangers, certainly, but they do not seem to be inescapable; and its practical results have been prodigious beyond anything in previous human experience.

2

The English furnished their full share of the early navigators, cartographers and geographers—John Smith and John White were notable examples—and valuable observations were made throughout the colonies by all sorts of people, travelers, governors, planters, clergymen. Harvard brought over to this country various learned men, some of them Englishmen, who established certain intellectual disciplines, especially in languages and mathematics.

But the first really significant impact of English science on American life occurred probably about 1725, when Dr. Pemberton, secretary of the Royal Society, and Bernard Mandeville —English by adoption—took an interest in an obscure but engaging American boy then in London and gave him a glimpse of the world of "natural philosophy." The boy was merely a craftsman, but extremely intelligent and the savants made an impression on him that he never forgot, for they awakened in him the intellectual curiosity that was to carry him far indeed. He was Benjamin Franklin.

Franklin was so prodigiously American that in the course of the centuries he has become a sort of national archetype, and we are accustomed to think of anything he touched as bearing an American impress. For this reason it is all the more important to note the part the English played in moulding him. It was in the role of scientist that this many-faceted personality owed most to England, and competent authorities * assert that it was precisely as a scientist that Franklin was most himself, most completely an integral personality, without a trace of the smiling skeptic discernibly lurking in every other role he played.

Franklin was great enough to earn a rather special place in

---

* Notably Carl L. Becker in his brilliant article on Franklin in the *Dictionary of American Biography*.

the history of science in America, not only for his achievements, but also for the spirit in which he worked. He was at once successor to Rolfe and predecessor of Einstein; he could, and did, go after either tobacco or truth with equal zest; he is conspicuous in both applied science and pure research. He could invent the lightning rod, a stove and a gadget to lift down books from a high shelf; and he could also determine experimentally the eleven essential phenomena of the condenser. Also, he could negotiate a treaty, make a fortune, write a "Dissertation on Liberty and Necessity, Pleasure and Pain" and seduce a woman, all with great aplomb.

Franklin has always been admired by Americans, but always a little uneasily. He is not quite credible. He is too much like the men of the Elizabethan age who could sack a city or construct a sonnet with the same workmanlike precision. He served with Jefferson on the committee to draft the Declaration of Independence and at the time he had much the greater reputation as a writer, but the work of framing the document was intrusted to Jefferson, because, as Becker notes, his contemporaries feared that if Franklin wrote it he would conceal a joke somewhere in the midst of it. Americans can understand a comedian and they can understand a solemn fellow; but a man who is neither soda-water nor sauterne a philosopher with bubbles rising through his thought, confuses and slightly alarms them. Franklin was champagne in everything except science; and so he has remained a little suspect.

It was a scientist that he wished to be. All his many other activities were thrust upon him. He made himself into one of the shrewdest business men in America because he was born poor and had to have money in order to acquire leisure; but he abandoned business at forty-two, because by then he had an assured income of a thousand pounds a year, which he regarded as enough. He made himself into one of the most popular writers in America because his business was publishing and good writing is the basis of successful publishing; but he never wrote for the delight of artistic creation, always to propagate an idea, and the moment the idea seemed to be successful he quit writing. He became a diplomatist, first because Pennsylvania had to have a representative in London and no one else was available, then, later, because the infant republic had to have a representative in France and he was sixty-nine years old, therefore of no use to the army; but he dropped diplomacy as soon as it was decently possible for him to resign.

All these things were interruptions and frustrations. They have combined to make him remembered as one of the greatest of Americans, but they were not what he wanted to do. Only at intervals could he indulge in his real passion, which was to push forward a little the boundary of knowledge. After nine terrific years in France, years in which he had contributed immensely to winning the war of the Revolution and in so doing had become perhaps the most famous man in Europe, when he was at last relieved he spent his time during the long voyage home in writing. But not memoirs, not reflections on the stupendous events in which he had played always an important and frequently a central part, not a philosophy of politics, or a guide for the future conduct of our foreign relations—instead, he turned out two papers, one entitled "Maritime Observations," the other "The Cause and Cure of Smoky Chimneys."

The first important organization of scientists in this country, the American Philosophical Society, was largely Franklin's creation, a fact fittingly recognized by his election as its first president. But the Society was far indeed from being all Franklin, and still further from being all English. One of its conspicuous ornaments, Benjamin Rush, although English by blood, was Scottish as far as his scientific training went, for he was a product of the great medical school of Edinburgh; and the one member who overtopped Franklin as a scientist was

David Rittenhouse, whose great-grandfather's name had been spelled Rüddinghuysen.

Yet the Society, formed in 1758 when America was still placidly British, did maintain close contact with the Royal Society in London and its members followed the work of English scientists with careful attention. Even Rittenhouse is said to have formed his mind—and ruined his health—by mastering Newton's *Principia* at an incredibly tender age. The scientific truth that the American Philosophical Society examined and expounded was not English; it was the common property of the Enlightenment, which transcended national boundaries. But the attitudes and opinions developed in England were swiftly and easily transmitted to America through the Society. In that sense, therefore, it may be described as an English influence on American scientific thought.

In 1758 the bishop of London made a minor appointment which he may not have remembered for an hour since it filled one of the more obscure posts included in his patronage. He chose a professor of natural philosophy for a struggling college overseas. The clergyman who held the post, with two other faculty members, had become involved in a dispute with the local Board of Visitors, had been suspended and had come to England to appeal to the bishop. No doubt the bishop was annoyed by the whole business, but he had to appoint someone to act while the ousted professors' appeal was pending; perhaps it was to express his annoyance that he named for the chair of natural philosophy not another clergyman but a layman, and a Scot, at that. Almost certainly he had no idea that the act would be of any future importance.

But when he sent William Small to the College of William and Mary, in Williamsburg, Virginia, the bishop of London set in motion a train of events that would affect profoundly the development of American science. For among Small's pupils was young Thomas Jefferson, and it was Small above any other individual who aroused Jefferson's intellectual curiosity. After a few years Small, in turn, came into collision with the Board of Visitors, refusing to admit their claim to the right to dismiss faculty members at pleasure. The outcome was the Scotchman's withdrawal to England where he remained for the rest of his life.

But he had touched Jefferson and through Jefferson he touched America. Small taught his pupil enough mathematics to enable the young man to gain some appreciation of the subject as a science and not merely as a sort of mental calisthenics. Jefferson's ability to brush up on the subject half a century later, in order to instruct his grandson, he ascribed to Small's ability as an educator.* But it was not through formal classroom instruction that Dr. Small produced his greatest and most lasting effect; it was through his extra-curricular activities.

There were in Williamsburg at the time two extraordinary characters with whom Small soon developed friendly personal relations. One was George Wythe, later to be Chancellor of Virginia, Signer of the Declaration of Independence, and the first professor of law in the United States. The other was Francis Fauquier, lieutenant-governor of Virginia—actually governor, since the two men successively appointed to that office, Lord Loudon and Sir Jeffrey Amherst, never took over administrative duties. Small introduced his favorite pupil to both and he became a regular attendant at their informal meetings, which frequently took the form of dinner-parties at the governor's house.

Francis Fauquier was a member of the Royal Society, but he was far from being a scientist, as Small was, or a scholar, as Wythe was. He was a member of what the English call the upper middle class. He was the son of a director of the Bank of

---

* To his friend Madison (the Reverend James, not the great little Jimmy who became President) Jefferson wrote in 1811 of his refurbishing his math, "thanks to the good foundation laid at college by my old master and friend Small, I am doing it with a delight and success beyond my expectation."

England and both he and his wife had kindred among the nobility, although he bore no title himself.

The important thing is that he was a typical product of the Enlightenment, a gentleman with no pretensions to profound scholarship, but with an alert and inquiring mind, delighting in the battle of ideas. Wythe knew more law and Small more mathematics, but Fauquier was no fool in those fields, and was capable of giving either man an argument that would test his wits sharply. In this company the young Jefferson for the first time witnessed the rapier-play of keen minds and began to understand the delight of toying with ideas for their own sake, rather than to win a lawsuit or to extirpate a heresy.

Without Small, the other two might have kept their intellectual gymnastics in the field of classical learning, perhaps with some excursions into theories of law and government. The talk then would have been much like that in other Virginia houses. But the presence of the professor of natural philosophy insured the injection of ideas that were stirring the world of science. Sitting listening to them the young man who was to become one of the most important moulders of the future republic learned something little suspected by most of the Virginia aristocracy of his day, namely, that a gentleman is well repaid for his time if he learns something beyond the management of estates, or even of states along the lines of ancient Greece and Rome. He discovered that the world at his door is more intricate than the syntax of the cloudiest schoolman and the history of *genera* both harder to trace and more important than the history of empires.

Wythe, under whom Jefferson took his professional training after leaving college, helped make the youth into a statesman; but it was Small who did most to turn him into the author of *Notes on Virginia,* a book of no small worth in its philosophical and political parts, but superb in its long section on natural history. It was Small who made him not merely the patron, but the eagerly and intelligently interested friend of every man of science who came his way. It was Small who started the process of growth that made him a suitable third president of the American Philosophical Society, after Franklin and Rittenhouse. Small, therefore, unquestionably had something to do with setting the pattern of American life in the field of science.

If it be objected that this was a Scottish, not an English influence, two excuses may be pleaded for listing it here. In the first place, Small was sent to America by the bishop of London. In the second place, the great strength of the influence that shaped Jefferson's scientific thought was not Small alone, but Small plus Fauquier.

It is safe assumption that Francis Fauquier never deliberately undertook to shape anyone's mind. He would have laughed at the suggestion and been, perhaps, secretly a little scandalized by it. He was at the farthest possible remove from what we now call an uplifter, and if he had known how strongly he was influencing his young acquaintance he might have been embarrassed, not to say aghast.

But he had fine manners, as well as a fine mind. He came from a sophisticated circle in London and the stamp of London was upon him. To a youth from a remote outpost of civilization he must have seemed brilliant, even dazzling. Add to his superficial polish real intelligence—Jefferson in his greenest days could not be fooled about that—and courtesy based on good-will, not on etiquette, in other words genuine courtesy, and the combination is enough to explain why the country boy was captivated by the governor.

It means much that the first model of a well-bred English gentleman encountered by Thomas Jefferson was a man with a keen and informed interest in the scientific thought of his day. It is no rash assumption that in 1760 Jefferson believed that anything Francis Fauquier took up was worth the attention of a gentleman. Fauquier was interested in contemporary science (in law, too, and necessarily in government, which was his duty, but that was to be expected). Therefore the young man, still uncertain about the ways of the great world, could rest assured that his own interest in such matters ought to be given free rein.

In later years political opponents made great sport of Jefferson's interest in "whirl-a-gig chairs" and mould-boards with which a plow might turn earth with least resistance. But ever since as a boy he had met Governor Fauquier he had had no doubt that all men of high intelligence are interested in science; so he was little perturbed by the ridicule, recognizing it for "the crackling of thorns under a pot," the laughter of fools.

3

It is conceivable, although far from self-evident, that if Benjamin Franklin and Thomas Jefferson had not been such great men, pure science might have fared better in America.

The enormous prestige both acquired in letters and statecraft certainly tended to reinforce their influence in whatever field they entered, including the field of science. Whatever they were known to have done inevitably bore a cachet of approval in the eyes of later Americans from the mere fact that Franklin and Jefferson did it.

To an ancient Zoroastrian, reverencing fire, there might have been a touch of degradation in mastering the laws of thermodynamics in order to "cure" a smoky chimney. The early Pythagoreans might have scorned to study the properties of the plane surface in order to make a plow move through the soil more easily. But since two very great Americans applied knowledge in such ways the American inventor can dignify his work by distinguished associations.

As men of the Enlightenment, both were inveterate foes of mysticism, particularly scornful of the Scholastic metaphysics that long survived in many European universities to give a touch of sanctity to abstract thought. Jefferson, in particular, found the Platonists unbearable and in his estimation scientific research was more likely to be invalidated than authenticated by a tinge of Platonic philosophy. Franklin was a lifelong protagonist of the theory that every man owes to his own generation some reasonable explanation of his presence in the world and his claim to a share of the fruits of the earth. Neither was an exponent of the principle of being rather than doing, and while both appreciated knowledge for its own sake they did not ardently urge its acquisition for that reason.

Nowhere else in the western world were two figures of comparable magnitude such vigorous exemplifiers of the utilitarian view at the moment when modern scientific thought was taking root in the national soil. It is incredible that they should have had no effect whatever on the development of that thought, and it is easy to believe that their influence was on the side of applied science.

But it is still easier to give too much weight to that influence. After all, Jefferson and Franklin themselves, like all their American successors, were thrust in the direction they took by the conditions under which they lived. The United States has always been and, to a larger extent than any other great nation with the possible exception of Soviet Russia, still is a fluid society, and it is characteristic of the fluid society that it offers unrivalled opportunities for the prompt application of new ideas. In thirteenth century Europe the reward given Roger Bacon for undertaking to apply new ideas did not include a large salary and a gold medal; instead it was nine years in prison. What wonder, then, that he turned to reflection, rather than invention?

To this day venture capital in Europe is far less venturesome than it is here. Even Harold J. Laski, surely no admirer of capitalists, grants American business men one admirable trait, to wit, the boldness to risk money on new ideas.* A scientist may as well confine his studies to general principles if he is aware that a suggestion for a specific application of those principles has little or no chance of immediate trial; but if he knows that facilities will be provided for a prompt and thorough test of any new and promising technique, he is inevitably attracted to that sort of endeavor.

This is the situation in modern America and it was true also in the time of Franklin and Jefferson. So much needed to be done, and there were so few hands to do it! This has been the handicap upon the development of abstract thought in America from the beginning; but it is hardly fair to call it an English influence, even though the two men—disregarding Rolfe—who set the pattern were of English extraction and strongly influenced by Englishmen. It is more nearly exact to call it the influence of time and circumstance.

There is one phase of American scientific thought that may much more justly be attributed to England, although it is scientific, rather than English. This is its supranationalism. This is a better term than internationalism, or supernationalism, for one connotes a mingling of nationalisms and the other a superior nationalism, whereas the true scientific spirit, like the true religious spirit, recognizes no nationalism at all.

This spirit was fostered first by the Royal Society of London. It is, to be sure, not distinctively English; it is the spirit of modern science the world over, but it came to us from England, where the Royal Society has always been conspicuous among the protagonists of the universality of knowledge. The fact that fifty of its memberships are open to men of science who are not English is less important than its hospitality to the work of any

* He asserts that in this the American is without a rival and to this he attributes the superior vitality of American capitalism. See his *The American Democracy*, published in 1948.

man, of any nation, or any race, who contributes to the advancement of knowledge.

For example, Benjamin Franklin needed no other introduction to the Royal Society than the originality of his ideas and the fact that his experiments could be repeated and verified by others. When his work on electricity proved to be interesting and stimulating, the Royal Society gave him credit publicly and made his name known to its members and to all its correspondents abroad. Franklin's experience with English statesmen included a depressingly large share of frustration and humiliation; but among English scientists he was accepted on the basis of his knowledge and in exact measure as that was sound and extensive he was accorded honor.

Jefferson, in his turn, abated his anti-British prejudices where English scientists were concerned, for with them his only arguments were rigidly intellectual. His early championship of Joseph Priestley was certainly because of his membership in the Royal Society rather than for his theological views, although even they were somewhat attuned to Jefferson's thought. That famous chemist, by the way, probably had more influence on theology than on science in this country. He did isolate carbon monoxide in America, but his principal productions after his arrival were fulminations against doctrinal, rather than scientific adversaries.

The case of Thomas Cooper, on the other hand, was an adverse influence in that it revealed that even the Royal Society was not immune when public hysteria swept the land. Cooper was proposed for membership, by Priestley, but he was blackballed, not for lack of scientific attainments, which might have been justified, but because of his unconcealed sympathy with the French Jacobins who were as unpopular in England then as Communists were to be in the United States a century and a half later. Cooper also was backed by Jefferson and became an eminent American, but as a pamphleteer and controversialist,

rather than as a scientist. Yet, notwithstanding this conspicuous exception, the Royal Society did establish in this country
the ideal that in the realm of the mind there are no national or
racial boundaries and men there are to be judged by what they
know and can do, and by no other standard.

This is a figure in the pattern set by the English that Americans have followed faithfully until our own times. It has been
one of the most valuable, beyond a doubt, and its threatened
abandonment would be a serious loss of our intellectual heritage. No thought of abandoning it was seriously entertained
until the increasing militarism of the twentieth century dragged
science into the service of death. It is something forced upon
the world, not by scientists, but by men whose preoccupation
with nationalism makes them incapable of comprehending the
scientific attitude.

In 1662 the Royal Society * and, following it a hundred years
later, the American Philosophical Society, associated science
with growth, as Geoffrey Chaucer had two centuries earlier:

> For out of olde feldes, as men seith,
> Cometh al this newe corn fro yeer to yere;
> And out of olde bokes, in good feith,
> Cometh al this newe science that men lere,

and if its function were to be the fructification of the old earth
for the benefit of mankind, the more widespread its influence
the better for all concerned. Yet in our times scientists have
been denounced for their very success. Grave citizens ** have
argued seriously for laws to restrict scientists before they produce an instrumentality powerful enough to destroy the human

---

* Its full name is, significantly, the Royal Society of London for the Advancement of Science. Charles II., who made it royal by insisting on being en-
rolled as a member, envisaged the organization as an ornament, but hardly as
a bulwark of his realm; it was not expected to advance England, but to advance science. Charles, naturally, had no inkling of the advancement of rapine
that might be effected by jet propulsion, plant pathology and atomic fission.

** Lewis Mumford, for example, who advocates an international moratorium
on research in nuclear physics.

race; the shocking implication being that given such an instrumentality the race would inevitably use it.

This is tantamount to an assertion that science should revert to its position in the days of Friar Bacon, who did not reveal the secret of the manufacture of gunpowder, or even to Callinicus, the seventh-century Byzantine, who is supposed to have invented Greek Fire. The Byzantines guarded the secret more successfully than the United States has guarded the "secret" of the atomic bomb, but eventually their empire fell, just the same. It wasn't destroyed by what foreigners learned from them; it was destroyed by what they failed to learn for themselves, namely, the art of governing for the benefit of the whole empire instead of for the benefit of a few favored persons.

The difference between the England of Roger Bacon and the England of Isaac Newton was that the latter had converted astrology and alchemy into astronomy and chemistry, which were not English, but the property of mankind. It was the spirit of seventeenth-century England that was brought to America by the first men of science who worked in this country, and that was preserved and fostered by their successors down to the present generation. Under that influence American science flourished prodigiously. In medicine, including the whole group of sciences dealing with the treatment of disease and the prolongation of life, its success has been particularly brilliant; and medicine is precisely the science whose devotees are most zealous about making every particle of their knowledge known quickly to anyone and everyone who can make use of it.

This is emphatically not an assertion that American medical science is primarily, or even largely, English. It is not. It has drawn upon the whole world and is perhaps more heavily indebted to Germany and France than to England for the improvement of its materials and methods. But in its disregard of national and racial lines it reflects faithfully the spirit of English scientists at the moment when they were laying their part of the foundations of modern science.

The English did set the pattern, and if that pattern is now to be abandoned because science moves too rapidly for state-craft to keep up, science will be turned back toward necro-mancy, and statecraft will not profit. No Byzantine empire can be propped up by secret weapons. The way to survival is to see to it that the empire does not become Byzantine in the worse sense, that is, a government controlled by eunuchs and log-othetes, with a frozen social system and a petrified intelligence.

Say what you will of the English, that sort of thing is no part of the pattern they set for us.

Our debt to them in this department of life is perhaps less extensive than in most others. But what there is of it is almost completely free of dross. In the language, the laws, the faith, and the arts that we inherited from the English we have in-herited debits as well as credits. In all those departments parts of the pattern they set have been, or might be, abandoned to our advantage. But in science the important thing we received from them was devotion to truth regardless of man-made bar-riers of any kind, what Jefferson embodied in a magnificent phrase—"eternal hostility against every form of tyranny over the mind of man."

This we shall abandon at our peril.

Chapter VI

∞

THE PHILOSOPHY

1

Biographers of various eminent Americans, especially biographers of Jefferson, have spent incalculable time and energy endeavoring to trace exactly the influence upon American thought exerted by the man the Founding Fathers described as "the ingenious Mr. Locke." It has been a curiously baffling endeavor, for no sooner has one biographer proved to his own satisfaction that Locke's impress is plain upon a certain passage of the Declaration of Independence, or the Constitution, or the *Federalist,* than another rises to prove that the passage in question derives from some other source.

It is perhaps a field in which no one but a specialist has a right to an opinion, for the evidence has been sifted down to points so fine that none but a specialist knows of their existence, not to mention their precise significance. But the savants agree that John Locke, like every other philosopher of high importance, collected the ideas that were in the air breathed by his generation and sharpened them into pointed phrases that penetrated because they expressed clearly what many men had been thinking vaguely. The ability to do this has always been the secret of eloquence and it was as true in the seventeenth century as at any other time.

To say, for example, that the bedrock on which the whole American system rests, the notion that sovereignty resides in the people, was original with Locke is a manifest absurdity.

That is shown by a glance at the ancient Roman equivalent of the "U. S." on American military equipment; it was "SPQR," an abbreviation of *Senatus populusque Romanus,* "the Senate *and people* of Rome," irrefutable evidence that some conception of popular sovereignty antedated Locke by two thousand years.

But it is incontestably true that in his *Two Treatises on Government* he did bring sharply into focus ideas that had been floating vaguely through many minds. Therefore to deny that Locke had any influence upon the shape taken by American political institutions would be fatuous. His influence was present everywhere and very powerful—none the less so for being so diffused that it is impossible to locate it by chapter and verse.

Yet one is driven to wonder where was the Locke of the *Two Treatises on Government* when the Locke who was secretary to Lord Ashley was drawing up the scheme of government that the Lords Proprietors tried vainly to fasten upon the Carolinas? In that cast-iron regime was little suggestion that sovereignty, or dignity or any vestige of an inalienable right, rests in the people. It is not enough to say that this was simply a case of a philosopher afraid of losing his job and therefore determined to please his boss, regardless of truth; for the Proprietors had specifically commissioned him to outline for them the form of government that was theoretically the best, with no deference to precedent where precedent was in conflict with reason. The Fundamental Constitutions, therefore, should represent the practical application of the pholisopher's principles; and the only possible inference is that the philosopher had only a vague and uncertain notion of what those principles implied.

It is true that Locke's adventure in constitution-making preceded the *Two Treatises* by a quarter of a century, and in the meantime he had felt the heavy hand of governmental oppression, which may be supposed to have modified his ideas appreciably. Nevertheless, the incident has furnished ammunition to many generations of skeptics who hold that the nature of power cannot be deduced by the subtlest reasoning and therefore the philosopher who talks of government without ever having governed is a blind man discussing color.

It is true, also, that such ideas as the framers of the American system may have credited to Locke are not necessarily what he meant, but what a later generation thought he meant. It is a matter of record that every President of the United States who has done anything at all has been accused of deserting the principles that he proclaimed before he was elected. It is unlikely that all did anything of the kind, consciously, but all have been accused, and the fact is evidence that power reacts upon the wielder, substantially altering the structure of his thought.

So it is arguable that Jefferson, his predecessors and his successors, may have been influenced by Locke when they were doing things, as practical wielders of power, that theorists, as theorists, cannot possibly reconcile with Locke's expressed opinions. Grover Cleveland's somewhat plaintive explanation, "It is a condition which confronts us—not a theory," touched upon a mystery profounder than many people who have not staggered under the responsibility of power are inclined to believe.

On the other hand, it is incontestably true that experience has revealed to Americans ways of applying Locke's theories that never crossed Locke's mind. We are perpetually applying to philosophy John Marshall's constitutional doctrine of implied powers. Marshall had more effect upon the Constitution than the Constitution had upon Marshall; so one suspects that we may have attributed to Locke's philosophy implied meanings that never entered the philosopher's mind, and that might have shocked him profoundly if he had heard them expressed.

It is much easier to see the impress upon the American mind of that other great English philosopher of the period, Thomas

Hobbes. The doctrine that peace among men is essentially nothing more than an interruption of the normal state of war has been powerfully reinforced by the experience of the bloody twentieth century; but it had its adherents, some frank, but more unacknowledged, long before the twentieth century began. By war Hobbes did not mean exclusively the collision of armed men on the field of battle; the economic struggle was in his eyes very definitely a form of war, and that phase of his philosophy had pervaded large sections of American thought from the first settlements.

Alexander Hamilton's famous dictum, "Your people, sir, is a great beast!" was extorted from him in a moment of irritation when he was not carefully considering his words. Had he been cooler, he would not have said it; but he believed it. So did the rank and file of the Federalist party. Everyone knows that now, but what we are slower to concede is that Jefferson, within certain limits, believed it, too. No one felt a deeper horror of a mob, and no one knew better how easily an assembly of people may be converted into a mob which is, indeed, a great beast. On that point there was unanimity of opinion among the men who framed the Constitution. The document was designed, first of all, to prevent the American government from degenerating into mob rule.

The peculiarity of the men who, consciously or unconsciously, followed Hobbes was that they had no real hope that the people could ever be anything but a great beast. Make that admission, and a state of war is normal, or at any rate desirable, for incessant war with the beast is a condition of civilization.

Men with a profound distrust of democracy have always been numerous in the United States and they are especially numerous among those who hold positions of power and prestige. It could hardly be otherwise. By the time a man has battled his way to a really high position he is usually in late middle age or elderly and has taken so many unexpected blows that wariness has become his second nature. What is really difficult to explain is the arrival at comparable positions of a certain number whose confidence remains unshaken and to whom the Hobbesian position is unrealistic.

But such men do show up in positions of leadership now and then, and they are extremely attractive to youth and to the unsophisticated in general, so they can always command a large minority and not seldom a majority. They have appeared with sufficient frequency to maintain the theory of majority rule as the dominant principle of the republic. Indeed, they have maintained it so consistently for so long that a direct, frontal assault upon it is almost unheard-of by this generation. Its last open and powerful enemy was John C. Calhoun, who has been dead almost a hundred years.

Perhaps the most complete American Hobbesians are to be found among those who are unaware that the man existed and who do not know that the name *Leviathan* was ever applied to anything but a mythical sea-monster and a transatlantic liner. For his argument is not without much supporting evidence in the experience of every man, or at least of every man who has lived long and actively. Like Locke's, his influence is pervasive, not sharply defined, but that it exists is proved by the fierceness of the conflict that has been maintained between radical and reactionary throughout American history.

Locke and Hobbes were the two English philosophers roughly contemporaneous with the English invasion of America and who were of sufficient importance to exert a definite influence upon the thinking of their times. Their successors, of course, were studied in America perhaps more carefully than they were in non-English-speaking countries, although that would be hard to establish. But as far as formal philosophy is concerned, that is, the sort of thing that is studied and discussed in the schools and among the highly-educated, it is generally conceded that the Germans had more influence after the Revolution than did the English, and the French and Italians perhaps as much.

There was one conspicuous exception. For a time Herbert Spencer came close to dominating the field in America. His synthetic philosophy, which many Americans construed as a justification of whatever is, coincided with the swift, almost explosive, sweep across the western half of the continent. The exploiters as a rule had little time for philosophy and not much interest in justifying themselves; but their academic and clerical hangers-on, the pastors of fashionable churches and the presidents of kept universities, found Spencer a godsend.

For even the exploiters, like Nebuchadnezzar the king, had occasional nightmares that damaged their complacency and which they expected the Chaldeans and soothsayers attached to the court to explain away. For this purpose Spencer was admirable. He was a master popularizer who could not only make Darwinian biology partially comprehensible to the semi-literate, but could transmute it into a system of ethics admirably suited to the requirements of the great industrialists, railroad builders and financiers of the latter half of the nineteenth century.

He was misinterpreted, of course. All philosophers are. He would have been staggered by the imputation that he believed God had decreed that John D. Rockefeller should have a billion dollars, or that George F. Baer should stand *in loco parentis* to labor.* But he did postulate, or seem to postulate, a teleological element in the process of organic evolution. If, then, the survival of the fittest tended toward the improvement of the species, clearly the fittest were the best, and those who survived were the fittest. It was abundantly clear that Mr. Rocke-

---

* "The good Lord gave me my money," said Mr. Rockefeller. "The rights and interests of the laboring man," said Mr. Baer, "will be protected and cared for—not by the labor agitators, but by the Christian men to whom God in his infinite wisdom has given the control of the property interests of the country."

feller and Mr. Baer had survived, and the Chaldeans and soothsayers were not slow to point out in mellifluous tones that according to the reasoning of the great philosopher, Herbert Spencer, this was proof of their moral excellence.

Spencer thus flourished as the dominant philosopher until the economic system under which the exploiters prospered began to crack and so to incur increasing doubt and suspicion; but with its collapse in the first third of the twentieth century he was buried under the rubble and disappeared.

Yet the philosophy that is printed in books is of importance mainly to people who live in books to a greater extent than they live in the world outside of library walls. Philosophers and economists are infinitely clever at the business of explaining the event after it has happened. They are much less successful at predicting the event before it happens, and that they ever cause anything at all to happen is extremely difficult to prove. Locke, Hobbes, Herbert Spencer, John Stuart Mill, Malthus, Ricardo, Adam Smith and the rest are tremendously important Englishmen to students and professors in colleges, to lawyers writing briefs and judges writing decisions, to campaign speakers seeking votes, to newspaper editorial writers and to anyone else whose business is explaining what has already happened, either to justify or to condemn the men of action who precipitated the event. But the philosophy under which the bulk of the people live from day to day is something different. It is not bound between covers. It is no respecter of logical systems. It is a vast complex of memories, prejudices, inclinations and emotions with which the discipline of the schools has little to do. Its interpretation, therefore, is pretty largely guess-work, and the determination of the influence that the English, or any other specific nation, had on it is so uncertain that no man's dictum on the subject should be accepted as authoritative. Yet, if it is understood that these opinions are advanced tentatively, something may be said.

2

The American people, as the twentieth century approaches its halfway mark, are certainly not English. This seems to be a matter of perpetual astonishment to Englishmen who live at home and they are still incredulous despite a multitude of witnesses. The Frenchman, Crèvecoeur, told them so a hundred and seventy-five years ago; but if they reject him as full of Gallic prejudice, they have the evidence of an impressive list of British observers, beginning with Lord Bryce, including Arnold Bennett and H. G. Wells, and coming down to John Buchan, D. W. Brogan and Harold Laski. All agree that the American is something quite different from the Englishman.

But what is he? The question puzzled Crèvecoeur in 1782, and it puzzled Laski no less in 1948. His name may be Roosevelt, contracted from Martenzen van Rosenvelt, which is emphatically non-English, he may have French, Italian, Flemish, Swedish and Scottish blood, and yet be so nearly the model of an English gentleman that his enemies will accuse him of being practically a subject of the King; or he may be named Best, a native of a State with almost no intermixture of foreign blood, and yet be imprisoned for adhering to the common enemy of the United States and England. Obviously, the racial origin of an American doesn't tell much about him.

From this uncertainty has sprung in recent years a theory that since the country is no longer predominantly English, therefore it isn't English at all, or not to any important extent. It is a theory held tenaciously and hopefully by all who for highly emotional or severely rational reasons consider English influence derogatory to the country.

Statistically and theoretically there is a good deal to support it. For two generations before the quota system shut it off the great flood of immigration had come from non-English-speaking countries. Add twelve million Negroes and statisticians arrive at a figure of about fifty-one per cent for the non-British part of the population, and the British figure includes the Scotch, Welsh and North Irish elements.

But there is an imponderable factor that doesn't appear in statistical tables. It is the English power of transmutation, which is very considerable indeed, the indefinable process whereby a Swedish-French-Italian-Scottish-Flemish-Dutch combination touched by English influence may become so remarkably like an Englishman as to command the enthusiastic loyalty of the English. During his wartime visit to London, Wendell Willkie was equally popular in West End clubs and in Limehouse. German-American he may have been by blood, but he was a good enough Englishman to be acceptable in London, whether among the aristocracy or among the proletariat.

It does not follow that when an American, affected by this power of transmutation, takes on some English coloration he is necessarily improved. We assimilate their bad qualities as well as the better ones; in particular there is only too much reason to believe that we are pretty well saturated with the worst of all English traits, one which is as conspicuous in them as it is in the Germans and the Jews and which has made all three groups bitterly hated.

This is the deadly heresy of the *Herrenvolk,* the Chosen People, the race whose merits are so conspicuous that even God is forced to recognize them and to take the race under His special protection. It may be argued with some plausibility that the English are worse infected with this disease than either the Germans or the Jews, simply because they proclaim it less vociferously. Their relative silence on the subject is attributable, not to any doubt of their own superiority, but to a confidence in it so sublime that they tacitly assume that all the world shares it. This assumption was never made by any other group that cherishes the same delusion of its own superiority. Therefore the others insist on proclamations that lay them open to ridicule, while the Englishman is so blandly certain of his membership in the Master Race that he considers it not worth while to make any effort to impress "lesser breeds, without the law."

A hundred years ago Americans developed a virulent case of this malady and it is interesting to note that one of the correctives applied consisted of the comment of English writers, notably Charles Dickens, Harriet Martineau and the female Trollope. The satire in *Martin Chuzzlewit,* like many strong poisons, had a powerful germicidal effect when applied to a nationalism already inflamed and threatening to turn gangrenous.

The infection subsided for a while, but it has never been wholly eliminated and two conditions of modern American life are favorable to another flare-up. These are the simultaneous possession of great wealth and great military power. It would be fatuous to deny that it is easily possible for the American people, in the years immediately ahead, to generate an arrogance which would make that of the British seem almost a virtue by comparison.

But we are to some extent aware of the danger, and there is in existence some disposition to resist it. If the pattern of our national life is set by influences we know we should resist, then we are a failure as a nation. What is better worth considering here is the influence of those factors that are accepted and approved, sometimes unwittingly, but never consciously resisted.

In Scripture it is written that "as a man thinketh in his heart, so is he." As a rule, a man thinketh in his heart in the terms that he acquired when he first began to think at all, that is, in his youth when he was under formal instruction by professional educators. If he is an American, that formal instruction was given in the English language, and English literature was the medium used to give shape and expression to his notions of the sublime and the beautiful. Poetry he first learned as English poetry and even non-English thought, the philosophy of Plato, for example, came to him in the words of Benjamin Jowett.

His forefathers may have lived in Hungary, or Japan, or Mexico, or anywhere else, yet "if there be any virtue and there be any praise" in the thoughts of his heart and if these things come to him expressed in the English language, he is somewhat English regardless of race, or nationality, or residence in the midst of the Mississippi Valley. We are not English and our minds are not English minds, but as long as we can pick up a book of verse from London and be stirred instantly "there is some corner of a foreign field that is forever England."

The fact is immutable. It may be regretted, but it cannot be changed and it is folly to ignore it. That is the philosophy that really counts. The writings of the learned doctors may agitate the schools and fill the columns of the reviews and the more stately newspapers, but what moves the people is the intangible influence of a thousand years of English thought and English struggle. To attempt to measure it with any degree of precision is hopeless, for the people are not aware of it and cannot report it to others. As far as their conscious thought is concerned they may be anti-English and consider themselves anti-English to the bone; but it is not true.

Walking up Charles Street in Baltimore in the spring of 1939 I encountered a crowd of rather dilapidated youth streaming out of a church and into busses decorated with large cloth banners denouncing war and British imperialism. The young people were singing a dismal chant and bored-looking policemen stood around keeping the sidewalks clear.

"What goes on?" I asked the biggest and most bored.

"Some sort of pacifist outfit," he answered, twirling what elsewhere is called a nightstick, but in Baltimore an espantoon.

"That's all very well," he added suddenly, "until old England gets in trouble again, but then—" he spat and twirled his espantoon and looked silently down the street, closing the interview.

Not six months later the war was on and his words were justified; but to assume that the policeman was bribed by British gold, or deceived by British propaganda, would be nonsensical. He simply recognized the power of British tradition, which is for the most part English tradition, and knew what it could do.

There is no reasonable doubt that Woodrow Wilson in 1914 sincerely believed that neutrality, not only in deed, but in word and thought, was the right course for the United States to pursue. There is abundant evidence that he made desperate efforts to pursue it. He was not English; he was of a Scottish family that had lived for generations in Ireland. He was not an enthusiast, but a historian, trained in critical examination of evidence. He was not a traditionalist; on the contrary, ever since he attacked the eating clubs at Princeton, before he entered politics, he had been known as a great iconoclast. So when the first World War broke, for a time he could hold aloof, but that was the utmost of which he was capable. It was as impossible for him to accept the German concept of the all-inclusive state as it was for him to change the color of his eyes. All the weight of English tradition was against it, and in the end it thrust him, as well as the great mass of his fellow-citizens, into the English side of the fight.

President of the United States or patrolman pounding a beat, all Americans are under the pressure of that tradition and are shaped and moulded by it. Americans of the first generation are probably more acutely conscious of it than those of the tenth; but they are all moved by it. Some rejoice in it and some, as far as their rational processes go, resist it; but it exists and there is no understanding America without taking it into account. Nor should anyone think he has taken account of it when he attributes it to some slight and transitory cause—bribery, or threats, or snobbery, or deceit.

It is a curious fact that some of the people who have most completely misunderstood the nature of this influence have been visiting Englishmen. They make the mistake of assuming that the force whose existence they recognize has its source in the organized state named England, which is the capital and nerve-center of the British Empire; and when they discover that American enthusiasm for that state is, in fact, quite languid, they are puzzled and sometimes exasperated. In the other direction, German observers, including diplomatic agents, observing this lack of enthusiasm for the government of the Crown, have twice mistaken it for a deep anti-English feeling, and twice the mistake has led to the ruin of Germany.

Americans threw off allegiance to the Crown in 1776. The act was final, definite, irrevocable. Since 1814, when a group of misguided Federalists in New England seem to have imagined that they could take their States back into the empire, no American leader above the tenth rate has seriously suggested a return to monarchy. The chance that such an effort will ever be made has been diminishing steadily since the Declaration of Independence and is smaller today than ever before. Even those enthusiasts who are hottest for world federation, or a federation of western democracies, do not propose that the institution of monarchy should be revived.

Primogeniture, the basis of a permanent, hereditary aristocracy, is even more definitely out. The American trend, far from favoring inheritance by the oldest son, is distinctly in the direction of the abolition of all inheritance. Inherited money commands servility and sycophancy in America as money commands them everywhere in the world, but genuine respect for inherited wealth is probably at a lower ebb at this moment than it ever was before. This is evidenced not merely by the fact that inheritance taxes tend to increase rather than diminish, but also by the attitude of politicians and publicists, notably newspaper writers. Fifty years ago the doings of what was known as "Society," composed largely of people with inherited money, were given an immense amount of space in the newspapers. Today "Society" is relegated to relative obscurity and the large space is given to "Café Society," which is a different thing and in nothing more conspicuously different than in its independence of inherited wealth. Notoriety is a better passport to Café Society than any kind of wealth.

Imperialism is another matter. Imperialism is an insidious idea, capable of assuming countless forms, including the form of anti-imperialism. William McKinley took over the Philippine Islands in the name of anti-imperialism, and the assumption that he was hypocritical about it is not backed by substantial evidence. Mommsen declares that the Roman people, even after they had brought all Italy under their control, were strongly isolationist and the conquest of Sicily had to be effected under all sorts of subterfuges to avoid a popular uprising against it.

No prudent commentator, therefore, will assert flatly that the American people have definitely and permanently rejected imperialism. But it is safe to say that if and when it comes it will not be recognizably British imperialism. For one thing, the nation has not been fecund of great proconsuls. There have been many honest and earnest American governors of subject peoples, and a few reasonably efficient ones, but no American has arisen remotely comparable to Cecil Rhodes, or even to Warren Hastings.

Our experience has been in the diametrically opposite direction. Our worse failures have not been by way of sending out men like Gaius Verres, terrible scourges of mankind, but nincompoops. There is a faint but perceptible air of the comic about the history of American colonial administration and comedy was ever the ruin of glamor.

In addition to our unhappy experience in governing other peoples, efforts to create an untouchable Ark of the Covenant called the national honor have not been notably successful for a long time. Their last memorable achievement was precipitation of the Spanish-American war in 1898. Since then the trend has been in the other direction until at present the danger is less our truculence than our disposition to assume that every national collision must be a War of Jenkins' Ear, a case of unblushing aggression.

So the most that can be said is that we are not admirers of British imperialism, but that can be said definitely. The thing may creep upon us—there is no lack of pessimists who aver that it has already crept upon us—but if and when it comes it will not be in the form that has been familiar to the world since Elizabeth's sea-dogs made the Spanish treasure fleet a bad insurance risk, and the expansive Samuel Argall, agent of Virginia, thought it moral and praiseworthy to blast the Jesuits out of what is now Bar Harbor, Maine, and compel the Dutch at the mouth of the Hudson to swear allegiance to England.

Monarchy, aristocracy and British imperialism, three pillars of the English state, are out as far as America is concerned, and no one who ignores the fact can understand the country.

3

But monarchy, aristocracy and imperialism are not England.

To an American it seems strange that a fact so obvious should be worth mentioning, but the writings of some English commentators on America are evidence that they have not realized it or at least that they assume that these things are inseparable from England and that wherever English influence is felt they must be operative.

The England that still holds a powerful grip upon the thoughts and acts of the American people, including those of non-English origin, is not the realm of the English king, nor the institutions created by the English people. It is nothing so tangible, nothing definable in materialistic terms. It is a story, partly history, partly legend, largely poetry and drama. It is the struggle of a thousand years through which the common Englishman was transformed from the crook-backed serf who was sold with the land into the labor leader who stands before the King as his Prime Minister and whose will the King cannot gainsay.

The struggle is not unique. It has been carried on in every country in the world and in some it has been carried on successfully. But the version that we know best, the only one that we know at all well, is the English version; hence it is the one dominant in our lives.

The never-ending struggle has always and everywhere the same objective. It is simply to place the common man in a position where he may call his soul his own. But while the struggle is the same, it has been carried on against opponents of various types at various times and in various places. Autocrats, theocrats, aristocrats, plutocrats have fought it and demagogues have betrayed it, so the story is never exactly the same in any two nations.

One of the conspicuous characteristics of the English version is gradualism. In England there have been no such sudden surges forward as were represented by the French and Russian revolutions, not any such backward thrust as the Thirty Years' War in Germany, or the revocation of the Edict of Nantes in France. The English story is bloody enough, but the blood has usually been shed drop by drop, rather than in torrents. Bloody Mary was an English Queen, but she is unique; and even her butcheries were rather slight as compared with those of, say, the Duke of Alva in the Netherlands. As a rule English martyrs to liberty met death singly. As a rule, liberty advanced in England step by step and not in leaps and bounds.

This gradualism is so conspicuously a part of the American story that, although we have been under democratic rule continuously for a longer period than any other great nation, we are at this moment politically the most conservative of the great nations. We have outdone the English themselves in the matter of proceeding with caution.

This is a severe trial to the spirit of impatient idealists, who deprecate this English influence as hobbling social amelioration in America without any compensating advantages. But they are wrong, not about the hobbling, which is obvious, but in denying the advantages. It is precisely because we have been going slowly that no important reform in the United States of America has ever been undone. The Alien and Sedition laws, an effort to undo the First Amendment to the Constitution, lasted two years. Lincoln suspended the writ of *habeas corpus,* but only momentarily in time of war, and even that remains the principal blot on his memory. Wilson's attorney-general harried radicals, but eventually the courts put a stop to it under the existing law.

Once, indeed, we plunged ahead rapidly on what we thought was the road to reform, and had to fall back in confusion. That was in the adoption of the Eighteenth Amendment, prohibiting the sale of beverage alcohol. It failed because it wasn't in fact a reform, but an invasion of liberty.

After every great war it seems that we develop a panic fear of liberty and indulge in an orgy of crimes against it. But Reconstruction in the South after 1865 and the witch-hunting after 1918, were perpetrated not by repealing the guarantees of liberty but by monstrous violations of them. The slow judicial process at length will almost certainly reveal that much of the reactionary hysteria following 1945 was equally lawless. Americans are no more exempt from criminal tendencies than are other nations and when they are sufficiently terrified they give way to the same mob instincts. But the fact remains that American law as it is written after due deliberation—undue deliberation sometimes, without a doubt—has moved steadily toward enlarging, rather than restricting the liberty of the common man.

If not one of his important rights has been snatched away by law in the course of nearly two hundred years, it is in part because he has not won his rights too soon. No great popular leader—not Jefferson in 1800, not Jackson in 1828, or Lincoln in 1860, or Wilson in 1912, or Roosevelt in 1932—has come to power without evoking anguished screams from those who were convinced that these men were bent upon giving the people liberties they were incompetent to hold.* Yet when the dust had settled every important reform effected by these leaders was embraced by the opposition party and remained a permanent part of the American system.

Perhaps because the enlargement of English liberty proceeded for a thousand years so slowly that the effect of one step could be measured before the next was taken, it has developed in the nation a strong belief in fair play. In politics fair play is justifiable only on the theory that the opposition may be partly right. That idea is utterly rejected by partisan campaigners, as the assailants of every strong President abundantly prove, but it

---

* "The ties of marriage . . . are severed and destroyed; our wives and daughters are thrown into stews; our children are cast into the world from the breast and forgotten; filial piety is extinguished, and our surnames . . . are abolished." This is a description of the state of the nation made by Theodore Dwight in an oration at New Haven July 7, 1801. This interesting situation, it seems, was attributable to the election of Thomas Jefferson as President the previous November.

"The bill . . . applies force to the judiciary and . . . would undermine independence of the courts. It violates all precedents in the history of our government . . . The theory of the bill is in direct violation of the spirit of the American Constitution and its employment would permit alteration of the Constitution without the people's consent or approval; it undermines the protection our constitutional system gives to minorities and is subversive of the rights of individuals." This is the opinion, expressed 130 years after Dwight by a Senate committee, of President Roosevelt's proposal to take measures to guard against the Supreme Court's ever being composed of judges the majority of whom are senile.

has never been abandoned by the mass of the voters, who have always taken fervid partisans somewhat humorously.

It must never be forgotten that what is now the United States remained part of the realm of the English King through the hundred and seventy critical years that saw the transition of the monarchy from Tudor to Hanover. These years included the English Civil War with all the tremendous emphasis it laid upon the dignity of the individual. They included a vast amount of experimentation and cogitation in government; and they included also the discovery, in the course of this experimentation, that no political reform is ever exactly right. Reformers, being human, invariably either overshoot or undershoot the mark, which means that the initial success must always be followed by precise adjustments to correct errors.

This knowledge was not passed on to the Americans. It was acquired by them along with the English when they were still a part of the English political system. But it is part of the influence that the English have exerted upon American life. Upon it is based the American principle that the ballot as a political instrument is always preferable to the bullet, because your opponent of today may be a useful supporter tomorrow, if he is alive, but can be of no possible further use once he is dead.

In one instance only have we departed from the tacit understanding that whatever happens, nobody will shoot. That occasion was after the election of 1860, when the defeated minority did appeal to arms. The result was a war that cost more American lives than both World Wars, and left wounds that have not yet healed. It was a powerful reinforcement of our old belief that the English system of gradualism and no shooting is the best method of effecting lasting improvements in our political, social and economic institutions.

The American valuation of the capable man also has in it more of English tradition than we sometimes think. We like to believe, and Frederick Jackson Turner and his followers have strengthened the belief, that the frontier, not the English, taught us that skill and energy yield precedence only to honesty among the human qualities that command respect; and we have not always given first place even to honesty.

But the idea had begun to permeate English society as far back as the reign of Elizabeth. The seaman, Francis Drake, was knighted by a queen who coolly ignored the scions of many noble houses. He had skill and energy, so he became Sir Francis while barons' sons went untitled. Long before that, indeed, the English had begun to restrict inheritance to a single line. If a nobleman's younger sons wished recognition, they had to earn it. Earned honors, furthermore, were regarded as no whit less honorable than those inherited. Two centuries later Wellington, who started as an untitled younger son, became not merely a perfectly genuine duke, but the Iron Duke, compared to whom dukes by inheritance were but poor stuff.

With such ideas in their heads the English settlers could find a certain reasonableness in the granite law of the frontier that crushed all but the able in body and mind; and finding it not without reason could adapt themselves to it with better grace than men trained in the belief that there was a certain divinity in blue blood for which ability was no equivalent. From this it was a short step to the theory that a combination of brains and character constitutes the only genuine superiority, which theory is the foundation of democracy.

Finally, "a nation of shopkeepers" unquestionably had something to do with implanting in us the belief that the producer and trader is the true conquistador. This inheritance has its sordid side, as no candid man can deny. We have never been able to make a clear distinction between the commercial instinct and the acquisitive instinct, so we have failed many times to differentiate the man who makes money from the man who grabs money. The result is that over and over again we have followed the leadership of Gadarene swine who repeatedly—as in 1873 and in 1893 and in 1929—"ran violently down a steep place into the sea . . . and were choked."

But civilization has made a step forward in any community when it makes up its collective mind that the way to deal with an intruding stranger is to cheat him and not to shoot him. Civilization has made, not a step but a long stride forward when it is decided to make a fair deal with the stranger. A fair deal presupposes a profit at both ends; and while it is true of late years that there are extremists who equate "profit motive" with all evil, it is nevertheless much preferable to the homicidal motive. The English taught us to exalt the trader, and while it is a teaching not without flaws it has unquestionably tended to soften manners and restrain manslaughter. Incidentally, it has built up an economic power that is now the most formidable in existence.

Locke's empiricism, Hobbes' materialism and Spencer's eclecticism are elements of English philosophy that have agitated American schools and still furnish matter for gentle and joyous debate among the learned doctors. But most of the people never heard of any of them, and if they heard would promptly forget. The English philosophy that still sways the thoughts and acts of the millions who never saw the inside of a college is none of these. It is English faith in gradualism linked with compromise, English faith in ability as at least equal to heredity, and English faith in commerce as a better instrument of conquest than war.

The pattern that the English set is not perfect. In many ways it has proved to be so imperfect that it had to be abandoned and a new pattern devised. Many English ideas have given way to ideas brought from some other country because the non-English idea was superior. Many English methods have been less efficient than other methods and have been abandoned.

Nevertheless, so much of the pattern has survived that a relation unique among nations exists between the United States and Great Britain. Nearly three hundred and fifty years after the first settlement and nearly a hundred and seventy-five years after the political separation the English pattern is still followed. England probably never sent more than four or five millions of her people to this country; other countries have sent more than thirty millions; yet the English pattern survives.

It is true that the English, coming first, multiplied so prodigiously that the millions pouring in later could not overwhelm them. Nevertheless, the impact of thirty million aliens is a terrific test of any culture. The English pattern had to be good, very good, to survive that test. It is hard to think of any other except the Chinese that has stood up under an equivalent strain, and the eventual triumph of Chinese culture was very much slower. The English pattern in America has not been subverted even temporarily. Many times its end has been announced, but the announcement has always been premature. After a short season it has become plain that the new idea had not really taken hold.

It is possible that it is nearing its end now. It is being assailed with tremendous vigor by what is probably the oldest concept of government in existence. This is what we are in the habit of calling the Fascist-Communist concept, or totalitarianism. But only the name is new; totalitarianism is simply despotism "writ large." The despot may claim his authority by the grace of God, or by the grace of "the leadership principle," or by the grace of the proletariat, but he is a despot still. He has had more names than Proteus had shapes, but only one nature. As Nero he was not essentially different from Genghis, as Caligula he was basically Hitler, and as Attila, as Abdul, as Bonaparte, as Franco and as Stalin he is recognizably the same.

As John he ruled England for a while, but eventually his claws were clipped. As George, a singularly feeble avatar, he provoked an explosion of the English spirit that snapped our political bonds with England. As someone so far without a name, but probably much resembling Huey Long, he may yet dominate this country, and then, indeed, the English pattern will be rubbed out, its promise belied and its significance gone.

For in spite of its multitude of intricate, interwoven figures and its bewildering variety of colors, the pattern that the English set is in its main outlines a simple one. It seems complicated only because there is movement in it. Time being one of its dimensions, it alters from day to day, and thereby confuses observers whose perception is slow.

It is the figure of the stooping serf, himself a part of the real estate, straightening, slowly standing up, raising his eyes from the clod to the plant, to the flower, to the furrow and then the field beyond, at last to the face of the King. In the panel being woven now he stands erect and eyes the King with level gaze, and the King cannot gainsay him.

What is the next panel to be? It is a question not to be addressed to the English, for although they gave us the outline they are no longer weaving the web. Their responsibility ended with their dominance, many generations ago, and the pattern henceforth must be American. Others have contributed to it colors and figures unknown to the English, and the artistry, or lack of it, of Americans as a nation will be proved by their capacity to make these new contributions enrich the original design without obliterating its masterly strokes.

We have no lack of pessimists who are certain that the work is beyond us. The development, they say, has come to its logical conclusion, the wheel has made its full turn, and retrogression is all that may be expected. The next panel that comes from the loom of Time, they prophesy, will show the level-eyed citizen beginning to quail before the glare of a dictator, beginning to stoop again, and to sink his gaze toward the earth.

Others say no, that the pattern set by the English, far from having run out, is only now ready for its development with richer fabrics, more gorgeous hues and more daring designs than its originators ever possessed. Weavers as industrious and skillful as their fathers, and far more splendidly endowed, will carry the moving figure on, and the man who is the center of the picture little by little will raise his eyes from the face of the Ruler and turn them toward the stars.

But that is for the future to reveal. That, as the yarn-spinners like to say when they don't know what comes next, is another story.

THE END

Index

Abbey, Edwin Austin, 204
Adams, Brooks, 156
Adams, Henry, 98, 156
Adams, John, 156
Adamson, J. W., 53 fn.
Alien and Sedition Laws, 57, 142, 239
Allen, Ethan, 128
Allston, Washington, 203
Amadus, Philip, 20
American Philosophical Society, 211-12, 215, 220
Anti-Saloon League, 162
Architecture
  English influence upon, 196, 197, 198
  materials used in, 196-97
  types of in English colonies, 194-99
Argall, Captain Samuel, 39, 46, 89, 237
Arminius, Jacobus, 171 fn.
Arthur, Chester Alan, 178 fn.
Asbury, Francis, 173

Bach, Johann Sebastian, 190
Bacon, Sir Francis, 13, 82, 124
Bacon, Nathaniel, 93
Bacon, Roger, 82, 133, 217, 221
Baltimore, Lord, *see*
  Calvert, Cecilius
  Calvert, George
  Calvert, Leonard
Bancroft, George, 134
Baptist
  church government of, 165
  history of, 166-68
  ideology of, 168-69
  influence of, 166
  migration of, 165
Barbados, 9
Barlow, Arthur, 20
Baxter, Richard, 78
Bayly, Lewis, 65 fn.
Beecher, Henry Ward, 161
Becker, Carl L., 209 fn., 210
Becket, Thomas à, 192

Bennett, Arnold, 230
Benton, Thomas H., 204
Berkeley, William
  and education, 56
  contributions of, 90
  religious intolerance of, 91
  rise to power of, 89-90
  second administration of, 92-93
  tyranny of, 92-93, 94
Beverley, Robert, 36, 38, 39, 43
Bible, King James Version of
  creation of, 127-28
  influence upon American pattern of, 128-31
  reflection of English prose style in, 126, 128
Bigod, Roger, 138-39
Binyon, Lawrence, 184 fn.
Bonaparte, Napoleon, 150 fn.
Boswell, James, 110
Bradford, William
  as administrator, 95, 96
  compared to William Penn, 99
  contributions of, 97-98, 99
  philosophy of, 97, 98
Brinsley, John, 55
Brogan, D. W., 230
Brown, John, 161
Brown, Mather, 203
Bry, Theodore de, 184
Bryan, W. J., 108, 130
Bryce, James, 230
Byrom, John, 77
Buchan, John, 230
Buchanan, James, 177 fn.
Buckingham, Duke of, 69
Buckland, William, 57, 198
Bunyan, John, 78, 165 fn., 167
Burke, Edmund, 110, 201
Burleigh, First Earl of, *see*
  Cecil, William
Butlers, "gang of," 15
Byrd, William, 186, 189

Calhoun, John C., 156, 227
Calvert, Cecilius, 49, 59, 70, 71, 72, 101
Calvert, George
  characteristics of, 68
  charters granted to, 70, 72
  contributions of, 71, 80
  religious beliefs of, 69-70
  religious tolerance and, 71-72, 73, 74, 158
  rise to power of, 69
Calvert, Leonard, 72, 73
Calvin, John, 171 fn., 173
Carroll, Charles, 72
Carroll, John, 158
Carteret, John, 108 fn.
Catholicism
  attitude toward religion, 60
  English influence upon, 159
  in Maryland, 71, 72
Cause and Cure of Smoky Chimneys, 211
Cecil, Robert, 21, 24, 68, 69, 71
Cecil, William, 21-22
Cervantes, Miguel de, 55, 125
Charles I, King, 69, 70, 89, 92
Charles II, King, 79, 92, 93, 167, 220 fn.
Chatham, Earl of, 151
Chaucer, Geoffrey, 82, 124, 220
Churchill, Winston, 82
Clarendon, Edward Hyde, 133
Clay, Henry, 105
Cleveland, Grover, 225
Clifford, John, 145, 146
Code Napoléon, 141
Coke, Edward, 142
Colonists
  class of English, 9, 10
  clergy among, 10
  comparison of Spanish and English, 24
  contemporary attitude toward death rate of, 39-40
  England's purpose in sending, 9
  factors influencing death rate of, 29-31
  recruiting of, 47-49
Comberford, Catherine, 192 fn.
Concessions and Agreements, 79
Constitution, 223
Cooper, James Fenimore, 32
Cooper, Thomas, 219
Copley, John Singleton, 203
Cortez, Hernando, 25, 36

Crèvecoeur, 106, 230
Cromwell, Sir Oliver, 63, 64, 74, 75, 78

Dale, Sir Thomas, 10, 25, 37, 87
Dante, 125
Dare, Ananias, 183
Dare, Ellinor, 183
Dare, Virginia, 183
Declaration of Independence, 141, 223, 235
Delaware (de la Warr), Lord
  contributions of, 48, 49
  influence on recruiting of colonists, 47, 48-49
Delaware, Lady, 88
Descartes, Renée, 66
Dickens, Charles, 232
Dickinson, John, 177 fn., 177
Dictionary of Music, 190
Discourse on Method, 66, 206
Dowland, John, 186, 189
Drake, Sir Francis, 18, 19, 21, 82, 242
Drummond, Robert Hay, 202
Dryden, John, 126
Dunning, William A., 63 fn.
Dulany, Daniel, 57
Dwight, Theodore, 240 fn.

Edison, Thomas A., 208
Education
  attitude of indentures toward, 57
  English attitude toward, 53
  factors influencing spread of, 53-54, 56
  in Middle Ages, 53
  in Virginia, 56
  influence of merchants upon, 54
  influence of protestant reformation upon, 54-55
  Spanish attitude toward, 55
Edwards, Jonathan, 64, 67, 161, 177
Eighteenth Amendment, 143, 237
Elizabeth, Queen, 12, 14, 15, 16, 21, 25, 76, 132
Emerson, Ralph Waldo, 161
England
  area of interest in New World, 20
  as "ruler of the seas," 18
  "dignity of labor" in, 25-27
  early emigrants from, 9, 10
  factors influencing emigration from, 27-29, 76-77
  influence on religious affairs in New World, 159-62, 181

piracy of Spanish ships, 18, 19
religious sects contributed by, 158-59
Encyclopedia Britannica, 139
English Language
  ambiguity of, 122-24
  character of, 116, 121
  distortion of history due to, 131-36
  dominance of in New World, 117-20
  scope of, 116
Episcopalianism
  effect on American Revolution, 179-80
  influence of, 178, 179, 180
Eugene, Prince, 108
Essex, Lord, 16, 21

Fauquier, Francis, 213-14, 215, 216
Federalist, 223
Ferguson, Donald N., 186 fn., 187
Fielding, Henry, 124
Fitzgerald, "gang of," 15
Fosdick, Harry Emerson, 165
Fourteenth Amendment, 154
Fox, George, 78, 79, 101
France
  in New World, 20
Frobisher, Martin, 18
Franklin, Benjamin
  contributions of, 85, 209-12, 215, 216
  Royal Society of London and, 219
Fugitive Slave Laws, 142, 143
Fundamental Constitutions, 74, 107
Fulton, Robert, 203

Gainsborough, Thomas, 201, 203
Gardiner, Rev. Dr., 193
George II, King, 244
George III, King, 103, 202
Gibbon, Edward, 133
Gilbert, Sir Humphrey, 15, 19
Glass, Montague, 122
Goldsmith, Oliver, 110
Grant, Ulysses, 123
Granville, Lord, 100, 108 fn.
Graupner, Gottlieb, 192 fn.

Hakluyt, Richard, 183, 184
Hamilton, Alexander, 226
Hamor, Ralph, 195
Händel, Georg Friedrich, 185, 186
Harding, W. G., 123
Hariot, 184
Harrison, Benjamin, 177 fn.
Harrison, William, 54, 178 fn., 194

Hawkins, Sir John, 18, 82
Healey, J., 65 fn.
Henrietta Maria, Queen, 70
Henry IV, King, 73
Henry V, King, 82
Henry VIII, King, 25, 165
Hermansen, Jacob, 171 fn., 173
Hewitt, James, 193
History of the World, 13
Hobbes, Thomas, 226-28, 243
Holland
  in New World, 20
Holmes, O. W., 147 fn.
House of Burgesses, Jamestown, 41-42, 53
Howard, Lord Charles, 82
Hutchinson, Anne, 68

Indentured Servants
  attitude toward education, 55
  characteristics of, 52-53
  influence of, 58
  recruited by London Company, 57-58
  value of land to, 57-58

Jackson, Andrew, 177 fn., 240
Jackson, George K., 193
James I, King, 14, 16, 36, 69, 176
James II, King, 102, 167
Jamestown, 35
Jefferson, Thomas, 49, 68, 85, 98, 141, 142, 156, 179, 180, 198, 205, 210, 213 fn., 213-14, 215, 216, 219, 222, 223, 225, 226, 240, 240 fn.
Jews
  first appearance in New World, 45, 159
John, King, 82, 138-39, 244
Johnson, H. Earle, 193 fn.
Johnson, James, 201
Johnson, Samuel, 65, 110, 193, 201, 202
Jonson, Ben, 14
Jowett, Benjamin, 233

Key, Francis Scott, 192
Kipling, Rudyard, 143, 146

Las Casas, Bartolomé, 23-24, 25
Laski, Harold J., 217, 230
Latrobe, Benjamin H., 198
Law
  American attitude toward, 142-43
  canon law, 155
  commercial law, 155

corporation, 154
development of common law in America, 140-41, 144-45, 146-48, 155-57
development of common law in England, 138-40, 144, 145
effect of frontier upon, 146
law of property, 150-51, 152-54
legal position of man and woman, 155
marriage and, 154
right of security, 151-52
trial by jury, 148-50
League of Nations, 123
Legate, J., 65 fn.
Leicester, Earl of, 15, 21
Leiden, John, 165 fn.
Leslie, Charles Robert, 203
Lewis, Sinclair, 190 fn.
Lincoln, Abraham, 98, 239, 240
Literature (English)
effect of on American, 124-25, 126
in America, 124
Locke, John
influence upon American political thought, 74, 96, 223-26, 227, 229, 243
scheme for government of Carolina, 74, 106-08, 110
London Company
attitude toward education, 55
attitude toward religion, 60
class of colonists recruited, 46-47
corporation of, 154
indenture and, 50, 52
motive of, 44-45, 85
pattern established by, 51
pilgrims and, 62
propositions to attract colonists, 47-51
religious tolerance of, 45
Lorent, Stefan, 184 fn.
Lost Lady, 90
Luther, Martin, 165
Lyon, Matthew, 57

Macaulay, Thomas, 50 fn., 100 fn.
Madison, James, 178 fn.
Madison, Rev. James, 213 fn.
Magna Carta, 138
Malthus, Thomas Robert, 28, 229
Mandeville, Bernard, 209
Maritime Observations, 211

Marlowe, Christopher, 13, 188
Marshall, John, 156, 225
Martin Chuzzlewit, 232
Martineau, Harriet, 232
Mary Tudor, Queen, 18, 238
Maryland
founding of, 70
success of experiment, 73
Mather, Cotton, 67
McKinley, William, 105, 236
Melville, Herman, 125
Mencken, H. L., 115, 116, 130
Mercantilist Economic Theory, 28, 75-78
Methodism
church government of, 170
contributions of, 66-67, 174-76
development of, 170-73
founding of, 111, 170-71
ideology of, 173-76
Whitefield, George and, 171-73
Mill, John Stuart, 229
Mills, Clark, 200
Mills, Robert, 198, 200
Milton, John, 82, 124, 125, 128
Moody, Dwight Lyman, 190 fn.
Monroe, James, 178 fn.
Morrison, S. E., 194 fn.
Morse, S. F. B., 203
Morton, Thomas, 66, 98
Mumford, Lewis, 220 fn.
Music
character of English, 189
English hymnody in America, 189, 190
English influence on American, 180-93
history of early English, 185-89

New World
effect of environment on colonists, 31-34
effect of environment on English pattern, 106
English development of, 26
Spanish exploitation of, 26
Newport, Christopher, 29, 30, 32, 33, 34-35, 38, 84, 124, 128, 185
Newton, Thomas, 201
Nicholas II, Czar, 167
No Cross No Crown, 79
Notes on Virginia, 214
Noyes, Alfred, 160 fn.

O'Carroll, Ely, 158
Oglethorpe, James Edward
  administration of, 109, 110
  characteristics of, 108
  Charles and John Wesley and, 111
  contributions of, 111-12
  in Georgia, 109-11, 190
  religious tolerance of, 109
Opechancanough, 39, 85-86

Pablos, Juan, 23
Paine, Tom, 179
Painting
  contributors in America, 203
  English influence upon, 204
  influence of Benjamin West upon, 203
Palladio, 199
Pandects, 137
Parrie, H., 65 fn.
Peale, Charles Wilson, 203
Peale, Rembrandt, 203
Pemberton, Dr., 209
Penn, Admiral Sir William, 79
Penn, William
  attitude toward Indians of, 100, 104
  Cecil Calvert and, 101
  characteristics of, 102
  compared to William Bradford, 99
  constitution of West Jersey, 80
  contributions of, 94, 99-100, 102
  early life of, 79-80
  George Fox and, 79
  Philadelphia, 74, 99, 100
  policy in Pennsylvania, 103
  and Quakers, 80
  religious freedom and, 80-81
Piers Plowman, 27
Pilgrims
  in Netherlands, 61
  and London Company, 62
Pilgrim's Progress, 77
Philip II, King of Spain, 22, 24, 25, 132, 183
Philosophy
  influence of Thomas Hobbes upon, 225-28
  influence of John Locke upon, 223-25
  influence of Herbert Spencer upon, 228-29
  characteristics of American, 230-46
Pierce, Franklin, 178 fn.

Pizarro, Francisco, 25
Pocahontas, 11, 87-89
Powell, William S., 65 **fn.**
Powers, Hiram, 200
Powhatan, 83, 85
Presbyterians
  ideology of, 177
  contributions of, 177
Priestley, Joseph, 219
Principia, 212
Property
  value of to English lower class, 50-51
Purcell, Henry, 185, 189
Puritans
  as theorists, 63-64
  characteristics of, 63-66
  concept of religion, 60
  growth of movement, 62-63
  influence of movement, 63, 64
  influence on education, 67-68

Quakers
  characteristics of, 100, 101

Raleigh, Sir Walter
  as captain of the guard, 14-15
  character of, 13-14, 17, 48
  and Elizabeth, Queen, 16
  and James I, King, 16-17
  navigator, 18, 19, 20
  reputation of among contemporaries, 14, 16
  rise to power, 15-16
  rivalry with William Cecil, 21-22
Randolph, John, 89, 150
Relation of the Right Honorable the Lord De-la-Warre, Lord Governour and Captaine Generall of the Colonie, planted in Virginia, 48
Religious Freedom
  as motive for colonization, 60
  and Catholics, 59, 60
  in Maryland, 72, 73
  influence of Cromwellian Revolution upon, 72
  planting of, 80, 81
  and Puritans, 59, 60, 61
  and Quakers, 59
Reynolds, Joshua, 201, 202, 203
Ribton-Turner, 29 fn.
Rittenhouse, David, 212, 215
Rolfe, John, 38, 84-85, 94, 205-06, 218
  and Pocahontas, 87-89
Rolfe, Thomas, 88

Romney, George, 203
Roosevelt, Franklin Delano, 105, 178
    fn., 240
Root, Elihu, 123
Royal Society of London, 218-20
Rush, Benjamin, 211

Salisbury, Earl of, *see*
    Cecil, Robert
Sankey, Ira David, 188 fn.
Sargent, J. S., 203 fn., 204
Savile, Henry, 127
Schmoltz, Benjamin, 191 fn.
Science
    American attitude toward, 207-08
    English influence upon, 220-22
    influence of Benjamin Franklin on,
        210-12, 216, 217, 218
    influence of Thomas Jefferson on,
        216, 217, 218
    influence of John Rolfe on, 205-06
    influence of Royal Society of Lon-
        don on, 218, 220
Scotus, John Duns, 82
Sculpture
    English influence upon, 200-01
Securities Exchange Commission, 149
Separatists, *see*
    Pilgrims
Seward, William H., 68
Shakespeare, William, 13, 48, 75, 82,
    124, 125, 126
Shurtleff, Harold R., 194 fn.
Slavery, 43
Small, William, 212, 213, 214, 215
Smith, Abbott Emerson, 9 fn., 29 fn.,
    39 fn., 57 fn.
Smith, Adam, 229
Smith, John, 37, 47, 83, 84, 96, 209
    influence on recruiting colonists, 47-
        48
    in Virginia, 25, 26, 30, 33, 45
Smith, John Stafford, 192
Spain
    as land power, 19
    attitude toward Indians, 23
    colonial administration of, 22-23
    cultural contribution of, 23
    "dignity of labor" in, 25-27
    holdings in New World, 22, 23
Spencer, Herbert, 228-29, 242
Spenser, Edmund, 17
Standish, Miles, 35, 66, 98
Stuart, Arabella, 16

Stuart, Gilbert, 203
Stukly, Lady, 88
Sully, Thomas, 203

Taft, William H., 123
Taylor, Zachary, 178 fn.
Thomson, Charles, 57
Thornton, Matthew, 57
Tooke, Horne, 150
Toynbee, Arnold J., 63 fn., 63, 134 fn.
True Relation, 47
Trumball, John, 203
Turner, Frederick Jackson, 146, 242
Two Treatises on Government, 224
Tyler, John, 178 fn.
Tyndale, William, 82

Universal-Konversations-Lexikon, 117

Vanderdecken, Captain, 43
Van Rensselaer, 108 fn.
Venables, General, 9 fn., 10
Victoria, Queen, 189
Virginia
    first clergy in, 10
    influence of success of Jamestown,
        35-36
    religious tolerance in, 46
Virginia Statute of Religious Freedom,
    141
Voltaire, 160

Walpole, Horace, 110
Washington, George, 49, 98, 106, 178
    fn.
Watch and Ward Society, 162
Watts, Isaac, 190
Weber, Karl von, 191 fn.
Wellington, Duke of, 134, 242
Wesley, Charles, 108, 111, 190-91
Wesley, John, 108, 111, 170
West, Benjamin
    contribution of, 201-02
    early life of, 201
    in England, 202
    influence on American painting, 202-
        04
West, Thomas, 47, 48
Whistler, James Abbott McNeill, 204
White, Father Andrew, 83, 158
White, John, 182-85, 191, 201, 209
White, Thomas, 55
Whitefield, George, 67, 111, 170, 171-
    73, 191
Whitman, Walt, 125

William III, King, 50 fn.
Williams, Roger, 61, 68, 158, 160, 165
Wilson, Woodrow, 98, 105, 128, 177
  fn., 234, 239, 240
Winthrop, John, 64, 95, 96, 97, 105
Wister, Owen, 146 fn.
Witherspoon, John, 177
Woelfkin, Cornelius, 166
Wood, Grant, 204
World Almanac, 162, 163

Wren, Christopher, 198
Wright, Orville, 108 fn.
Wright, Louis B., 53 fn., 54 fn.
Wycliffe, John, 82
Wythe, George, 213, 214

York, Archbishop of, 180 fn.

Zimbalist, Efrem, 188 fn.